MLJ/4

CAN9989 £3

CW01481151

READING AN ERASED CODE

MICHEL DESPLAND

Reading an Erased Code: Romantic Religion and Literary Aesthetics in France

UNIVERSITY OF TORONTO PRESS
Toronto Buffalo London

© University of Toronto Press Incorporated 1994
Toronto Buffalo London
Printed in Canada

ISBN 0-8020-0578-0

Printed on acid-free paper

University of Toronto Romance Series

Canadian Cataloguing in Publication Data

Despland, Michel, 1936–
    Reading an erased code : romantic religion and
    literary aesthetics in France

    (University of Toronto romance series)
    Includes bibliographical references and index.
    ISBN 0-8020-0578-0

    1. Romanticism – France. 2. Christianity in
    litertaure. 3. French literature – 19th century –
    Hitory and criticism. I. Title. II. Series.

PQ295.R6D48 1994   840.9'007   C94-930972-9

University of Toronto Press acknowledges the financial assistance to its
publishing program of the Canada Council and the Ontario Arts Council.

This book has been published with the help of a grant from the Canadian
Federation for the Humanities, using funds provided by the Social Sciences
and Humanities Research Council of Canada.

Contents

vi   Contents

Acknowledgments

Conversations with colleagues at Concordia University and elsewhere have aroused and nourished interest in the literary and historical issues discussed in this book. More formally, I must thank Frank Paul Bowman (University of Pennsylvania), who was kind enough to read the Chateaubriand chapter in an earlier form, produced by a novice in the field; his comments set me on a good track, and I hope I profited from them. John Laffey was also helpful with his comments on this chapter. The chapter was later presented in a joint Concordia/UQAM departmental colloquium, and I thank my colleagues in religion for the spirited discussion that ensued. Bill Crouter (Carleton College), Ibrahim Khan (Trinity College, Toronto), and Robert Martin (Université de Montréal) read the whole manuscript at an early stage; their comments, coming from specialists of nineteenth-century German, Danish, and American texts, were encouraging (sometimes at decisive junctures) and helped me focus my issues and handle them in a way that might be of interest to a variety of readers. Three readers' reports enabled me to improve on my efforts. For secretarial help, Elizabeth Maclean and Faye Trecartin were thoughtful and efficient.

Chapter 1 includes material found in a previous publication: 'A Key to 19th Century Critical Attitudes toward Religion? The Work of J.-J. Rousseau,' in Jack Lightstone and Michael Oppenheim, eds, *Truth and Compassion* (Waterloo, Ont.: Wilfred Laurier University Press, 1983), 55–74. Chapter 2 was published in an earlier form in *Religion and Literature* (Summer 1989), 19–44. Some of the material in chapter 3 was used in an article with the same title in *Papers of the 19th Century Theology Group* of the American Academy of Religion (1989), 1–10. Chapter 4 is a revision of an article published in *Annals of Scholarship* 6–4 (1989), 397–415, and, in French translation, in *Studies in Religion / Sciences religieuses*, 17/4 (1988), 421–42. Chapter 5 is a translation by Jill Capri of the French original published in *Etudes théologiques et religieuses* 4 (1989–4), 535–60. Her competence was also put to the test as she revised my laborious translations of the longer texts cited from Nodier and Nerval. All translations from secondary material are my own.

READING AN ERASED CODE

Introduction:

New Writing, New Reading

And it shall come to pass afterward,
that I will pour out my spirit on all flesh;
your sons and your daughters shall prophesy,
your old men shall dream dreams,
and your young men shall see visions.
Even upon the menservants and maidservants
in those days, I will pour my spirit.

Joel 2:28–9 (RSV)

Students of English literature are familiar with these biblical verses and can usually quote a list of writers who did not hesitate to place themselves in this open-ended line of prophecy. To mention only the most famous, Milton began *Paradise Lost* by invoking the same heavenly Muse that inspired Moses; did the seventeenth-century Puritan really claim for his epic inspiration equal to that of the Pentateuch? Blake was bolder yet; he wrote his visions in direct prophetic style (and their content countered what passed for Christianity in his day). By the time Wordsworth and Coleridge had completed their work, English Protestants were quite prone to see in their literature an entirely legitimate outgrowth of their religion; an heir rivalling Scripture, or replacing it; or perhaps simply a continuation and fulfilment of its age-old spiritualizing and democratizing tendencies. They could draw a smooth line of succession from medieval to Protestant to romantic religion. Victorian literary criticism and theology were deeply intertwined. Theologians stressed, not without some apologetic intent, that the interpretation of poetry raised inescapably religious questions.[1]

When the holders of such views looked at the European Continent, the towering figure of Goethe appeared to confirm their account of the development of the human spirit. The sentiment thus got widely accepted that in the modern era, literature is destined to become the main nourishment for 'spiritual' needs formerly met by religion.[2] (That the meaning of 'spiritual' had undergone a vast shift from what it was in traditional Christian theology was commonly overlooked.) France, however, seemed to be different. But the fact that the French were Catholic and had been caught up in the excesses of the Revolution could account for that. Romantic religion in France thus appeared to be both less important and less interesting and the génie of French romanticism became commonly ignored or misrepresented.[3]

The first objective of this book is theoretical: to counter the views that place literature (from the nineteenth century on) in too direct a descent from the older religion. Even though it may be helpful when discussing English romantic poets, the idea of a prophetic mantle passing from traditional religious shoulders to modern literary ones seems to me, as a general rule, rather misleading. Two points require closer attention here. First, literary aesthetics in the romantic era explored many new avenues and the new literary practices disrupted established modes of relationship between literature and dominant religious beliefs. Second, religion did not just disappear in the nineteenth century to be 'replaced' by literature. It rather developed along new lines. As we shall see, the new aesthetics invaded the religious field and had an impact on religious life. (This may help define what is new about modernity in religion.)

This brings me to my second objective (which is more historiographical): to introduce consideration of French material into the current discussions of 'romantic religion,' or of the new rapport with religion that appears among the writers of the late eighteenth and early nineteenth centuries. French romantic literature seems especially helpful to those who want to stress the cultural innovations of modernity.[4] I also hope that those who have read some of the recent translations from French theorists will welcome an increased access to the literary tradition imbibed by such authors.

My attempt to redress the balance will however use only part of the available evidence.[5] I will look only at the French *literary* history (and even, as we shall see, only at some aspects of it). I will limit myself to five authors who read the Bible – and handled general religious issues – in ways that exhibit a clear break in continuity between what, in brief but vague and ambiguous terms, I shall call the older, religious and the newer, literary reading of Scripture. (In French, only a capital separates 'Scripture' from 'writing': *Ecriture, écriture*. The gap is nevertheless wide.)

Fortunately the basis for any study of the transformed place of Scripture in the Western world has been excellently laid in the now-classical book of Hans Frei, *The Eclipse of Biblical Narrative*. (The singularities of French cultural history are not such as to rule out considerations of it that place it in the context of broader, European phenomena.) This 'eclipse' was the sort of civilizational 'event' that took a century to occur and left no one untouched. Christians had practised a 'realistic narrative reading'; the narrative found between the covers of the book, from Genesis to Revelation, told 'facts.' This 'sacred' history was the only one; all other narratives were inscribed within this meta-narrative. This 'history' is a record of proleptic types and verified prophecies. It is thus a record of fulfilments; it sets a pattern for connected, understandable, oriented history. But this manner of reading the Bible receded under the impact of a variety of factors, historical criticism being first among them. As Frei puts it, 'The narrrative became distinguished from a separable subject matter' which was deemed to be more important.[6] Critical and hermeneutical techniques taught that what the Bible told was not necessarily what 'really' happened; or that the 'real' moral meaning was to be found out behind the surface or apparent meaning; or, finally, that what was in the author's mind was different from what his words irresistibly convey to us now. In each case this other, separable subject matter, the one retrieved by the capable reader, became seen as the only possible source of the true, abiding, 'meaning' of Scripture.

One of the newer readings of Scripture was particularly influential. Robert Lowth (1710–88) published (in Latin, 1753) a series *Lectures on the Sacred Poetry of the Hebrews*. He found 'sublime' poetry in the Hebrew Bible, described its stylistic characteristics, and linked this sort of poetry to 'primitive' culture. The text was translated into most European languages (English 1787, French 1812).[7] Herder read him, of course, and wrote the equally influential treatise *The Spirit of Hebrew Poetry*. In the mind of this Protestant minister, the religious authority of the Old Testament rests on the merits of its poetry, 'the oldest, the simplest, and the most sublime that can be found.' These poetic texts also provide the key to the march of things divine and human.[8] Herder's works too were widely translated (into French by Edgar Quinet in 1827). As Frei puts it,[9] the meaning of the Bible has ceased to be the product of a 'cumulative narrative,' but is the result of the impact made on the modern reader by the ancient spirit of its most potent pages.

One can also add to the influence of this new romantic literary view the broader thrust emerging from the deist tradition and its interest in moral meaning. In response to the increasing shift to an autonomous view of morality, one that did not rest its case on belief in divine commands and sanctions, some interpreters began to allege that what they found in the Bible was a pure, abiding morality. The Ten Commandments, for instance, were said to embody the principles of natural morality. Other interpreters, less soberly rational, preferred to find in the Bible, in the Gospels especially, a 'sublime' morality, which moved and transformed the human heart by expanding its vision. Bayle coined memorable phrases, contrasting flattering and unflattering versions of the divine agency: it is clear to him that when God wishes to instruct mankind, he does not send comets, but virtuous persons, with 'the brilliance of excellent virtues.'[10] Bayle probably meant prophets but Jesus was soon to be included in the list of such messengers. These new sentiments set vast shifts in motion. God does not speak through the events of creation, fall, and redemption narrated in the Bible (a narrative structure that provides a key for reading all subsequent chaotic and disturbing congeries of events), but in morally impressive persons that make an impact on our minds and hearts. The process of reading Scripture is thereby emancipated from its letter, not to be made obedient to the Holy Spirit, but to be placed in a new venue, the human spirit and its historical dynamics.

Some features of the great transformation are conspicuous. Biblical chronology, for instance, is shattered. Chinese and Egyptian dynasties must, inescapably, be dated before the date theologians had commonly set for Adam. Some pieces of literature are older than anything found in the Bible; the impact of this discovery was most potent in the last third of the nineteenth century when the deciphering of cuneiform found flood narratives clearly antecedent to the biblical one. All history used to be confined in biblical history; now biblical history is just a slice of world history. But what can perhaps be called the psychological shift is equally pervasive, and for our purposes, more important. Readers of Scripture are less guided by tradition; they now respond to the 'meaning' they find in the Bible, and the construction of this 'meaning' is the result of new processes occurring, in the historical present, in the readers. The 'value' of the Bible has shifted to the subjective realm. That 'understanding' is an event in self-presence becomes the unquestioned assumption of the new hermeneutics.[11]

But these sweeping, broadly European phenomena do not suffice to characterize what happened to religious reading in France. Three factors are very specific to this country.

1 The definition of classical standards around 1640 effectively drove the Bible out of polite literature. Biblical topics and biblical references became rare or disappeared, as the imitation of the Ancients gained complete sway.[12] With the exception of Tasso, European literature of biblical and Christian inspiration was ignored. *The Divine Comedy* was translated only in 1784 (by Rivarol) and *Paradise Lost* in 1836 (by Chateaubriand). With the Romantics, the Bible made a comeback, after a quasi-absence of at least 150 years.

2 Throughout the eighteenth century, the intense activities of academies and salons strengthened an older trend toward socialization and secularization of the processes of writing. Writers became aware of their public, a critical public. Christian concerns (such as could be voiced by either laymen or clergy) were singularly absent from all the lively literary circles. (Worldly abbés do not count, of course.) Rousseau, who is from Geneva, and wears his religious sincerity on his sleeve, is out of tune in all *salons*. The ability of theologians to lead discussion, or share in it, which Bossuet believed he had and which Fénelon had to some extent, has completely eroded. A tradition of erudition goes on, but chokes with repetition. Likewise with the apologetic tradition; the last, brave attempts are by Protestants, Abbadie (in Amsterdam) and Vernet (in Geneva).[13] As a matter of fact, the only new and intelligent argument Catholics come up with rests on the practice of silence. Abbé Dinouart published in 1771 *L'art de se taire. Principalement en matière de religion.* There is too much talking and writing on religion, he argues; all of it is flawed, impertinent, and useless. When the subject comes up in polite company, only silence is fit.[14]

3 After the Revocation of the Edict of Nantes (1685), France no longer had in its territory learned Protestant voices to bring the Bible to bear on contemporary issues and maintain a public tradition of inquisitive reading of Scripture.[15] The art of civil commentary on the Bible henceforth waned; the ground was abandoned to a rigid alternative: authoritarian commentary (like Bossuet) or purely erudite, historical-critical study, aimed at a small élite of scholars (like Richard Simon). In other words, what is missing is the line of Protestant mediating theologians that can be so amply documented in England and Germany, transitional figures who pour new wine in old wineskins, thrive on elaborat-

ing mediating positions that promote the new under the guise of the old, and insensibly achieve a shift, visible for all to see, from authoritarian to liberal reading of Scripture.

It follows that when the French romantic writers read the Bible and write on it, they renew a lost contact and write with a freer hand; they land more quickly upon radically new positions. Unlike that of their counterparts in England, their relationship to Scripture lacks the constant and intense moral earnestness, the traditional tone of righteousness, that characterizes the Victorians. Matthew Arnold, who allowed that his fellow Britishers were sometimes Philistines and had too much Bible, was sure he was making an important moral and civil statement when he wrote that 'more Bible would do no harm' to the French.[16]

Our study will focus on five French 'romantic' writers: Jean-Jacques Rousseau (1712–78), François-René de Chateaubriand (1768–1848), Charles Nodier (1780–1844), Alfred de Vigny (1797–1863), and Gérard de Nerval (1808–55).

At the outset, let me voice a caveat on their 'romanticism.' English-speaking readers are accustomed to a notion of romanticism that can readily be illustrated only with examples from British and German (and American) literature. Romanticism in France is something else.

As an explicit literary movement romanticism started later in France than in Germany or England.[17] Rousseau is only an honorary Romantic. In the French context it is more helpful to think of him as a Swiss outsider, a revolutionary innovator who introduces new literary themes and practices. (Of our five authors, he alone was born outside of France, citizen of a free republic and raised a Protestant.)

French romanticism is also distinctive in three further aspects. 1. The revolt against classical standards of taste and literary canons could not be a revolt against a foreign yoke, since the French themselves had defined these canons since the seventeenth century. Romanticism thus was not linked with a national revival, and the return to regional roots was only a minor theme. It also had to coexist with a strong and continuing classical tradition. When Victor Hugo articulated in the 1820s the ground for revolt against classical norms, he blamed them for being 'hieratic' while romantic literature was 'demotic' ('democratic' would have been too provocative a term in those years). 2. The French Revolution was not an exciting foreign spectacle to French men and women. They, or their fathers and mothers, had brought it about and struggled through it. The moments of national exultation had been followed by a hard education in political and military realities. Most French Romantics were highly politicized. 3. The travail of democracy was repeated in 1830 and 1848; the political situation remained apparently open and the French commonly felt they had gone farthest (for better or worse) and suffered most in the search for modern social and political institutions.

Our sequence of five authors also makes up a sequence of five generations, even though their dates of birth are not equidistant. (After 1789, the pace of history quickened.) The place of each is defined by his relationship to events in the Great Revolution. Rousseau was idolized during the Revolution (his ashes were transferred to the Pantheon), but in 1793, the year of the execution of the king, he had been dead for fifteen years. In 1793, Chateaubriand was twenty-five; he saw the revolution unfold as a young but grown man. In the same year, Nodier was an impressionable thirteen and witnessed capital executions. When Vigny was thirteen, the year was 1810; French troops were then galloping through Europe, overthrowing feudal structures, redrawing boundaries on a national basis, and imposing the new civil code. (Napoleon stopped short of emancipating the Russian slaves; even when he was in Moscow, a stroke of his pen might not have been enough to do it, but Tolstoy invented a character who wished he had tried.) When Nerval was an adolescent, the epic years were over; he grew up in the dull, prosaic Restoration years. The one exciting political event of his youth was the bourgeois revolution of July 1830; he was then twenty-two, but, like all young men of his generation, he could not be excited by a revolution which, he felt, merely replaced a gerontocracy of old reactionaries with a gerontocracy of aging liberals.

I stress the impact of the Revolution on these literary people not just because of my belief in the importance of the social and political context, but because the Revolution was also a major event in the history of language. What began with the intent of reforming the constitution, promptly undertook to *write* the constitution and embarked upon a flurry of writing new texts with momentous significance. Instead of interpreting law, or revising it, the National Assembly and especially the Convention simply wrote law. For the first time in European history, a group of people consciously emulated the Original Legislators, Lycurgus and Solon (commonly deemed better models than Moses). The Déclaration des droits de l'homme et du citoyen of 1789 is the most notorious text they produced. It is an expansionist, militant statement of universal significance, charting a path for political progress for the benefit of all humankind; in contrast, the American Bill of Rights is a defensive statement: a group of Americans establish ways of protecting themselves against the new government they have just set up.[18] The Revolution moreover witnessed numerous outbursts of political rhetoric. The noises of a new orality filled the air.[19] That the Revolution gave voice to the people and, even more so, to people who claimed to speak on behalf of the people, that it did new and exciting things by just saying them, was bound to give thought to writers – and it flung a challenge to them.[20]

Two of our writers were aristocrats, Chateaubriand and Vigny; both of them as writers broke from those of their class who pretended to go on talking – and writing – as if nothing or little had happened. Rousseau was the only relatively assured commoner. Nodier, in time, did what had to be done to pass in the legitimist ethos of the Restoration years. Gérard de Nerval, the last in our sequence, experienced a worsened form of the estrangement known by Rousseau, but took a nom de plume that sounded aristocratic.

I have selected these five authors because each one of them wrote on or about religion in innovative ways. They were not the only ones of their era to be deeply interested in religion, far from it. Voltaire was obsessed by it, and hardly ever left the subject alone. Balzac held intense views on it. Stendhal was a subtle observer of its political and moral ramifications, and a connoisseur of fine religious sentiment. Baudelaire proclaimed that nothing is as interesting as religions. But my five authors remain singular because something in their literary innovations and experimentations seems intimately connected to their own religiosity, their own attempt to make sense of religion and enlighten their readers on this topic.

Their innovativeness goes back partly but not exclusively to Rousseau's *Confessions*, which gave new impetus and new orientations to the art of autobiographical narrative. Completed in 1770, the *Confessions* was part of a rising trend. Authors offered a new sort of contract to the public: read me, they said in effect, and you will get to know the real me.[21] The real me, emphasized Rousseau, is a religious me; his religious feeling and convictions were sincerely exhibited, and featured as realities that were commonly not properly acknowledged and appreciated, but that could fortunately be made manifest through the practice of complete autobiographical writing in the intimate tone. Rousseau was read by all, and his new linking of intimate voice with expression of religious conviction became pervasive. Chateaubriand, Nodier, and Nerval also wrote autobiographically; they too placed some presentation of their religiosity at the heart of what they had to say about themselves.

Such intrusion of a personal autobiographical voice into religious writing should not be conceived as merely the addition of a new theme (or even of an expansionist new theme) into religious texts. I shall argue that it brought about a profound transmutation of religious writing. It all happens as if the new writers undertake to displace an old and, for some reason, unsatisfactory text. Rousseau does it with a plebeian and Protestant assurance: he knows his heart, he reads his Bible; he never doubts that the old text as read by the orthodox is merely letter and that the rewriting he does is entirely legitimate. Chateaubriand also does his rewriting with some assurance. However, his confidence is not Protestant, but rather aristocratic and enlightened.[22] Men of letters had presented a hostile and garbled account of Christianity. Revolutionaries had tried to abolish the cult, so he reads histories and presents an account of what Christianity is all about, hoping to displace in the minds of educated French men and women accounts that were fragmentary, biased, and ignorant. The Protestant from Geneva and the Catholic from Saint-Malo differ in many points, but each feels able to replace something like an old, decrepit, and misshaped text with a more readable one.[23] Nodier, Vigny, and Nerval write at a time when it is obvious that none of the rewritten texts can take the place which the old one used to have. And yet they try to read the old, lost code and reconstitute something legible.

But there are further innovations, of a more technical sort. Chateaubriand inserted fictions inside a treatise to make a religious point that expository prose seemed helpless to convey. Nodier wrote eccentric and fantastic tales and theorized on the importance of these new genres in an age without belief. Vigny experimented with narratives inside narratives to provoke an interiorized, free examination of beliefs. Nerval included in his *Voyage en Orient* numerous meetings with foreign narrators; each time a new voice presents a different narrative. Not only does Nerval capitalize thereby on what was becoming a popular genre, but also, and more important, he strives to bring about a meeting with foreign civilizations that were becoming known to the public only through colonial wars. He also undertook to write the story of his own coping with insanity and thus to set down the stories that invaded his distraught mind. So the work of our French Romantics in the religious area has an experimental or innovative quality and openly demands literary treatment, and a focus on form rather than content; these authors touch upon old problems but they clearly produce new sorts of texts.

Their innovativeness is particularly evidenced by the fact that they take up religious themes in prose. Rousseau did not write verse. That of Chateaubriand is pitifully bad. (This Enchanter could not chant, or, rather, he sang in prose.) Nodier's few verses are occasional, negligible pieces. By excluding a consideration of verse, we do not lose anything with these three. Some of the best work of Vigny and Nerval was in verse. We will present, therefore, only a truncated view of these two writers. But they wrote in prose what matters to our argument.[24]

First and foremost among the new procedures introduced in the discussion of religion was the art of inserting stories within stories; the authors thereby encouraged a certain distance (which was rapidly to increase.) In their writing little by little myth became more outside than inside the main text.[25] Such authors were thus able to break with the sort of mythical alchemy that traditionally occurred in verse. With their new kind of prose, I will argue, the five authors did not just restate the code as they wrote. (Neither did they just give it new content.) Instead, they achieved a new sort of narrativity, the one, I submit, which became dominant in the modern era and shaped individual relationships to all codes. This study then may help handle one large question raised (but not answered) by Frei's book: What sort of narrativity emerged in the literary spaces opened up by the decline of the biblical narrative?

There is another sort of eighteenth-century development that needs to be mentioned briefly here besides that so ably analysed by Frei. As the Bible lost its use as a narrative of true events, something happened to all prose narratives. Indeed the rise of the novel can be said to have changed all the reading economy. Readers now admit they enjoy reading fictions.[26] Both new developments undermine the belief in the veracity of straight narrative. While biblical readers are informed that as history the Bible is inaccurate and that its narrative is not the really important message it brings, readers of novels accept in some sense the 'message' of narratives but do not necessarily assume thereby that what is narrated really happened. In both cases, the reader of the text does not take the framing of life offered by the narrative entirely at its face value. The 'meaning' of the text is not lodged in its referential value but in the mental events it elicits in the reader. Readers of novels first of all enjoy. If pressed on the issue of truth, they might say any number of things, one of them being that these fictions are truer than truth.

The period around 1800 can indeed be given as the watershed in the history of reading. More people read. Didactic books became fewer; religious books too. The proportion of novels in what people read leaped forward. *Paul et Virginie* and many other novels were best-sellers to a degree that *The Gallic War* never was.[27] People also began to read privately. One might even say reading became an intimate affair. Solemn, liturgical reading aloud of Scripture in church, before the bowed heads of those who hear a law they are expected to practise, ceased to be the model of attentive reading (or hearing). Books lost their status as authorities.[28] Reading practices also relaxed (or lost) the bonds forged in the eighteenth century with public social practices; one ceased to read books to be able to talk with their authors in a salon, or to converse with fellow readers. Solitary cuddling with a 'good book' replaced the older ideals: attention became individual absorption.[29] (Rousseau read his Bible in bed, a form of piety neither Calvin nor Francis of Sales ever condemned, because they did not imagine humans might ever try it.) And attention did not lead necessarily to the public expression of opinion, and certainly not the publishing of learned commentaries.[30]

The shift in the reading of Scripture occurs within a broader shift in reading practices. But the nature of the shift remains along the lines indicated by Frei. The Bible used to be indispensable; it became religiously meaningful.[31] Communally obedient reading of authoritative books (and production of obedient commentary for subsequent readers) gave way to a new form of attention: the individual reader pays heed to the text, either to learn what it reveals about the mentality of past ages, or to consider the way in which it resonates in his or her heart; if readers comment on their reading, they will discuss the history the text documents, or will attempt to express their own subjective responses with sincerity. What they have ceased to do is stay automatically within the representations established by the book, in order to assimilate directly its lessons and apply its teachings; their knowledge *of* the book no longer merges with knowledge gained *thanks to* the book. The book used to be part of the homogeneous territory of knowledge. As a map it was deemed so reliable that it was not seen as a useful contrivance interposed between the knower and the territory. With the new reading, the book becomes a map which one knows is 'only a map'; the knower becomes aware of the gap between map and territory. The reader begins to be in a position to evaluate every book when he or she is finished with it. Knowledge of the book becomes knowledge gained by placing the book in another, presumably broader context of knowledge or experience. The language of the book used to be mainly substance; it has become visible form as well. Reading used to be a largely didactic affair; it has become more of an aesthetic one. Books henceforth do not convey information as much as provide understanding. Clearly much has changed in the reception of books.[32] What readers expect of most of them now is a measure of help in the task of representing life. (And irony becomes a frequent feature: starting with *Don Quixote*, there is a tradition of writing books to show that life is not what books say it is.)

Some might suggest that in the first case the book is read with belief (or faith), while in the second case it is not. There is some merit in the contrast: it used to be taken for granted that reading a book instructed readers and led to their moral improvement. With the new reading, this becomes an open question: do books really change the real, public lives of those who read them?[33] The contrast between faith and unbelief does not, however, tell the whole story. A new sort of belief is at work in the new distanciated reading of the book. The meaning garnered by the reader undoubtedly holds some sway in his or her mind. Therefore, what happens around 1800 should rather be presented as a shift in the meaning of belief.

The French romantic texts we will examine have the advantage of making it clear that moderns must work with a very broad definition of belief, to include even those notions which are but fleetingly entertained in privacy. In an age of political and cultural crisis, of warring among paradigms, credence is not granted only to what is traditionally shared and socially confirmed. Individuals may become completely absorbed in some short-lived and passionate episode. Enormous credence (of some sort) may be granted to the most fleeting notion. True, systems of belief still exist; now they rival each other more manifestly than before and relativize each other – if one can look at them all dispassionately; they may be defined as sets of propositions purporting to define reality and mobilizing individual energies for the handling of it. But besides these systems, beliefs exist also as fragmentary, temporary emotions and motions. These should receive a minimalist definition: they may be described as any disposition to accept a certain way of phrasing things as appropriate. Each time a verbal utterance is opposed to the silent way things have of being what they are, some belief is involved, some bond forged by the self between himself or herself and the way he or she thinks things are or ought to be, and some contract ventured: things will (or may) turn out to be what the enunciator says they are.[34]

Romantic writers explore these practices of belief, which commmonly undermine the vast system of belief established in the ancien régime. The semantic field for the word is thus no longer that established in the eighteenth century by the polarity between what the Church teaches (or what the Bible says) and what sensible opponents object to it. In other words, the phenomenon of belief ceases to be limited to Christian or religious belief. When Rousseau writes that 'the human mind prefers to err rather than not believe anything,'[35] he creates for the word 'belief' a semantic field crowded with everyday beliefs (social, political, philosophical, scientific, religious, and above all 'personal') which rival systems of belief will strive to sort out, organize, and legitimate, if they can.[36] But clearly they can't. The utterance 'I believe' has a very peculiar feature: it can express assurance or doubt, depending on tone and context.[37] The observer of other people's beliefs is commonly prone to attribute to them an opacity and a solidity which they frequently do not have in the lives of those who hold them (or are held by them). The unbeliever believes that the believer believes in God; to most believers, things are a bit more complicated. In any case, Catholics and Protestants in the sixteenth, seventeenth, and eighteenth centuries were not labelled believers, and they did not think they had beliefs as they went about their business of obeying God and having faith in him. So the 'belief' elicited in the course of aesthetic experience must be considered to be only a distant cousin of the 'beliefs' one ordinarily attributes now to religious people. But that there is a family resemblance may be an idea worth keeping.

The prose texts we will examine all strive to keep up with and orient these minute phenomena of belief. With them, the power of a text begins to rest on its tellability rather than its assertability. But this does not diminish the importance of the text, because the discovery – or production – of tellable texts has become of enormous moment. (Autobiographical texts should suffice to establish that.) As the selves lose their location in universal sacred history, they must find their location among the shifting sands of the troubled history that engulfs them along with their contemporaries. This new dialectic between self and history works itself out by means of tellable stories.[38] Through them, individuals figure out what to believe at least about themselves, and come thereby to some understanding of the story of their own, unique lives. Thus through the examination of my five authors, I hope to update, or illustrate in the new conditions of the nineteenth century, this statement of Montaigne: 'We are, I don't know how, double in ourselves, so that what we believe, we don't believe it, and we can't get rid of what we condemn.'[39] Or this statement of Pascal: 'Man is naturally credulous, incredulous, timid, bold.'[40]

I have argued three points so far: the place of the Bible as narrative had clearly changed by the nineteenth century; our five writers introduced innovations in their way of writing about religion (a degree of distanciation being an important part of this); and readers started reading books in a new manner, with new interests. These affirmations lead me to a fourth point, which I phrase as a question: Did these changes in literary practices and aesthetics lead to changes in the religion ordinarily lived by ordinary people? Did the literary voices have an impact on the public religion, on such religions as historians of nineteenth-century France might wish to write about?

Much in fact happened to public religion in France in the aftermath of the Revolution. The principles of 1789 emancipated Protestants and Jews, enabling them to organize and take their place in the national life. (With Protestants the redress had started with the 1787 Edit de tolérance.) The Catholic Church was split during the Revolution by the Civil Constitution of the Clergy; some accepted it, others, the non-jurors, did not. During the persecutions of 1793 martyrs were numerous among the non-jurors; this halo and papal support resulted in a tendency to vilify the memory of the jurors.[41] In the 1820s began a struggle between a new ultramontane outlook and the older, restored Gallican one. The Gallican side suffered many handicaps: the hierarchy was highly aristocratic until 1830, subservient to the state until 1848, and taught a sombre piety.[42]

But all this is institutional history. Let me recall that what is striking about French religious history is the indigenization and territorialization of the sacred. The Crusades brought back important relics from the Holy Land and scattered them throughout French territory. There were numerous indigenous saints, and they were found in peasant families as well as in the Capetian lineage. Embattled and persecuted, the Protestants nevertheless remained loyal to the national king. Kings performed miracles at each coronation, with institutionalized regularity. The nineteenth century was highly aware that the Pope was in Rome, but the Virgin kept appearing in France.

What therefore is most interesting in the aftermath of the Revolution is the new look at religion as a social and civilizational reality.[43] Deep concern for religion as public reality received fresh formulations (and new urgency) with Rousseau's provocative pages on civil religion, which he tended to think could flourish only in small republican states. It also received new life with Rousseau's persistent illustration of religious feeling as an inescapable anthropological fact. Chateaubriand gave a great shove to all minds by presenting Catholic Christianity as a civilizing force. Finally, religio-social theories flourished with all the post-revolutionary ruminations on the rupturing and rebuilding of social bonds and on causes of civil violence and ways to prevent its return.[44] Our five authors, each in his own way, handled the whole sweep of such public religious issues.

But our authors also contributed to the rise of the new, private, romantic religiousness. Rousseau is again the precursor and founder of a new religiosity (at times somewhat weepy) among those who read books. Chateaubriand, who praised popular religiousness and folklore, contributed to a rebirth of Catholic religiousness (and kept some distance from it). Nodier, Vigny, and Nerval settled in a stance that was mainly some version of distanciation. Meanwhile the ultramontane movement, intransigent in it opposition to the state and to liberal ideas, was more tender with individual consciences and introduced a gentle piety. But it would be a grave mistake to see our authors as contributing to the torrent of religious sentimentality that swept the century. They were learned, and they were serious. They tried to tell the story of their lives; they also saw it as an austere task in difficult times, requiring much thought. It is in such a context, I believe, that they drew upon religious language.

It is worthwhile to note that most of their conscious departures from classical norms involved them in religious issues. They rejected the rigid choice between silence on one's hidden weaknesses and the veiled couching of them in the traditional terms of a Christian confession of sin; thus they made admissions of malaise that transgressed previous canons of propriety and taste. They also ventured into more vivid portrayals of passion, more tormented expressions of despair and negative feelings, and other topics that were kept off-limits by the classical authors with their religious and aesthetic standards. They pointed out that these very themes are those handled by the Bible (and Shakespeare). Thus they could claim, with entire good faith, that they were more Christian, or more attuned to Christian realities, than the classical or eighteenth-century authors. (A few priests took pen in hand to endorse these views, even though the Gallican hierarchy took its cues from the French Academy and stayed staunchly faithful to the classical canons of style.)[45] So it is their boldness that brought the romantic writers into biblical territory. Once there, of course, they handled the themes in their own way.

But as our writers position themselves somewhere within the terrain of French religious life, they do it in a literary manner. They invade the public religious scene not just with their beliefs, but also with their aesthetics. The notion that there is a stable (Christian) paradigm for telling what happens in the course of lives recedes rapidly. Rousseau is confident that he writes his confession in the biblical vein, but he interprets the Bible in the light of his own experience, an experience the like of which has never been narrated before. (He also gets involved in the attempt to effect a shift in public opinion: he wants to discredit misleading accounts others give of him; he wants to wrestle with the uniqueness of a misunderstood case. Inevitably readers are asked to choose which of the two parallel stories they wish to believe.) Chateaubriand writes movingly of admirable features of Christianity, but breaks his panegyric with poignant expressions of estrangement. The poet's intimate voice, we hear, cannot echo all the great biblical affirmations.

The Revolution projected such a conflict of stories on a grandiose screen. After 1789–93, French writers were accustomed to rapid narrative clashes. The new revolutionary discourse tried to establish itself as a new canon, a secular, worldly canon charting the path to political and social progress. The Restoration tried to repress this rhetoric. Reactionary writers tried to establish a counter-rhetoric. In vain.[46] The liberal press kept a muted form of it alive. The three of our authors who heard the revolutionary speeches and saw the popular impact of the new rhetoric (Chateaubriand, Nodier, Vigny) considered the speeches to be sources of illusions. But they did not try to silence these voices from the past, or establish a new dogmatic narrative. The experience of a rapid succession of incompatible stories led them to a stance toward narrativity. They tried to produce an alternative, more reflexive style of address.[47]

Because our writers chart their paths among the conflicting accounts of history and find their voices in writing about things earthly and heavenly, the literature they produce can indeed be styled a new religious text. Matters of belief are being reconstructed, from the ground up. Human writing, which usually disclaimed any revelatory content, becomes intrinsically revelational (even though our authors reject any

notion of revelation dogmatically held or buttressed by authority).[48]
What therefore may become manifest in our sequence of five writers is
the sweeping extent of the religious transformation that occurred in
Europe – and the need for redefinition of the word 'religion,' the very
word used in this preface with such apparent confidence. The contrast
drawn between pre-romantic religion and romantic religiosity remains
helpful, but only if it prefaces an examination of the actual romantic
texts and a look at the relationship they tried to establish with the
reader.

Among the many transformations that occurred, perhaps the most
profound is one not immediately visible: the privilege of promulgating
the interiorized command, of giving the inner revelation, ceases to belong to God alone. The French moralists had, ever since the day of
Montaigne, great confidence in their ability to convey through constant
observation how all things human should be handled. Rousseau and
his followers extend this confidence to some of the things divine. Here
too they find the key to insight within themselves. There is in Balzac a
brief text that expresses in a nutshell the new, full extent of the authority attributed to the self as narrator of all things in heaven and on earth:
'I read somewhere that God brought Adam the Giver of Names into the
world saying: *Thou art man!* Might we not say that he also brought the
Teller of Tales into the world saying: *Thou art Tale!*'[49]

There is in *Emile* an autobiographical page that can be treated as a
parable of this new self-image as heroic coiner of tales.[50] Discussing the
fear children usually have of the dark, Rousseau tells how one evening
in Bossey he was given the key and challenged to go into the church
next to the Lambercier's home and fetch the Bible left in the pulpit. In
spite of his considerable fright, he succeeded. He was alone in the dark
but he had the key, and the Bible was there. Our next four writers are
not children of the manse and do not have quite the confidence to enter
the sanctuary. And, with the exception of Chateaubriand, they are not
sure there is anything worthwhile left in the temple. And yet, somehow, they strive to emulate Rousseau's feat. They fear the dark but
fancy there is some code somewhere that could be got hold of. There
can be a book (or there will be a book) that is worth working for.
Writing a book – and reading a book – becomes then a metaphor for the
very process of making sense of life. In this way our modern writers
begin to write in such a way as to proffer themselves the words of
comfort that Deuteronomy attributes to God, gracious words which
displace any notion of the divine commandment as a distant law,

always measuring us and finding us wanting, words which also convey to readers that they have the taste for truth in their own hearts and mouths:

For this commandment which I command you this day is not too hard for you, neither is it far off. It is not in heaven that you should say, ' Who will go up for us to heaven, and bring it to us, that we may hear it and do it?' Neither is it beyond the sea, that you should say, ' Who will go over the sea for us, and bring it to us, that we may hear it and do it?' But the word is very near you; it is in your mouth and in your heart, so that you can do it.   (Deut.30: 11–14 [RSV])

1

Confession without Confessor: Rousseau

The work of Jean-Jacques Rousseau (1712–78) is, for many reasons, an indispensable starting-point for an examination of the interplay between literary aesthetics and religious belief. His 1761 novel, *Julie ou la Nouvelle Héloïse*, presented the domestic life of middle-class Protestants and shook up a reading public accustomed to fictitious characters who lived in a Catholic world, decent aristocrats, or adventurous commoners. All his books were promptly read all over Europe. Kant hailed their influence on his thinking, indeed on his behaviour: Rousseau taught him, he wrote, 'to honour men.'[1] At the other end of the Continent, Jean Ranson, merchant in La Rochelle, eagerly purchased every one of Rousseau's books and wrote effusively on what these books meant to him; but his form of praise did not entail stating exactly what difference, if any, they made in the visible part of his life; most probably they helped him shape his conjugal and family life.[2] It is thus clear that, besides the new themes that found expression in Rousseau's work, a new voice helped give expression to vastly shared tendencies of the age. This chapter has accordingly four parts: I first give an exposition of the relevant content in Rousseau's work; in the next two parts I focus on unique features of his style and of his religiousness; finally I attempt to draw some conclusions on the significance of his work for subsequent religious writing.

'Man is born free; and everywhere he is in chains.'[3] With such a sentence Rousseau announces as obvious fact something that, in reality, was a recent discovery: Europeans had just seen – or started to believe – that culture is a historical phenomenon. Man, they now think, is living in a man-made environment and is shaped by it. A radical question is also asked about the quality of this environment, and Rousseau undertakes to say how it came to be. His new ways of looking at man, his nature and destiny, is articulated by means of a story. Man used to be a certain kind of being; he then became different. Five original themes emerge in Rousseau's narration.

1 The hiatus between nature and freedom: 'The principle of any action is to be found in the will of a free being.'[4] With this affirmation of human freedom Rousseau destroys the world in which ethics, politics, and religion, as well as literature and philosophy, were traditionally cast. Man is invited to become aware of his will (rather than contemplate and submit to a necessary order). Freedom ceases to be primarily associated with a certain type of political constitution, the states which have 'free' citizens as well as slaves; it ceases to be associated with complicated philosophical or theological discussions of the 'freedom of the will'; it becomes an immediate power of individual self-assertion, taken as self-evident. The unity and coherence of Rousseau's work hangs upon this affirmation of an existential freedom proper to man. The animal is enclosed in his nature but man is not. The ancient view of human nature as a dynamic, end-oriented norm is replaced by an entirely new one: human nature amounts only to a simple, animal-like functioning, which can be posited as existing in the origins of man but does not hold the key to an understanding of man's present condition. The essence of man is rather to be seen as a negative freedom: men differ from animals thanks to the absence of instinctual determination for their conduct. The new vision of man has something exalting. 'It is a great and beautiful sight to see man coming out of nothingness so to speak by his own efforts, and lifting himself above himself.'[5] It is easy for us to point out that the state of nature rejected by Rousseau is not what the ancients meant by life according to nature. The contrast made by Rousseau nevertheless takes hold upon the mind; what men freely make of themselves and of each other becomes the paramount question.

2 Historical becoming: Rousseau undertakes to show how human beings made innovations in their behaviour. The need to work, the birth of society, and the development of reason are presented as simultaneous occurences. Social man is denatured man. Human beings *became* rational. Socialization is a genuine metamorphosis of man.

One must first of all stress the convincing power of this description of the basic metamorphosis: 'amour de soi,' self-preserving affirmation, is being overlaid with 'amour propre,' that is, the 'fureur de se distinguer.' Man in society has an image of himself, which he compares with his view of others and which he 'needs' to protect; there is henceforth a quality of strain and competitiveness in self-love. There is no telling what desires human beings may develop in their competitive social situation and what they may make of themselves as they pursue their desires. Free human beings are perfectible; they can also deprave themselves. Rousseau offers numerous such genetic analyses of human development. A penetrating one is that of the birth of language. Starobinski draws attention to this momentous innovation: 'Rousseau presents as "oeuvre humaine" what the tradition had defined as original gift of nature or of God.'[6]

3 The genesis of moral evil: The account of the birth of reason and of the rise of society also includes an account of the genesis of moral evil. Man in society lives 'outside himself'; he has lost himself. While Rousseau uses the word 'alienation' with the meaning it had acquired in jurisprudence, namely, the sale or surrender of a piece of property or of a right, he is the first to start the analysis of social alienation that was to be a recurrent theme of modern intellectual life. He even launches most of the basic themes. Property causes man to put himself in the things he appropriates. Social life causes man to accept the opinion which others have of him. The master and the slave deprave each other. The effort to dominate over others stems from a desire to compensate for a lost happiness.

Rousseau thus always holds that the social condition is both a development and a maiming of the human potential: rationality itself is an ambiguous achievement. The very crises he observes in his society are symptoms of a conflict which ruins mankind; social life secretes moral evil.[7] 'L'être' and 'le paraître' are at odds with each other. Life in society includes dissemblances *necessarily*. Rousseau tells a story of loss of innocence, of fall into man-made suffering and human oppression.

Let us note here that Rousseau is making use of biblical metaphors. (There will be more discussion of this later.) But he is not prevented thereby from breaking with a whole tradition of Christian interpretation of the biblical account of the origin of sin: his letter to Christophe de Beaumont makes clear that he has no use for the idea of original sin. How then can Rousseau reconcile his belief that man is 'naturally good' with his perception that 'everything degenerates in the hands of man but not in his heart'?[8] The self thus suffers evil rather than commits it. Rousseau has such confidence in this permanent goodness of the heart that, commenting on the story of Genesis 3, he excuses, even commends, the spirit of revolt: the divine command is said to be 'a useless and arbitrary prohibition,' and to kick against it is not vicious in itself but rather 'in conformity with the order of things and the good constitution of man.'[9]

There is of course no devil in Rousseau's scenarios. The fall is entirely man's work, and man can undo it. Man is captive but can break loose. So the Rousseau who can give to social vices the appearances of inevitability can also write that 'these vices do not so much belong to man as to badly governed man'.[10] And Rousseau clearly distances himself from all the 'déclamateurs' who repeat that society is corrupt by claiming to have unveiled the cause of its corruption. (He believed that his own social marginality made him a privileged observer.) The account of a fall from a state of nature into a state of culture includes the key to the moral ascent of man. (The state of innocence is therefore amoral or premoral rather than properly moral.) In social life, conscience is aroused and man begins to judge his society.[11]

4 The account of division and separation can also show the road toward reintegration. Baczko argues that Rousseau analyses the contradictions which tear social man apart, in order to overcome them.[12] Gouhier finds Rousseau asking a new question: Shall we have the history we have had so far, or shall we have another one? It seems somehow that mankind entered into the wrong history accidentally, not unlike a traveller who takes the wrong turn.[13] There is thus a new emotional climate in Rousseau's work: man is invited to undertake afresh the realization of missed opportunities. Schiller goes clearly beyond Rousseau's explicit meaning, but he remains within the same climate when he writes that mankind acts now as if it had to start its existence afresh.[14] Rousseau believes in regeneration: a currently powerful moral evil can be defeated by a moral conversion. To the destructive social denaturation must succeed a creative and moral denaturation.

The 'vision of Vincennes' (1749), which launched Rousseau upon his authorship, climaxes in the expression of a dominant passion, which is enthusiasm for 'truth, freedom and virtue.'[15] Virtue is the key notion: freedom introduced turbulence, moral virtue will restore unity. The dynamic movement, started when man broke from nature, goes on: freedom is not curbed, but the movement of expansion will, when virtuous, proceed without division. The permanent goodness of man manifests itself by a requirement for unity, by a longing for reunion which never leaves man.[16] Thus Rousseau believes he can 'derive from the evil itself the remedy which will cure it.'[17] Moral freedom will find the art of expressing itself and of limiting itself. In the age when freedom and laws cooperate, man is morally transformed so that he can be happy in society. Henceforth men make history knowingly, consciously.[18]

The prodigious effort to overcome the evil suffered – and committed – by social man takes a first form in active, civic virtue. Law and education will allow man to prosper in association with his fellow man. The *Social Contract* offers the formula for resolving at the political level the tension between human nature and social convention. *Emile* then offers a plan for social redemption through reformed pedagogy.

There is, however, another side to Rousseau: deterioration is so far gone that he despairs of restoring republican virtues and republican happiness in most societies. His hopes are really robust only about Corsica, Poland, and the more remote valleys of Switzerland.[19] There is also in him a tendency to substitute 'personal apology' for 'speculative thought.'[20] Virtue still recaptures the lost unity, but virtue in this second form becomes withdrawn, private, even hidden. Social alienation remains entire, but the self recaptures itself wholly in confession and reverie.

5 Providence: In a famous passage Kant announces that Rousseau, along with Newton, 'justified' the providence of God. 'Rousseau was the first to discover in the variety of shapes that men assume the deeply concealed nature of man and to observe the hidden law that justifies Providence.'[21] Rousseau himself is quite aware that his account of the genesis of evil resolved the problem of theodicy in a new manner that completely shunts aside the complex solutions so carefully worked out by Leibniz. God and man alike are innocent. 'Providence made man free, not for him to do evil, but for him to do good by choice. Moral evil is undoubtedly our work.' 'Take away man's work and all is good.'[22]

Evil is thus an accident of history; it is not the fault of 'essential man.' It results from a passion on the part of man for that which is exterior, but man can always go back to himself. And, *mirabile visu*, this very phenomenon of fall and corruption initiates the reascent or return to innocence. Fallen man is perfectible man. Society corrupts man, but like Satan in the book of Job, society never ceases to be an instrument of moral good. In society human beings are moralized, either in discovering their rational will and civic virtue or in discovering each other's genuine hearts and withdrawn virtue. Becoming is the magic key. Man who has a history is man who has lost himself – and who is in the process of finding himself again. 'Let us derive from the evil itself the remedy that will cure it.' Moral evil is being made into an instrument for a greater good. In this moral universe the very idea of God's being morally inadequate is as preposterous as it was in the days of Job (more preposterous even, since now we *know* how God made Leviathan).

This new theodicy manages to proclaim the innocence of God by making history a radically contingent affair. Evil in history is a human fact which men can remedy to their advantage, and it is only that. It is not a crisis in a divine plan. Man for Rousseau has no divinely appointed destiny, only a history. No providential God watches over – and manipulates – his progress. The problem of theodicy is solved because God lets men write their own history. There is an important correlate: Rousseau has no faith in history; progress is not inevitable.[23] And there is a significant departure from biblical views: man can become, through his own virtuous efforts, something other, better than what he 'originally' was.[24]

Once launched by Rousseau, these five themes pursue a brilliant philosophical career. The works of Kant and Hegel are evidence enough. But what I want to stress here is that Rousseau offers a new, compelling story, and that a story is all that can be offered as theoretical answer to the problem he set for himself. Furthermore, his story does not result from a painstaking survey of all known historical facts. It results from an act of intuitive penetration; an act of imagination, a fictitious account, is given which, brilliantly, instantly, makes apparent sense of all the facts known to the minds of concerned people.[25] How else can one theorize about contingent, free development in time?[26] This work of imagination is profoundly satisfying, and not just for epistemological reasons. Man was provoked (instinct, desire, opportunity); he invented a response, which was disastrous; he lost all control over the consequences of his behaviour – but he remained innocent through it all, captive but not guilty. Society, a creature no one before Rousseau thought of placing in the dock, is responsible. As Rousseau accuses society, he absolves himself.[27]

We also find in Rousseau a new account of the power of the imagination, because he is quite conscious that he lets imagination preside over the elaboration of his account of God and man.

At the outset, Rousseau is aware that the imagination has highly ambiguous powers: 'Such is the power of imagination and its influence that it gives rise not only to virtues and vices, but also to the goods and the woes of human life and that it is the manner in which one surrenders to it that makes men good or evil, happy or miserable down here.'[28] The role of the imagination is seen to be particularly decisive in the area of theology, which has so many insoluble issues. 'Impenetrable mysteries surround us everywhere ... we think we have intelligence to pierce them, but we have only imagination.'[29]

Moreover, Rousseau is entirely aware of the imaginative nature of language itself, which is, by its nature, fictitious (Paul de Man would say aberrant[30]). He can describe semantic transfers and analyse the role of imagination in social relations. (His favourite examples are of erotic love – the feelings associated with which he compares with religious feelings – but as we shall see, the point can be extended to cover the mental life of large groups.) 'Love is but an illusion; it creates for itself another world as it were; it surrounds itself with objects that do not exist, or to which it alone confers reality; and since it expresses all its sentiments with images, its language is always figurative ... Just as the enthusiasm of devotion borrows from the language of love, so the enthusiasm of love also borrows from the language of devotion.'[31]

There is here a sweeping change; imagination to Rousseau is no longer what it was to all rationalists, namely, a disease, a sort of pollution of the mind by the senses. It is an unavoidable fact in the life of those who speak; better, it is a much-needed corrective to the mechanical nature of 'rational' mental operations. What reason argues is so neatly constructed that it never fits the realities of life. Those undertaking to write 'rational' autobiography would lend their narratives a false and artificial order.[32] This is well shown by 'The Venetian Story,' Rousseau's account (*Confessions*, book 8) of his days as a secretary in the French embassy in Venice; this autobiographer does not wish to narrate what was visible to all, or even what could have been visible to all, but to record his feelings, or tell the story of his soul; he thus writes the account of an interior life as organized by the imagination.[33] The imagination may also be employed consciously as a power that can create a world in which human beings finally become happy. Civilized man is highly reflective, self-conscious, torn. His loving aspirations find no support in the world. He experiences reality through conflicts and contradictions. But in his imaginative life unity is restored.[34]

We may well label this recapturing of unity as merely psychological magic. But to the imaginative person, to open doors to what lies beyond the real is to gain access to a 'spiritual' world that is real. Rousseau is quite firm: what is imagined tends to become real; to live in the imagination is to anticipate one's own immortality. This 'unreality' *is* reality.[35] When social fictions are seen for what they are, literature can be seen to be, as H.R. Jauss puts it, 'anti-fiction.'[36]

Rousseau is also quite lucid as to his own recourse to the imagination. Trust in the imagination is rooted in his temperament and lies at the source of his art. 'My stubborn head does not want to improve; it wants to create.' 'Nothing is beautiful except what is not.'[37] As a child, he became absorbed in reading, and his imagination caught fire in the reading of Plutarch. He seemed to become himself as he started to read. As he put it, 'It is from that time that I date without interruption my consciousness of myself.' As an older boy, he played comedies with his cousin; when tired of that, he moved on to composing sermons; he loved sermons, he tells us.[38] Rousseau is thus quite unrepentant: there is no self, there can be no self without imaginative life. And he gives a free rein to his imagination. *Les rêveries d'un promeneur solitaire* informs us that he narrated things forgotten, 'as they should have been.'[39]

What we find in Rousseau's work is thus a uniquely self-conscious invasion on the part of an individual imagination into philosophical and theological language as well as into autobiographical language. Rousseau does not merely launch new themes around the notion of human freedom, he uses a new freedom in writing and writes with a new voice. His talent, he says, lies in his heart, not in his pen. Writing, he keeps stressing, cannot be a *métier* with him; it must be the expression of a moral passion. This *homme de lettres* can write only under some urgent and intimate pressure.[40] Thus readers find in his pages a new, vibrant appeal to intimate experience, and a desire to move by invoking it. It in a nutshell, we hear in his work the voice of sincerity.[41]

Numerous factors contribute to the making of this new voice. Rousseau enters the field of political theory with a lower-town Genevan background and therefore a plebeian egalitarian passion. His first major publications, the *Discours sur les sciences et les arts* and *Discours sur les origines de l'inégalité*, recaptured the power of ancient, public eloquence. (His sincerity is never clumsy.) A sharp moral demand is made: the social order is to be shaped in such a manner as to allow full spiritual authenticity to all. This demand is sounded by someone who will suffer no compromise. If society cannot 'provide' such authenticity for all, Rousseau wants nothing of it and will withdraw from it. As he tells us later in his life, his soul got accustomed to leaving the place where his body was located; he ended up 'nourishing his heart only with his own chimaeras.'[42] Rousseau speaks of 'justice for all' with the rigour of one who would rather have authenticity for himself alone than modest improvements for the many. A significant text from a fragment on public happiness puts the matter well: 'Make man one and you will make him as happy as he can be. Give him entirely to the State, or leave him entirely to himself, but if you divide his heart you tear him apart.'[43] The alternative is sharp: egalitarian order or romantic isolation. 'One must be absolutely like everyone else, or absolutely like oneself.'[44]

Frequently Rousseau prefers what we may call the withdrawn virtue to the civic one. (Ever lucid, he allows that, too lazy to be virtuous, his own wisdom lies in understanding his own self.) The sight of his own conscience, its undisturbed unity, is the sight of a world without shadows: it awards him the deepest satisfaction. His ever-renewed good faith justifies him. Writing is so soothing. His *Confessions* is an exemplary book, and he is confident that he can appear before the last judge with it in his hand.[45]

The sharpness of the contrast between the withdrawn and the civic virtue must not hide the dialectic relationship. For Rousseau solitude can be redemptive. The solitary self is released from the world of social 'appearances' and begins to find the way to man as he is in himself. When he emerges from his solitude his voice has the ring of sincerity but also the persuasive power of those who, ostensibly, have seen through social lies and pursue no selfish interests.[46]

His fiction was thus uniquely successful in establishing a sort of complicity between writer and reader, individuals who do not meet and yet privately understand each other. While his two *Discours* and *Le Contrat Social* nourished a whole new generation of philosophers, *La Nouvelle Héloïse* (six volumes) entered countless bourgeois homes. In this epistolary novel, readers become acquainted with the sentimental and domestic life of socially stable middle-class Protestants. Their status is secure, and so is the supply of money. (We understand that it is modest because the needs are modest; still, they have enough servants.)[47] Unlike in *Le paysan parvenu* or *Manon Lescaut*, the drama does not come from social ascension and downfall, but only from adventures that loving hearts (and bodies) can occasion for each other. Behind the torrent of overflowing interiority, we discern the already-familiar overall human story. Julie committed a sin of passion, but the blame for her fall is laid at the door of her despotic father; through her own effort, she reascends to marriage, acknowledged virtue, and domestic happiness. True sentimentality emerges as a new epoch-making norm: it offers the promise of happiness in what are acknowledged to be inevitably adverse social conditions.[48]

Emile starts ostensibly as a treatise on education. Someone speaks in the fist person; it could be the author of a *mémoire*. But the text insensibly veers toward the novel. In Book 4, the person saying 'I' introduces the testimony of a young Protestant who met with a wise priest in Savoy and inserts a long 'profession of faith' heard from the 'ideal' priest.[49] (Readers are explicitly informed that in being given the testimony of an absent priest and not of the 'author,' they are freer to assess as they please the sentiments set forth in the profession.)[50] In Book 5 this 'author' has become quite visibly a character, the pedagogue interacting with his pupil – and with the latter's fiancée. And in the end we are told that this account of a model education is 'le roman de la nature humaine.'[51]

Both these texts thus invite readers to meet people rather than ideas. But these fictitious people embody something that many wished to see represented. Darnton informs us that the Nantes merchant was very concerned to get the best edition, the *ipsissima verba* of his 'cher ami Jean-Jacques.' He also informs us that the Baron de la Sarraz ordered his household servants not to enter the room while he read *La Nouvelle Héloïse*; he wanted to weep at his ease. Such readers aspire to heart-to-heart communion with an author they don't expect to meet.[52] Darnton suggests that such readers come to read the novel, 'the most suspect form of literature,' 'as if it were the Bible.'[53]

Rousseau himself invites a new reading. He writes for *La Nouvelle Héloïse* two meandering, equivocating prefaces. First, he claims to be only editor of the letters (the conventional opening for epistolary novels) but then adds that he knows the area and has never heard there of people with the names of the protagonists, thus making more complicated the conventional question, Are these *real* letters or not? Then he tells us that in a less corrupt age, he would not have published the book, apparently catering to the views of those who see works of 'fiction' as immoral. But then he urges the reader to forget the author (or editor) and immerse himself or herself in the letters 'as if they were really the effusion of innocent hearts at the foot of the Alps.'[54] We cannot help but read the novel with the assumption that solitary identification with these (fictitious) people is, in the current circumstances of addiction to fictions, morally salutary after all. The reader who, like Julie, has fallen and needs the immoral stimulation of fictitious narratives, can, after all, reascend to virtue by reading proper sentimental fictions.[55]

The impact of this new content, new voice, and new reading is most powerful in texts handling religious issues. *La Nouvelle Héloïse* is in this respect devilishly clever – or beautifully crafted. French censors had a tough time with the young Protestants who interact in the novel. How could they expect them to utter only proper Catholic sentiments in matters religious? They are in Switzerland and the book was (ostensibly) published in Holland.[56] Catholic theologians and apologists were floored by what they labelled the seductive tone of this new enemy. Reading Rousseau was promptly seen as identical to reading libertine and licentious novels.[57] Not surprisingly there are in Rousseau's texts numerous expressions of sincere religious feelings. The opening page of the *Confessions* informs us of what Rousseau will say to God as he presents his book on Judgment Day: 'I have unveiled my inmost self even as Thou has seen it.'[58] An earlier age would have been horrified at the arrogance of this statement, or amused at the extent of the self-deception. Rousseau's reader somehow totally forgets that, traditionally, at the time of judgment, God (or Saint Peter) consults the great book in which the balance of our deeds is written. The soul of the deceased is confronted with the full and reliable account of his or her life; the soul is informed and does not do the informing. But Rousseau manages to achieve surreptitiously a complete reversal and still keep a pious feeling.[59] What he has just invented is the art of making a satisfactory confession without needing a confessor (or without requiring the public recitation of a confession of sins and the public listening to words of forgiveness). The very writing of the confession includes the presentation of the excuses and ensures the absolution. The salient feature is that the confession is *written* in the peace of solitude. Stendhal (and probably many priests) knew what to think of that: he told the story of an unusual penitent, a young man who came to the confessional with a written-out confession. After a while, his confessor grew wise to the practice and forbade it: 'You enjoy your sins a second time by writing them in this manner.'[60]

There is help in assessing this religious sincerity in Starobinski's analysis; he begins by referring to Hegel's pages on the intimate conviction treasured by the beautiful soul: 'The content of the language spoken by the good conscience is the self which knows itself as essence; its language expresses nothing but this.'[61] *Vitam impendere vero* becomes *vitam impendere sibi*. The autobiographical insight into oneself is a transposition of the divine search of the heart; through it all duality is gone and one is known (by oneself this time) better than one (ordinarily) knows oneself, and certainly better than other humans can know one. Conscience (or consciousness – in French the two words are the same) experiences, in itself, the source of its unity.

Nothing manifests this 'discovery' better than the literary voice of Rousseau's last work, published posthumously, *Les rêveries du promeneur solitaire*. The narration of his conflicts with other human beings moves into an account of his conquest of happiness. Others tried to make him miserable and forced him into solitude; but solitude became the occasion for peace and fulfilment. He discovered how sweet it is to converse with his own soul; by writing 'rêveries' of his happy moments, he can, whenever he reads his text, taste the enjoyment again.[62] The work was carefully composed, and written over a period of time,[63] but the fiction is presented that it is not at all a work of art but 'a sort of unpolished self-communion.'[64] And the fiction works: the reader feels privileged to enter into the inner communion of this individual. Speaking, or rather writing, becomes, apparently, an immediate experience as well as the means of a mediation. The writer communes with his inner source and meets the other human being with unfailing success; the singular acquires a universal significance. This language is not aimed at anything, or at any one. It *is* the authentic self authentically communing with itself and restoring its unity. 'One can say that [Jean-Jacques] has been the first to live in archetypal manner the dangerous pact of the I with language; the "new covenant" in which man makes himself word.'[65] We have only Rousseau's word that he is innocent and we are made to feel, confidently, that this is all we need.

Starobinski's severe judgment is probably justified: as he points out, Rousseau repeatedly proves himself incapable of accepting situations of reciprocity; showing himself 'as he is' is all he feels he needs to do; let the others draw the inevitable conclusion.[66] Paul de Man also shows how Rousseau manages to obscure the fact that while his misdeeds are empirically visible and public, his excuses are not; he writes them (for himself, for us) instead of presenting them to the people he hurt or harmed. Thus, on his excuses, we have only his word, and we are seduced into believing that by understanding them, we understand all we need to understand.[67] A sincere man is unbeatable; he plays by his own rules.[68]

In such pages, Rousseau manages to give a completely self-authenticating tone of religious seriousness to his assured and purely subjective sincerity. Like many others in his century, Rousseau frequently discovered an unbridgeable gap between the so-called rational demonstrative basis that was being offered to uphold religious belief and the unshakeable certitude characteristic of the earnest believer. Alongside what are to him the very shaky certitudes of the theologians, he always places, entirely distinct from them, the unshakeable confidence of the individual heart. And there is no doubt in the mind of this Protestant: genuine religion is to be found in what the heart feels and knows, rather than in the beliefs philosophers and theologians squabble about. (The Christian religion rests on so many good and persuasive reasons, the good priest from Savoy assures us, why should we excite ourselves to invent doubtful ones?)[69]

But what the heart knows is no longer what a catechized individual appropriated of the tradition; it is rather what the heart came to feel as it tried to make sense of its total life experience. (The distinction should not, of course, be absolute: there are some Catholic and many Protestant precedents for rooting the theological enterprise in the autobiographical one. It still remains true that with Rousseau 'what the heart knows' becomes exclusively rooted in biography as mulled over in solitude.) On her deathbed, Julie makes the only confession of faith that sincere people can require: she states that she may often have been wrong but says, 'I have always believed what I said I believed.'[70] No one is henceforth to blame the heart for not accepting shared belief, as long as the heart remains sincere. We are not responsible for what reason dictates to us or what beliefs we can hold, but only for what the will chooses. In the words of a letter addressed to a priest, 'I sincerely look for what is true and good. I do not believe but I want to believe, and want it with all my heart. Faithful to the faith, in spite of my reason ... I am more faithful than if I was convinced.'[71]

In command of an unyielding sort of sincerity, Rousseau can make some unusual statements, such as 'I am the only man in France who believes in God.'[72] He can also make some decisive interventions in the area of public religion. D'Alembert, he argues, committed a serious breach in writing that Geneva's ministers were Socinians: nothing they wrote or said publicly warrants such a label; and if the ministers have private sentiments, they should have the right to keep them quiet or express them in their own words. How can D'Alembert – or anyone else – undertake to state the faith of others?[73] Rousseau's letter to Mgr de Beaumont, archbishop of Paris, makes a powerful and systematic demonstration of the corruption arising from a required religious orthodoxy. Thus Rousseau's way of expressing religious feeling leads to a new method of evaluating religious doctrines and institutions. At the outset Rousseau sees much of what passes for religion as mere cultural trappings. Rousseau's 'discovery' of culture is therefore accompanied by a discovery of religion as 'only culture,' made up of human 'testimonies' and 'ceremonies.'[74] He debunks this historical religion, in the name of a vital link with God, as too human. Why should God have no other way to reach him except through books containing what men have said about what God had said to Moses?

The lived experience of the individual as narrated by the individual to himself or herself is thus seen to contain the near totality of religious phenomena. Religious themes become for all practical purposes a dimension of biography.[75] Sacred history becomes appropriated and monopolized by the self.[76] The sacred shifts to a new home: it becomes lodged in individual and unique experience. With Rousseau, who has suffered so much, the experience of restored unity, the communing with his deep nature, is experienced as a grace. Rousseau himself repeatedly speaks of it as of a gift of grace. For the traditional scheme of nature and grace, Rousseau substituted that of history and 'nature' – 'nature' this time meaning the essential goodness with which the self can commune in 'gifted' moments. What used to be called human nature in need of redemption is history. What used to be called grace is for historical persons the imaginative return to their own deep nature, which is an intimately felt unity. (The 'supernatural' is a 'super-historical' experience.) There is little in the Christian tradition that would warrant calling such experiences religious. Rousseau, however, convinces many that they are more religious than anything else that passes for religion.

The conclusions seem inescapable. Whether he is reconstituting the origins of inequality or confessing his faith in Providence, Rousseau is creating a literary myth. His imagination provides him with an account of the underlying unity both in the history of humankind and in his own biography. The real and the imagined are reconciled in literature, that is, in a manner of writing in which private language and common language merge. The very writing of the myth restores the unity. The nature of this literary activity is most manifest in the autobiographical writing, from the *Confessions*, through *Rousseau juge de Jean-Jacques*, to the *Rêveries*. His life is made into more than a novel; narrated, it becomes a virtuous model, a redemptive exemplar of lost and restored unity. The Rousseau of the *Rêveries* recaptures himself; he invents himself; he becomes entirely himself. (Apart from the act of writing he is lost, victimized, and beside himself.) As he writes, he keeps lying, or remaking himself into someone other than he was or passed as, and he keeps finding himself sincere – and happy – in the process. That is literature as we now know it, an expressive act which is privileged above all other expressions which the self gives of itself.[77] That is also the only genuine religion he knows: as Eigeldinger puts it, sacralization 'occurs in the affectivity'; it can be expressed only 'in a metaphorical writing that borrows the resources of religious language.'[78] Primarily expressive, such literature is also communicative, but its communicative act is one that lets the reader do the work of reading as he or she sees fit.

Rousseau rarely comments on myths. In his eyes (as in those of many of his contemporaries) traditional religion transmits beliefs, not stories. But he is most himself when he orients himself in reality by creating a myth. (To call this myth a literary one stresses its peculiarity: it is rooted in personal experience and it is couched in a book that will be read 'privately.') Once he has written, Rousseau knows who he is, and what others should be. Readers who have completed their reading know what they should be. Many of the parents who read *Emile* changed some of their practices; henceforth babies' limbs were left free. But what they mostly learned from Rousseau is a self-image.[79] Literary though it is, this myth does something of what the older myths used to do: it stabilizes belief and establishes identity.

The power of his literary myths and the sweeping powers of the writer can be tested by seeing how the new myth transmutes the significance of traditional Christian theological themes.

In the 'Profession de foi,' included in *Emile*, a priest from Savoy bluntly announces that he has left all books aside: there is nothing God wishes to teach us in any of them. But one page later we learn that one book still lies open on the table. 'The majesty of the Scriptures amazes me, the holiness of the Gospel speaks to my heart.'[80] Rousseau speaks most slightingly of the nonsense found in catechisms and of the persecuting bent of the church. (Such views were commonplace among the *philosophes*.) But he loves Christ and his love has genuine passion. 'I am Christian, not as a disciple of the priests, but as a disciple of Jesus Christ.'[81]

Two of the testimonies given by Rousseau to the person of Christ indicate exactly what he has in mind. The third of the *Lettres écrites de la montagne* examines the ethics of the Gospel and ends on a statement of what there is that 'charms in the character of Jesus.' The word 'charm' is to be interpreted strongly; Rousseau confesses himself overcome. There is in Jesus not only delicacy of mores, simplicity, but also ease, grace and even elegance. He did not shun pleasures and feasts; he attended weddings, saw women, played with children, loved perfumes and ate with financiers. His disciples did not fast; his austerity was not rude. He was at the same time indulgent and righteous, sweet to the weak and terrible to the wicked. His ethics had something attractive, caressing and tender ... Il avait le cœur sensible, il était homme de bonne société.[82]

This amazing portrait of agreeable, civilized sophistication attributes something winsome, even irresistible, to the life of Jesus. This moralist has a sternness that attracts whereas everywhere else sternness repels.

The *Morceau allégorique sur la révélation* suggests the source of this extraordinary power. In a dream a philosopher sees a dismal sanctuary centred around a veiled statue. The temple is a place of illusion and oppression; priests preside over a cruel ritual. The allegory then presents the intervention of three liberating heroes. The second clearly stands for Socrates; he tears away the veil from the statue, and the figure looks heavenward and tramples upon mankind. But the people in the temple remain caught in the illusion; they keep on worshipping the statue. A third hero, obviously Christ, is announced as 'son of man'; he topples the statue and takes its place upon the altar. 'He seemed to be taking his rightful place rather than usurping that of another.' He then speaks: the priests' power is broken, the people are seized with enthusiasm. 'He led all; everything announced a revolution.' His mere word confounds his enemies and all are moved by it. 'One felt that the language of truth did not cost him anything because he had the source of it in himself.' The achievement of Christ is surprisingly similar to that of Rousseau, or of any honest conscience. 'Goodness appears in the world through an I that is transparent to it.'[83] An immediate presence overcomes all distance, all dissemblance, all misunderstanding, all oppression. It spontaneously surges out of the self.

Mystics before Rousseau had spoken of an inner Christ contrasted to the official one. With Rousseau the writer puts on the mantle of the mystic. Furthermore – and this is quite new – the 'authentic' Christ is psychologically redeeming: his word brings just what divided post-enlightenment persons need. The door is open for a whole series of reconstructions of the consciousness of the historical Jesus that make of it a powerful cultural phenomenon, which overcomes the evil divisions belonging to human beings in their historical state of culture and which can be re-created by the writer who duplicates this unitive consciousness. So Rousseau does love Christ and the gospels. The 'creative' writer honours them, and on his own terms. He recognizes in them an achievement similar to his own as a sincere and passionate writer.[84]

Does this mean that Rousseau will discard the notion of revelation? The religion of conscience has such an intimate ring; its emotions seem so linked to sentimental piety, pantheistic nature mysticism, or 'spiritualité naturelle.'[85] But at the end of a study of what Rousseau has to say about his 'extases,' Gouhier concludes that even in the *Rêveries*, self, cosmos, and God are always kept distinct. The 'extases' are not a swooning of the self, but a heightening, a gathering of it.[86] Rousseau does not approve of petitionary prayer. His God is not one to give favours. He is, however, the source of gifts which must be acknowledged as grace. Those who contrasted a sense of the presence of divine immensity with the sense of God's presence as grace made a contrast where Rousseau saw none.

Rousseau can speak of grace and of revelation because he has experienced them. Rousseau, of course, like all the *philosophes*, brings discredit to the idea that God left a message (embodied in a code of laws or a body of doctrine) with some individuals of the past so that humankind is forever held to what was told then. On this point the priest from Savoy repeats the standard doctrines of the deists, with a new, modest ring, however: 'I do not teach my sentiment but exhibit it.'[87] But the letter to Mgr de Beaumont (signed by Jean-Jacques Rousseau, citizen of Geneva, and pointedly entitled *Lettre à Christophe de Beaumont*) has a new thrust. Attacked by Roman Catholics, Rousseau summons a more characteristically Protestant response. He tries to build his case on the principles of a sound theology, and writes one of the founding texts of liberal Protestant theology. And this time, he claims that he has never denied revelation.[88] The truth is that Rousseau rejects one type of revelation, namely, the reified body of truths to be forever believed (and in the name of which one can proceed safely to speak ill of all other religions and sects), and affirms another type, namely, the revelatory moment, where insight and certainty are received as given. Revelation and grace are thus acknowledged, not because the writer honours what they traditionally taught (what the tradition transmitted in the eighteenth century was, in any case, singularly distorted by rationalizing compromises), but because they are indispensable terms in describing the individual's experience.

Rousseau's pages on the public religion show that it too, like the private one, is subordinated to the dominant myth of the 'creative' writer. Rousseau ventured boldly into a discussion of civil religion. The problem was extraordinarily complex. Since the sixteenth century, religion in Europe had become intensely socialized, and moral norms had simultaneously been deeply internalized. Each European society acquired its profound and durable cultural unity by the shaping of a moral conscience among all levels of the population. This conscience was both social and religious. In the eighteenth century, the institutional strains caused by the religious elements of this consensus became bothersome to many; the costs of religious intolerance in particular seemed too high. Many, therefore, came to wish that the public religion would recede, or that the religious element of the consensus would give way to other elements of equal moral and social strength. D'Holbach and his friends emerge as complete secularizers: social unity will gain in strength as religion is shoved aside. Voltaire and d'Alembert are social realists: change cannot be sudden. Voltaire and d'Alembert are also class-conscious. They know that upper-class philosophical atheists are virtuous, but they are sure that religion remains necessary to keep the populace moral. They envisage therefore a slow ebb of the religious part of the national consensus. Meanwhile they promote among their own the sort of natural religion they believe in. They do not propose to inculcate it in the many, or legislate it into practice; they acknowledge that it lacks spiritual appeal for the masses. So they are happy to let the law buttress the authority of Christianity.

Rousseau sees the flaws in all these positions: they provide no basis for a genuine civil, national religion, and they maintain a dishonest compromise between the Christianity of the many and the atheism or enlightened religion of the few. The Genevan patriot wants to do better than that. To him religion and civil life are inseparable in a united, moral, egalitarian, national community. So the *Contrat Social* offers a new religious settlement: tolerance for all virtuous cults and a public religion established by law, with as few dogmas as possible and penalties for public dissenters. The apostle of religious sincerity and tolerance shocks all the *philosophes* by proposing, at the end of his discussion of civil religion, the death penalty for obdurate atheists.[89] The very private man, master of his own reality and of nothing else, sees himself as fit to be, on a few decisive points, master over others. There is clearly a side to Rousseau that welcomes the power he attributes to the legislators as they found the institutions of a people, the power 'to change, as it were, human nature.'[90] The qualification sometimes disappears when he speaks of his pedagogue: this human being 'steps in God's shoes' and 'makes a man.'[91] Indeed the pedagogue never reasons with his pupil; he forms his pupil's reason. With a sovereignty comparable to that of Plato's legislators, he organizes experiences that are appropriate to the child's needs and thus enables the child to 'learn by himself.' In Book 5 of *Emile*, the teacher, that paragon of sincere virtue, tells his pupil that his new love, Sophie, is dead. This lie is meant to teach him how to sublimate. Rousseau knew that all his ideas were in images.[92] His dominant ideas exercise at times a ruthless domination.

Rousseau's analysis of the problem of civil religion is one of the most penetrating ever written. The only weakness lies in the solution and its inherent contradiction. But Rousseau is forced into the contradiction because he sees the writer as a giver of unity. There is in his mind no happiness for a group of people apart from a deeply felt unity. A civil religion is the only way this Protestant republican knows toward such unity. He has not yet dreamed up the cohesive force of nationalism. He comes close to it, however; his plan for the rebuilding of the Polish state asks it to 'reveal to the Polish people the unique nature of their social identity' and 'to strengthen this identity through wise legislation which would establish bonds of affection among the Polish people.'[93]

The study of Rousseau provides, I said, an indispensable starting-point: it enables us to focus on the new links established between the expressions of religiousness and the practice of writing. Rousseau writes because he wants to be believed.[94] And what he offers as object of belief is not a package of second-hand affirmations, but his own feeling and writing heart. This new voice of sincerity is, after him, a lure for all. Before reducing him, however, to the position of initiator and precursor, and thus of just a means toward the understanding of other authors, I wish to make two further points that aim at giving him all his due.

First of all, this creator of a myth is not entirely bewitched by his own magic. He remains endowed with the virtue of moderation most of the time. He knows his limits: *Emile*, for instance, stresses that the pedagogue is not God and the pupil not king.[95]

Second, he remains a moving example of the courage and dignity of the human being who tries to think while living in conditions of mental distress. Rousseau struggles toward doctrines, truths, that will 'save' an otherwise difficult existence. And clearly existence was becoming difficult for others besides him. As H.R. Jauss puts it, after the breakdown of the old theodicy, humankind is reponsible for all evil in the world;

without a corporate identification with an old or a new Adam, the individual must bear the entire weight of evil; 'faced with the overadjudication of the reality of human existence man sought compensation by fleeing into a realm free of social and juridical consequence.'[96] We may well say that Rousseau's doctrine is the product of his disease, but should add, with Bénichou, that it is also the sign that he did not accept his disease.[97]

This being said, here are our hypotheses:

1 Rousseau starts a trend in literature, in which the author is somehow deemed more important than his or her book. The real object of passionate interest is the author's life experience, adventure, travail; the book matters only as testimony to that. Rousseau is 'one of the first writers who managed to make sonorous the silences around his pages'.[98] In autobiographical writing, concentrated in the latter part of his life, he keeps trying to overcome the misunderstandings created by his literary pen in the earlier years; hence the effort to go back to the deepest self, the purest source of his convictions.[99] The prestige of writing is thus both enhanced and undermined. Writing is a boon but having to write is a curse. Maurice Blanchot put it quite well: 'In a century in which there is hardly anybody who is not a great writer, who does not write with easy and happy mastery, Rousseau is the first one to write with *ennui*, with a bad conscience, with the feeling of a guilt that must always be aggravated in order to try to escape it.'[100]

In this manner of writing, the writer always seems to give a little bit more than the text says. This of course is particularly helpful if the writer wishes to convey something 'religious,' something that is deemed beyond ordinary perception, something to which ordinary language is not adequate.

2 The themes of culture and of imagination together provide a new, basic framework for the elucidation of religion. They lead readers to conceive of human life as lived out in a man-made historical social environment. The eighteenth century was highly aware that human beings can change their environment, and with this awareness came confidence. A return to simpler norms of nature was proposed. Rousseau announces that there are no such norms. He also discovers unfortunate by-products, unforeseen consequences, resulting from human cultural creativity. He shows to human beings that they do something to themselves as they manipulate the natural world and the social environment. Everywhere in chains! Man imposed a fate on himself as he exercised his powers! The moral confidence of the European who acts

confidently on the desire to master the world is shattered and a new moral anxiety is felt. The old Aristotelian distinction between *praxis* and *poiesis* becomes relevant again. *Praxis* (*actio*), the action of human beings upon society and upon themselves, must be critically examined and its ends established. *Poiesis* (*factio*), the action of human beings upon inanimate things, or the art of making useful things, offers no guidance at all when it comes to finding the art of living together with one's fellow human being.

Rousseau adds, however, that humankind can escape from the prison. Its imagination has wings; its flight to the transcendent can open the path to a new, harmonious reality. Imagination, which used to be seen as a faculty that warps judgments of reality, is perceived now as having an ontological role; it can be creator of a new reality. (*Praxis* then is no longer the coping for the best which Aristotle had in mind; it is envisaged as a dynamic, individual, or corporate self-shaping based on inward creative power.)[101] Rousseau challenges readers with a far-reaching question, aptly phrased by Paul Cantor, 'Why, when man has it within his own power to change himself, does he continue to endure a miserable condition ?'[102] *Emile* is indeed quite clear on the practical powers of the imagination: 'It is imagination that extends for us the range of the possibles, both toward what is good and toward what is bad, and therefore excites and nurtures our desires by giving hopes to satisfy them.'[103]

Rousseau's radical, 'ideal' answers were soon to be emulated at the public national level, with the revolutionary efforts to remake society.[104] Rousseau clearly showed the way; his hero Emile (in an unfinished sequel entitled *Emile and Sophie*) organizes a rebellion among slaves.

The discovery of culture precipitates humans into new depths of pessimism: we have maimed ourselves. The discovery of the imagination invites us to a new optimism: we can start afresh again. Nineteenth-century writing on religion can be radical because religion is seen as culture, as a product of human history. But with such disenchanting vision comes also the dream of a re-enchanting one; some critics are confident that the imagination of the poets – or of religious geniuses – can re-poeticize or re-religionize existence and thereby start a transformation of it. Culture and imagination have emerged as historical principles of reality, as time-bound sources of a sense of reality. What is oppressive is attributed to culture and the imagination is entrusted to guide humans to a happier order or a completely happy order. Mental inertia is denounced; human beings must deimagine before they can reimagine. The release of new energies is constantly invited. If humans have the power to change, why indeed should they continue to endure a miserable condition?

Many clearly saw in Rousseau the herald of the new dispensation. Hoelderlin compared him to the eagle that flies toward approaching gods, and Victor Hugo called him the rising sun of the new world.[105] Rousseau, I must stress, does not just launch a new anthropology; he launches a *powerful* new anthropology. Emile, the man of nature, is admirable, imitable (just like Achilles and Alexander were).[106] John Locke had spoken of the new, modern man but had never tried to paint him as a warm, attractive, obviously authentic human being. A new poetry suffuses politics too. Aristotle said that politics was a combination among the needy to meet their wants. Rousseau says that it is a combination among the suffering to overcome their humiliation and recapture corporate happiness.

3 The discoveries of the realities of culture and the powers of the imagination, the hovering between pessimism and optimism, keep placing readers in an uncomfortable position, on the brink of an indeterminate future. Rousseau advocates civic virtue; he also illustrates the withdrawn type of virtue. A duality is found in writing that corresponds to this tension with respect to virtue. Some writing re-conceptualizes social existence and issues a call to political action. The call was powerful, and was heeded; the French Revolution is enough evidence. Other writing evidences a very different sort of power: the book catches the reader in an intense aesthetic pleasure, the pleasure of being caught in totally absorbing reading; and the book leaves the reader quite free to decide what, if anything, he or she will do after coming to the last page and putting down the book. This second type of writing will require close watching. It pleases; does it thereby cease to instruct? Moral and political writing cannot eschew some sort of call to the practice of virtue in the real world. Can religious writing tie its lot to that of the non-authoritative voice, the voice of lyrical poetry and withdrawn communion with the intimate self?

4 As Rousseau writes the history of human beings as acculturated and creative beings, he borrows from Christian traditional symbols and theological concepts. He tells a story of fall and redemption. The Christian themes seem to acquire fresh relevance: never, it seems, had so many biblical themes been assimilated into human self-understanding. But the themes are subsumed under an entirely new heading: they are aids to an autonomous human self-understanding. Rousseau lays thereby

the basis of a new art: that of a friendly decoding of Christian 'truths' to let their 'profound' truth emerge. And that decoding is done by someone who offers himself as a sincere Christian undertaking to 'rescue the truth' in an age when priests have masked it.[107]

The new anthropology is thus accompanied by a new way of reading Christian doctrines. 'Ever mindful of my inadequacy, I will never reason on the nature of God, unless I be compelled to do it by the feeling of his relationship to me,' declares the priest from Savoy.[108] How this prudence contrasts with the confidence (presumption?) of the older theology! One may, however, ask whether the path has not been found to make of theology simply anthropology under another name.

At any rate, romantic authors exhibit a new mastery: they can manipulate Christian symbols to make them say what the artists want them to say. This is particularly clear among German authors. The procedures initiated by Rousseau seem to have become endemic there with both Romantics and Idealists. In 1786 Kant wrote his *Conjectural Beginning of Human History* and with apparent innocence stated that man's departure from Paradise was but the means of a desirable transition from 'bondage to instinct to rational control – in a word, from the tutelage of nature to the state of freedom.'[109] (In Christian theology, the *culpa* is said to be *felix* because it led to the dispensation of grace, not because it led to progressive moral self-perfecting.) In a famous passage (significant in both what it says and how it says it), Kleist announced that the gates of Paradise are now closed to us, guarded by an angel with a flaming sword; he added, however, that there is, perhaps, a back door. (He referred thereby to the powers of art.)[110] Hegel of course perfected the art of transmuting Christian statements; almost none was left untouched by him; but, again, the 'death of God' in his books does not mean what Golgotha meant in the New Testament.[111] In *The Sorrows of Young Werther* (1774), perhaps better translated as *The Passion of Young Werther*, the hero has numerous Christlike traits – among other allusions, he sees his suicide as a sacrificial act for the liberation of his friends. But it is also clear that Goethe intended the novel to be a critique of the religious sentimentalism which he believed was inseparable from Christianity; it is certain that he emerged from the writing of it a more confirmed pagan.[112]

One of the most respected critics of romantic literature borrowed a phrase from Carlyle's *Sartor Resartus* to entitle a major study *Natural Supernaturalism*; M.H. Abrams sees traditional religious ideas assimilated and reinterpreted by the poets 'as constitutive elements in a world view founded on secular premises.'[113] The nineteenth century abounds in authors who can use the Christian myth to advance their own. There are, of course, also those poets who are great admirers of Christianity and of Christian culture and spend much talent defending them. Kierkegaard, who knew something of the poet's ability to create a sentiment of existence, had a firm diagnosis about them: 'An admirer of Christianity is not a live Christian.'[114]

5 Perplexities thus abound about Rousseau's innovations. But there is something in them that does turn a page for ever, or make us pass beyond a point of no return. This is well illustrated if one has the patience to read Lamennais's laborious refutation of the confession of faith offered by the Savoy priest.[115] Lamennais undertakes to show that Rousseau keeps getting embroiled in contradictions – for instance, between the duty to adhere to truth sincerely and that of remaining in the church of one's fathers. Lamennais wants to force out of Rousseau the acknowledgment that there is and can be only one true religion; but Lamennais proves himself incapable of admitting that Rousseau could call a religion 'sainte' without thereby acknowledging it to be entirely true, and without requiring universal adherence to it. He cannot see how social conservativism might be coupled with theological relativism. Paul Hoffmann has put his finger on the source of Lamennais's persistent thickness of skull: he refuses to see that the conditions of human access to truth might be complex.[116] He does not see the numerous causes of error that may affect the operations of minds; neither can he allow that erring is inevitable when one speculates. And he cannot accept that error in one area (e.g., that of religious doctrine) might not inevitably lead to error in others (e.g., that of virtue). After 1800, writers who adhere to monolithic notions of truth and error, who believe that their reasonings can – at once and simultaneously – settle all matters of truth, dictate what others must hold in good faith, and prescribe how society (and religion, if the writers in question care about it) must be organized, run the risk of being branded naive ideologists, or fanatics. Lamennais has missed one new inescapable point: writing, besides conveying content, is the gesture of a fallible human being toward other fallible human beings and, as such, needs to become the object of some conscious care. The sincerity of the writer does not reveal everything about his or her condition and interest and thus may not be a completely adequate answer; but it has at least the merit of signalling the problem.

2

To Interpose a Little Ease: Chateaubriand

Views of François René de Chateaubriand (1768–1848) have ordinarily been fragmented. All church histories refer to his first major work, *Le génie du christianisme* (1802), and the role it played in the 'return' of religion in post-revolutionary France; they usually say no more about the author and his other works. Any treatment of French romanticism discusses *René* and *Atala* to illustrate the new style and mood. And history books make an obligatory reference to the defender of liberal ideas in the midst of the Restoration.[1] Chateaubriand's own books often suffered the fate of being read in anthologies; worse yet, the fragments were scattered into collections with different slants. Students in Catholic schools read sonorous pieces praising Christianity and Christian virtues.[2] (If one goes back into the nineteenth century, one finds Chateaubriand recruited for the most reactionary royalist and Catholic causes.) Captured by partisans, the man became known through clichés. Fortunately for his literary reputation, he also left us his posthumously published *Mémoires d'outre-tombe*, a work which found admiring readers in every generation.

This incurable Romantic was also a highly visible public man.[3] There were other tensions and apparent contradictions in his life. His pious Catholic readers were not informed of the life he led as he wrote *Le génie du christianisme*. The defender of Christianity against *les philosophes* was not living with Mme de Chateaubriand but with Pauline de Beaumont (who borrowed books from her father's library and wrote summaries for him). His friends in literary circles did not ignore this fact, and used it to undermine the religious value of the apology, composed in circumstances quite dissimilar to those of *The City of God* or the *Summa contra Gentiles*.

In this chapter I shall argue that we can discern integrity in this man as a modern sort of believer, or that we can discern genuineness in his religious development,[4] provided we do not look in his works simply for affirmations of beliefs (to be somehow evaluated as 'genuine' or not), but attempt to see how he occupies literary spaces opened up by Rousseau.[5] Thus, taking cues from literary historians, we will look for the growth of a distinctive style. His first published work, the *Essai sur les révolutions* (1797), immediately signals the importance of the literary voice. The book is ostensibly written by a *philosophe* who casts a disabused eye on religion ('religions are born out of our fears and weakness, spread because of our fanaticism and die in the midst of our indifference'), but the tone frequently betrays a previously unknown anxiety of feeling. 'What religion shall replace Christianity? The more one turns over the question, the more frightened one becomes.'[6] As one critic puts it, the essay proclaims that religion is obsolete and notes its durability.[7]

Chateaubriand's style has its origin in his discovery as a youth that history is mass murder. His older brother died on the guillotine; he saw the homicidal violence of Parisian crowds in 1789. He gained an important insight: 'Men are throat-cutting machines that are triggered with words.'[8] A clear and apparently constant political stance was to result from this; throughout his life he expressed a visceral dislike of violent governments.[9] As a young man with literary interests he also saw in these democratic massacres a major problem for poets. Traditionally, poets pondering death meditated on destiny in general and wove the brutal fact into a larger meaningful whole. This poet, however, was forced to realize that the dying was human-caused and that these deaths, brought about by fellow citizens and not by foreign or barbarian conquerors, cannot be made poetic. No meaning of the traditional (i.e., mainly epic) kind can be given to this sort of mass murder. No god holds the reins of the universe when *this* is taking place. 'Any one who wants to sing the modern age will have to banish truth from his work.'[10] The young poet also felt the incongruity of the sentimental, pastoral, 'republican' plays performed in theatres while the streets were red.[11] To mask the crimes is to renounce lucidity.[12] Chateaubriand thus does not keep company with the militant poets of the day (minor ones, I should add), who are quite happy to see the forces of the soul absorbed in politics and sing of the French triumphs in Europe, or of what has been (appropriately?) called the Napoleonic epic.[13] Reviewing this evidence, de Diéguez concluded that Chateaubriand finds his poetic voice as he sings of the universal sinking into annihilation: glorious and petty criminals, executioners and victims alike sink into the grave. History is a cycle of death in the light of which the most momentous revolutions are banal. The poet keeps a steady eye on the whole but remains alone as he sees history sink into silence. He creates the realm of art over a universal kingdom of decay and oblivion.[14]

De Diéguez, however, overlooks some of the evidence. Chateaubriand was not a spectator like the others. First, he was aware he was seeing a new reality, one without precedent, which he, with others, designated as such by calling it modern. In the *Essai* of 1797, he did not react to the fall of the monarchy as Augustine reacted to the fall of Rome – or not entirely. He did not say that empires come and go and leave it at that (since in 1797 he was not inclined to add that the City of God lasts for ever). He sensed a new force at work in this revolution, namely, the abstract idea of republican freedom. The melancholy pages on repetitious upheavals and universal decay were thus balanced by pages on the fresh energy displayed by the (interior) barbarians responsible for the fall.[15] Second, this spectator, while quoting Lucretius on the peace of those who watch a shipwreck from the shore, felt sympathy for those caught in the turmoil.[16] While down and out in London among the emigrés, Chateaubriand lived the life of the urban proletariat. First-hand experience of poverty marked him for ever.[17] Third, this spectator did not find his poetic response to murderous history right away and once and for all. His stance was uneasy and kept evolving. The *Essai* of 1797, for instance, articulated mainly a stock reponse – everything sinks into nothingness sooner or later – while the *Génie* in 1802 affirmed perfectibility and stressed the new path open to humankind.[18] A close look is therefore required: Chateaubriand's poetic style is a slowly evolving response to a history that stunned him.

De Diéguez also makes too short shrift of the fact that the young poet underwent a religious 'conversion.' Death was again very much in the background here. If we are to believe what he wrote in 1802, the news of the death (in jail) of his mother reached him in London, in 1797, by means of a letter from her sister, who herself had died by the time the letter reached its destination. The mother had voiced the hope her son would return 'to the religion in which [he] was brought up.' 'These two voices from the grave... struck me; I became Christian .... I wept and I believed.'[19]

The thinness of this account and its subjective character, along with the absence of any signs of joining any committed Christian group with common faith and discipline, have led to derogatory comments that the 'conversion' was largely, or merely, sentimental. Is his religiousness also a beautiful appearance poetically created in urgent recoil from sheer horror?

An examination of the poetic creation he launched in 1802 should lead to an answer. The main argument in *Le génie du christianisme* is that hearts and minds are dry without religion, that religion adds new strings to the soul. The Christianity presented there is moderate and non-polemical, if not ecumenical in the current sense of the word,[20] and, above all, literate, beautiful, and sensitive. Chateaubriand could quite rightly defend his work by saying that since Christianity had been presented for a whole century as tasteless, morally repellent, and artistically ugly, it was entirely appropriate to meet its enemies on this ground.[21] The powerful rhetorical device Chateaubriand perfected to this end consisted in the painting of highly visual scenes in which the writer allows himself a richer, more lyrical, freer vein.[22] The mysteries of Christianity are depicted rather freely: to cite an extreme, the section on Incarnation has one paragraph on the manger and two pages on the Virgin Mary. Wonders of nature are described and made to sing of God. Christian literature is surveyed. (The rehabilitation here was much needed: Dante and Milton, to mention only them, had been ignored in France.) The portrayal Christian authors give of human relations is analysed and favourably compared to classical Greek and Roman models. One example is not unexpected: discussing *La Nouvelle Héloïse*, Chateaubriand gives many citations and praises the happy blend of religion and love found in so many exchanges between the lovers. 'One would need to be insane to reject a cult which wrung such tender accents out of hearts, and added, so to speak, new strings to the soul.'[23] Another example is, again, a much-quoted extreme: the Christian hell is the only one where the demons themselves are seen to suffer; this (correct) observation leads to developments on the 'poetic advantage of our hell'; the 'poetry of torture,' Chateaubriand adds, reaches the highest terror in Dante. The contribution of all the visual arts is also recalled and exhibited, and numerous touching scenes of popular piety and folklore (again a commonly overlooked or merely ridiculed reality) are offered to our admiring eyes. The last book introduces a new theme, which was to grow in importance in the author's work: Christianity has rendered countless services to society. The 'proof' begins with an account of missions. 'Everywhere, civilization has fol-

lowed on the footprints of the Gospel.' The Gospel is eminently favourable to freedom. So Christianity will emerge triumphant from the trials
that have just purged it.[24]

The book literally *surveys* Christianity. A visually talented poet gives
its history a fresh look and offers a renewed description. To be sure, the
work confirms a century-old tendency to expatiate on Christianity, positively or negatively, rather than handle the topoi on God, Christ, humankind, and the church. It also confirms a tendency to talk about
religion rather than the church. But Chateaubriand's religion is not a
doctrinal or moral system, it is a civilization that produced art and
shaped mores.[25] He took here a decisive turn: being defined as a congeries of facts rather than a system of truths, Christianity is taken out
of the hands of authorities defending orthodoxy and handed over to
those most competent to *describe* it. He also decisively establishes that in
France the religious facts to be properly surveyed and correctly assessed include social and political facts. Christianity is a historical presence affecting the life of nations, not just some 'spiritual' force emancipating individuals. Thus Chateaubriand launches a description with
great and novel narrative qualities: Christianity has been a rich and
evolving historical reality, always a moral consolation and a civilizing
force. The description itself has persuasive power. This procedure recalls that of Rousseau, whose priest boasted, 'I do not teach my sentiment, but express it' (*Emile*, bk 4; IV: 581). This time, however, what is
set forth is not mainly personal conviction but an abundant and colour-
ful tapestry of Christian history and literature, and the poet acknowledges this history as his own. Between 1797 and 1802 Chateaubriand
did more than read books in order to write one; he joined a dynamic
history and thereby completed what had begun with his 'conversion.'

This apologia also contains a highly visible feature that has no precedent in religious works, the full implications of which, however, were
not really seen until the works of Pierre Barbéris (1973, 1974, 1976).[26]
Two fiction pieces, *René* and *Atala*, are inserted in the 1802 edition of *Le
génie du christianisme*. Such a device had recently been introduced in
literary works: a spate of late eighteenth-century books disrupted
convention by bringing about some sort of interpenetration between
reasoned philosophical exposition and pieces of fiction.[27] Barbéris
makes points so obvious one is surprised they were not made before:
René in fact undermines the didactic thesis of the *Génie* it supposedly
buttresses, or at least forces us to read the treatise differently.[28]

René, which Barbéris analyses in detail, is the story of an impoverished young aristocrat who experiences a triple exclusion: as a younger son he does not inherit from his father; as an aristocrat he cannot find a place in the revolutionized society and goes to wander in search of nature; as an alienated young man, he cannot live a natural life even with the Indians in the American forests, as his intense relationship with his sister makes it impossible for him to take an Indian spouse. René is immobilized: the past is gone, the present empty, and the future blocked. None of his desires can be fulfilled, so he makes himself into the hero of solitude and non-desire. He feels no affinity with any social order and cannot be captured by any.[29] One scene in the story is highly symbolic: he wanders on the beach alone between the walls of a convent (in which his sister is confined) and the ocean, between a hostile, impenetrable society and a vast, formless, empty space. Ostensibly this piece is inserted in the apologetic treatise to illustrate 'le vague des passions' and the unhappiness of anyone whose heart has not been reformed by Christianity.

What Barbéris points out is that *René* launches a manner of writing that enshrines revolt, while the *Génie* renews the manner of writing that sustains public order. But even in the didactic socializing treatise, the new Christian order does not entirely silence the voice of the solitary rebel. The story of *René* is included. And these pages are not the only breach in the texture of well-meaning didacticism. In the *Génie* Chateaubriand quotes, amasses proofs, pours out erudition; sometimes, however, his pen takes off. In such cases, he has style, and a personal voice. Unlike Buffon and the other countless theologians of nature, his descriptions of the beavers and the water-hens (meant to prove God) move us, because of the added vibrations of his personal sensibility: he has seen these animals, when he was far away in America, when he was young and unhappy, and this touched and appeased his heart. When Chateaubriand writes in this way, not only is he good in literary terms, but he also clearly transgresses against established, unsatisfactory (European) order: he keeps re-creating a yearning in the heart for something else, elsewhere. Any social order wants to be full, and to be seen as assuring the fullness of life. Now the literary voice undermines the official tone of accepted belief by evoking a perpetually hollow place in the self. While Chateaubriand wishes us to join a renewed social order (the post-revolutionary France of the first consul and his Concordat), his writing keeps inviting us to some interior emigration. His pen cannot be made subservient to any social or political project.[30]

So the *Génie* takes on the old apologetic task in a new way. To the insinuating language of derision and irony perfected by the *philosophes*, the work replies with a language that uncovers and stimulates the very source of poetry in the self, thus overcoming quite effectively the bent of most readers with literary taste toward a literature and a poetry that were frivolous. One might discern here a parallel with Pascal. Pages in the *Génie* evoke human beings as divided, mutable, and the prey of a thousand chimaeras; their feelings are incomplete, their thoughts inadequate, their hearts broken.[31] There is of course a comparable expression of anxiety, but this time the dizziness is not mainly cosmic-spatial (humankind caught between the immensities revealed by the telescope and the microscope) but primarily temporal.[32] The past provides no foundation for the future and the present is but a point, puny, lost in time. The old era is gone and no new age manages to be born that would elicit the loyalties of the heart. The self nurtured and organized during childhood by parents and other authorities finds out during young adulthood that the society for which it was prepared has ceased to exist. The self is alone, without a stable world around it. The social space being empty, it has to create its own world – with the help of the imagination.[33]

What we have arrived at is a truism: Chateaubriand is a Romantic. But the label should not be a cliché. Let us attempt, therefore, to characterize Chateaubriand's romanticism and grasp what there was in it that could unlock the inner springs of religiousness.

At the beginning of the nineteenth century, many came to conceive of the human mind (including its cognitive capacities) as an organic whole, obeying the laws or following the rhythms of a live organism. This new analogy became dominant and replaced the older one of a mirror reflecting eternal, stable ideas or changing facts.[34] Attention then focused on the dynamic or expansive aspects of the mind, seen as an organic whole encompassing the imagination and what used to be called character and the passions. Attention of course was also paid to what feeds and nurtures mental dynamism. Art and aesthetic representations received in this context a fresh, more positive evaluation.[35]

Chateaubriand's evocation of his wanderings, and all his subsequent writings, are a particularly obvious development of such imaginative dynamism, occurring in what must be pictured as some inner mental space, half way between the centre of the self and the outside world. Echoing Rousseau he referred frequently to his 'chimaeras.'[36] His friend Joubert referred to 'the immense space which is vacant between himself and his thoughts.'[37] In this mental space, images and forms take shape and feelings rise and dissolve; they are not the exact self, nor the direct products of the exterior world. Echoes of the encounter between self and world resonate in this inner space and are shaped by a brooding self. The self feels truly at home in this space only;   writing and reading occur in this 'aesthetic' space.[38]

The metaphor of a core of the self surrounded by an inner circle and then by an outer periphery keeps reappearing in romantic writings. The self is invited to gather itself, discover its own inner source, and then go out, stream out, create. Ethical activists like Fichte tell it to shape the world; others are aware that the inner circles are constantly invaded and disrupted by sensations and feelings: a battle then must be fought inside and some victory gained in there first. Whatever the nuances, the self is conceived as having an apparatus for forming images and a place for storing them.[39] The specificity of art (in its new modern sense) is that it works on this inner reality close to the self. Since the same can be said of sexual love and of religion, the stage, so to speak, is set for the romantic blurring of boundaries between the emotions of art, of sexuality, and of religion.

The significance of Chateaubriand lies, then, in the forging of a very powerful style that keeps drawing from this inner aesthetic space,[40] and in the fact that this voice, addressing similar inner spaces, is made to invade religious, apologetic, and didactic writing. As Joubert put it after reading the *Génie*, our friend is 'not a pipe, like many others, but a spring.'[41] This style and this stimulation of the reader are also linked to an emerging 'modern' reality and are believed to be henceforth necessary.

Thus Chateaubriand recalls his wanderings through war-torn France and upon his escape, wounded, to England; on the oceans and in the American forests. (To this repertoire of vast, open, unorganized spaces, he added, when older, the desert wastes and sands of the East.) Immense, equally disorganized spaces are felt to be inside, in the heart and in the mind. The experience of the world and of history has disrupted the old personal core and confused its identity. 'We are not the same Christians any more; we have aged in the world [*dans le siècle*] not in the faith.'[42] Chateaubriand's literary voice, born in the wanderings of the emigré, reaches the sensibility of his contemporaries, touches them to the quick, and gives an avowedly Christian (albeit poetic) structure to their disordered sentiment of life. To the old God who guaranteed the stable order of the world succeeds a new God who guarantees the permanence of an interior, personal centre in the midst of historical vicissitudes.

The *Génie* therefore reflects a disenchantment not just with eighteenth-century science and philosophy but with all traditional didactic prose. Hearts grow dry, circumscribed by a mass of exact knowledge and definite ideas. Distant, empty deserts are necessary to give them space.[43] The book is also marked by the author's early disenchantment with history. Human beings believed they were launching events; they were in fact suffering them. Man-made history turned into mass murder. No Providence guides human exertions but Fatality takes them over.[44] 'Who will tell us,' asks the *Essai* of 1796 rhetorically, 'the art of changing the nature of the soul using words and knowledge?'[45] In a work of his maturity, *Itinéraire de Paris à Jérusalem*, Chateaubriand muses on the difference between the young man and the older one: the former feeds on 'chimaeras'; the latter wants more solid food but has only souvenirs and history; unfortunately for him, history is a record of calamities.[46] So there is, in maturity, a second loss of innocence. The crisis of essences, or the realization that things are not what we thought they were (and were told they were), goes through a second turn of the screw. As Barbéris puts it, the classical writer, discovering existence and experiencing a crisis of essences, becomes a moralist (or a satirist) and writes to amend mores. The romantic writer, upon discovering existence, has, in the age of democracy, the opportunity to practise the new politics. He or she soon experiences a crisis of the new essences: political life does not unfold according to plan. When the writer writes, therefore, it is with the knowledge that the pen does not amend mores immediately.[47] But the writer cannot accept the cynical certainties voiced by the 'positive' minds who accept life as it is; somehow the interior person must reassert his or her rights.

One of his contemporaries wrote that Chateaubriand always created around himself a little atmosphere of which he was the sun. It was meant unkindly,[48] but it was, I think, to his credit. The point of an aesthetic space is that, starting there, the self can, pen in hand, begin to recreate its badly shattered inner identity. One should add that this manner of writing arose in an age when the usual grounds of literary appeal and persuasion were gone; there did not exist in 1802 any social consensus that could define taste and be a basis of appeal. To touch readers, a new spot, so to speak, had to be found. Individual experience sought to speak to individual experience, inner emotion to inner emotion. Indeed during this period reading became a solitary and silent activity.

The notion of inner aesthetic space and the exploration of its ramifications in literary style permit us, I believe, to unravel the old debate on the Christian merits of *Le génie du christianisme*.

The first Catholic response to the early *Génie* found the inclusion of *Atala* and *René* unbecoming.[49] The first Protestant response deplored the focus on aesthetic questions.[50] The same theme was taken up by the Genevan pastor Bost, who sought out, corresponded, and conversed with Chateaubriand during his sojourn in Calvin's city. 'You've spent your life playing with Christianity and seeing only the poetry in it.'[51] Sainte-Beuve summed up the case for the prosecution: Chateaubriand, he wrote, put the French religious restoration on a fatefully wrong track; he gave an exterior beauty to the faith and made it incapable of regenerating hearts. Christ, he added, cares only for inner beauty, as every good Christian knows. Sainte-Beuve also slipped in two sexual innuendoes about Chateaubriand's life and implied that he himself was a better Christian on the counts of both orthodoxy in belief and purity in morals.[52] Anyone today who knows anything about Sainte-Beuve will dismiss such insinuations as hypocritical cant. In any case moralistic belittling only clouds the issue. Proust gave Sainte-Beuve a blow from which he should not recover: 'A book is the product of a self other than the one we show forth in our habits, in society, in our vices.'[53] What is important to the history of Christianity is not the life of Chateaubriand (his sins had been committed before) but the new literary procedures the *Génie* introduced into religious discourse.

And here it must be admitted that the book contains imprudent statements. If *René* and *Atala* are religiously meaningful even though they are fiction and not truth, are we not led to believe that the surrounding pages on God and Christian virtues deserve our attention on grounds other than their truth?[54] And is there not too much self-indulgence in the book?[55] And what are we to make of the delicately erotic allusions to Christian virgins?[56] Is not Chateaubriand stretching too far the notion of proof when he writes that the power of religion is proved by *René*? (He does makes clear that we should judge *René* not on the maxims of the protagonist but on the impression the work leaves on the soul.[57]) Is he not courting ridicule when he writes of crocodiles 'proving Providence' since they eat fish who would die anyway? Often our author compounds with poetic licence the worst of the foibles of the old apologists who tried to prove too much.[58]

Clearly also the new aesthetic focus transforms everything this author touches in Christianity. Evidence of the shifts in meaning is not hard to find. He announces that he left for Jerusalem with the sentiments of a pilgrim, but adds two pages later that he travelled to the Orient to gather images for *Les martyrs*, the epic he had just undertaken to write.[59] His praise of cloisters focuses on the peace that is found away from the sorrows of the world rather than on salvation away from the perils of the world.[60] (His pages started a romantic fondness for hermitages and isolated chapels and aloofness from the old parish churches and the new, larger sanctuaries.) Religion is feminized: women are said to excel in it. Chateaubriand launched a theologically excessive but conscious poetic licence as he extolled Mary's divinity.[61] If Chateaubriand, like Schleiermacher, had to overcome the bent of deism and differentiate clearly religion from morality, did he have to encourage a confusion between religious and aesthetic feelings, especially the sentiment of the sublime?[62] De Diéguez, echoing Bossuet's statement that the universe is a performance God stages for himself, suggests that with Chateaubriand as poet, man becomes the creator of the performance. So we might also conclude with him that Chateaubriand poetically metamorphosed Christianity until it became a beautiful bravado flung to an immense and silent universe.[63] That the Catholic clergy welcomed the *Génie* in 1802 and afterwards, would only reflect their distress before the spread of the outlook of the *philosophes* among nearly all the educated French.[64] Any ally seemed good to a clerical and theological establishment that was intellectually flaccid, heir of the intellectual and ecclesiastical scene of the eighteenth century, not to mention the costs of the Jansenist crisis and the Wars of Religion. Thus they hardly noticed that Chateaubriand's Christianity was not that of tradition and common usage but rather some new thing he fashioned for himself – and for his contemporaries.

This reading, however, overlooks both the historical roots and the historical timeliness of the recasting of Christianity brought about by the *Génie*. Chateaubriand expressed aesthetic sentiments, but these were shaped by a reappropriation of the Christian past and of his Christian affiliation. The reappropriation was highly personal: he surveys his cultural roots with his René-like sensibility; but he also expresses the results publicly. His recasting, moreover, was informed and deep. In London he was close to Anglican circles and he felt there a deep Christian solidarity: the Anglican divines and pastors were shocked by the fate of Catholics in France and dug into their apologetic tradition to find and offer ways to counter the new militant atheism. He also had a chance to read some of the transactions of the Calcutta Asiatic Society before they were in print.[65] All this meant that he stretched and blurred the semantic boundaries of faith, a word which in ancien régime France had acquired an extremely definite edge, dogmatically and politically defined as it was. There were – and are – of course those who felt that he obliterated the boundaries. 'He finds the Gospel everywhere,' wrote a contemporary critic, 'just like the priest who saw steeples on the moon.'[66] In any case, faith again becomes an unrestricted attitude, linked with faithfulness and honour, with emotion and love, and also with yearning and hope.[67]

The time then may have come not only to set the poetic recasting of Christianity in its proper historical context but also to envisage its merits. This I propose to do by tracing some ramifications of the literary voice in apologetic and religious writing. (This, incidentally, should also help evaluate the contention between moralism and aestheticism that runs throughout nineteenth-century religious thought.)[68]

1 Chateaubriand ventured to speak as an educated layman when theological experts, such as they were, and few as they were, were silent or helpless. He takes for granted a proper division of labour: a layman should not presume to utter the truths of Christianity but can open a vigorous front on the issue of poetics.[69] He claims no authority but that of literary talent. When he announced he had been converted, he specifically avoided claiming that he had received supernatural grace or a vocation directly from God. His defence of Christianity claims no authority other than that claimed (and apparently earned) by those who attacked it.[70] In either the book or the defence we hear a private person speaking from the personal conviction acquired and felt while taking stock of what he or she believes. And these beliefs are firm. In 1802 Chateaubriand commits himself to a clear allegiance, and he does it with 'evangelical moderation' in an age of ideological polarization. ('Cut and dried opinions abound in this age which doubts nothing except the existence of God.')[71]

2 Chateaubriand's literary sensibility made him vigilant with respect to issues of freedom. Late in his career, he drew a contrast between the freedom known to the ancients and that found among the moderns. The former is 'the daughter of mores,' the latter is 'produced by enlight-

enment and perfected civilization'; in one case virtues give rise to freedom, in the other freedom gives rise to virtues.[72] His sense of the fresh requirements of freedom always prevented him from idolizing the past. He echoes feelings of admiration for ancient and aristocratic mores: they were attractive; the habit of authority (and of obedience) gave nobility to relationships. But, he adds sharply, the moral superiority of past ages was purchased at the expense of the liberty of the human race. Christianity has brought this freedom.[73] This historic role of Christianity remains as a leitmotif. (A secondary theme is that it is not true that Protestantism has been more favourable to freedom than Catholicism.)[74] In all his writings (save René of course) culture, civilization, enlightenment, freedom, nature, and religion go together. On this issue he openly broke with Rousseau: for human beings, the state of nature is the state of civilization.[75] This is his stable doctrine, and development only deepened his understanding of the links. In politics he wagered on those political forms that promised a life with fresh moral prospects and new possibilities.

He also came to see that he once gambled on the wrong horse. In 1804 he left the service of Napoleon, took on the pose of an opposition intellectual, and started creating his legend.[76] The change of regime in 1815 was a sign to him that rewards should be coming. But he could not countenance those who planned to return to the society that had existed before 1789. The ancien régime had been gone for only twenty-six years but to him it was gone forever. This past could only be mythical. So while loyal to Louis XVIII, he criticized his ministers and argued that a constitutional, legitimate monarch feels disinterested and secure enough not to fear freedom of the press. The Bourbons did not feel this way. He joined the opposition again. Twice after commitment came withdrawal. With him commitment could not be enslavement, withdrawal could not be silent isolation.

The oscillation between the two rejected poles of feudal loyalty and political absenteeism is clearly articulated in Chateaubriand's late writings. Les mémoires d'outre-tombe contain constant shifts between intimate recollection and past political action, or between present (public) distanciation and past (secret) emotion.[77] To him political enthusiasm and political irresponsiblity were equally impossible. Private chimaeras haunted him in his public hours and dreams of public life accompanied him in his private years. The denunciation of any complicity in the exercise of power between the spiritual and the temporal serves to prevent the enthusiasm, but the spiritual is not allowed to flourish alone. Chateaubriand sets up a permanent tension between the throne and the altar that no human can ignore and no Constantine can resolve.[78] There is, I believe, a link between such temperamental dedication to freedom and the discovery of the inner aesthetic space. An aesthetically aware self needs elbow-room to define and redefine itself and cannot find any peace in a system of obedience or any purely economic system. There is a self-shaping dimension in each life and political association must leave room for that.

3 The moral fruitfulness of the romantic self-shaping becomes most apparent in *Les mémoires d'outre-tombe*, a work begun in 1803 and completed in 1846. Style here serves to give content; this work, besides developing new autobiographical skills, contains Chateaubriand's most interesting contributions to doctrinal development. Starting from the initial insight into universal impermanence, the self of the writer seeks to subvert constant change by becoming the poet of his own existence. The layers of memories thicken: the ocean and forests of his childhood in Britanny are added to those of his travels. Memories and anticipations are organized in the inner aesthetic space in order to reconstitute an identity for the self and create a feeling of permanence in the midst of impermanence. Human life is thus a process that only the self can paint. Here the achievement of the self is clearly an aesthetic one.[79] But in these memoirs, personal destiny is always linked to the collective historical destiny of humankind. The pain of the changing self is exorcised by the sight of social transformations and the social transformations are made bearable by changes in the self.[80] This achievement is truly moral in nature: in the recalling and writing what was felt and done, a distance is taken and an active freedom adapts to an evolving destiny. Out of the disconnected times of Chateaubriand's life, private times and public times, the time of the *Mémoires* is slowly being built. A redemption of loss and evil is taking place in a new, textually constructed time that presents a future to the self.

This autobiographical time, one must stress, is also the time of an era. Besides the awesome, irreversible changes Chateaubriand notes the small, subtle, ambiguous, avoidable changes that precede and follow the big events. The Bastille did not fall in a day. (Has it finished falling?) The epoch is a fluid one, full of selves that, as they 'write' their history (in their heads or on paper), adapt to the necessity of change and gather strength and purpose to 'write' history in the language of public events. The individual and the corporate epic echo each other in this poetic prose that fails to see iron necessity anywhere. The self is not left untouched by historical change and public history is affected by transient selves who pursue intelligently their dialogue with time before they sink into eternity. On such a basis, *Les mémoires d'outre-tombe* proceeds to correct two weaknesses found in *Le génie du christianisme*: the memoirs slowly unfold a characterization of modernity; they redefine Providence and argue for a Christian view of progress. Each point requires a closer look.

4 Chateaubriand is among the first French authors who responded to the post-revolutionary situation by seeking to grasp correctly the 'modern' conditions of life, or the features of 'modern' society and civilization. Behind the demands of egalitarian republicanism, he feels the presence of actual, new forces. He thus ascribes to modernity the status of a fact that is here to stay, breaking from a trend that perceived the new developments as temporary aberrations, or fresh illustrations of an old tendency to decay. On modernity, he abandons the tone of the moralist to take that of the sociologist.[81] Like Machiavelli, who cast a cold eye on the operations of princely power, Chateaubriand casts a cold eye on the functioning of post-revolutionary society. But, unlike Machiavelli, he did not write plain prose purporting simply to tell things the way they are. As he contributed to the delineation of that momentous heuristic abstraction 'modernity,' he never let the modern 'facts' have the last word. The author of *René* could not settle his readers in a rejection of modernity (as a second fall which only religion can redress) or in an enthusiastic endorsement of it. The aesthetic vibrations are here to prevent us from reading him as a propagandist. The inner aesthetic space always contains an ambivalence about what the self acknowledges as real out there on the periphery. When we hear that Napoleon, 'the armed poet,' took God's place, seized the reins of the universe, and made and unmade kings, we are given insight into a fact that became a precedent, and we are made to feel that a transgression occurred; we also read that Napoleon's conquests were not inscribed in the designs of Providence. The *Mémoires* show the despot behind the legendary figure, but they are careful not to attack him in the name of some dead idea, only in the name of something greater than he, namely, freedom.[82] When we hear that the oceans now speak English and have become highways of trade, we feel the loss of a poetic refuge and remain uneasy with the implications of the commercial boom. Besides struggling against the legitimists who have not understood anything in history, Chateaubriand denounces those who have understood too well the direction of it, and want to mobilize it to their profit. Here his aristocratic

background serves him well. He is not dazzled by steamboats, locomotives, increased exports of manufactured goods, and the colonial exploits of European soldiers. 'All this is not civilization.' Bourgeois commercial ventures exploit the potentialities of modern society for their exclusive interests. Industrial leaders do not govern workers but use them. 'To excel in handling business, one does not need to acquire qualities, but to lose some.'[83] The economic liberals distort the meaning of liberty; when they argue that liberty will enrich the poor without impoverishing the rich they promote a false vision of progress.[84] Chateaubriand's political liberalism thus does not become what it so often became after 1830, namely, an annex of economic liberalism.[85]

The Revolution, we read in the *Génie*, has changed the core of character. Avarice, ignorance, and self-love present themselves in a new light. This new moral world cannot simply be accepted; it calls for a second preaching of the Gospel.[86] Chateaubriand thus acknowledges modernity but does not spread modernism as an ideology. Human beings nowadays, he writes, 'are less the slaves of their sweat than of their thoughts.'[87] In dynamic tension with the abstraction, 'modernity,' he sets up another abstraction, 'Christianity.' Religion is not the foe of modernity, nor its ally, but rather a seed of anxiety within it – and, increasingly, a ferment of moral progress.

5 The older Chateaubriand saw the early nineteenth century as one of the great creative eras in the history of Christian civilization. Unlike Pascal, he is a Constantinian, overconfident in 1802, chastened after 1804. While he was not messianic about the return of the Bourbons and had no illusions about Louis-Philippe, he kept seeing new historical possibilities and felt confident about the fresh theoretical insights into the march of history.[88] So we are not settled in a dichotomy between the (historical, political) world of violence and the (spiritual, literary) world of truth.[89] The recalcitrant world can, at times, be bent to good purposes. His journalism, writes Barbéris, occasionally has biblical force.[90] As French ambassador in Rome, he had the opportunity to address the 1829 conclave. 'Evangelical ethics,' he told the cardinals, 'supports the efforts of human reason toward a goal it has not reached yet: among modern peoples, after centuries of darkness and force, Christianity becomes the cause that moves society toward its perfection.'[91]

From approximately 1824 on, he argued that Christianity has the key to the true meaning of progress. The 1831 *Etudes historiques* develop the view according to which the history of modern society begins 'on our side of the Cross.' Christ the Liberator has sown the seeds that now finally bring forth political fruit: after freedom and equality, human-kind is preparing to proclaim fraternity. From now on, no man, no state, has rights on the life of any man.[92] The *Mémoires d'outre-tombe* tells how he would rewrite *Le génie du christianisme*: 'Instead of recalling past benefits and institutions of our religion, I would show that Christianity is the thought of the future and of human freedom; that this messianic and redeeming thought is the only foundation of social equality; that it alone can establish it, since next to equality it places duty, the corrective and regulator of democratic instinct.'[93]

Without Christianity, he stresses in the final pages of the *Mémoires*, the book of history remains closed. 'Anybody who is not a Christian cannot understand the future society.' These pages speak positively of Providence and link it with a democratic notion of progress.[94] We have moved far away from a (fatalistic) Providence that condemns and ruins universally.[95] We have also moved beyond the pale teleology of the *Génie*, which finds purposiveness in plants and animals. But we are not returning to anything like traditional orthodoxy. Chateaubriand has openly broken with Bossuet on Providence. The bishop of Meaux, he writes, neglects to get information on earth; he gets all his charts from heaven. Not all events can be encompassed within an inflexible Christianity.[96] Humankind is perfectible. Christianity, while stable in its dogmas, moves in its teachings.[97] What Providence has in store for us becomes manifest only as we struggle and progress in history.

6 Chateaubriand's romanticism thus does not fit our common cliché about Romantics. He lives in the oscillation between private withdrawal and public involvment.[98] Like many others of his generation, he discovered the sublime: the self, left to itself, feels and tests the awesome power of imagination to create worlds. An ensuing literary voice is born in solitude, in rejection of clichés and usage. There is no approving public left to dictate standards of taste, or if there are remains of such a public, the writer does not want to appeal to them. But the new writer cannot just dream a voice: he or she must find it, try it, write it, must shape his or her truth. Sincerely? Of course. Away from traditional artifice? Yes. But the writer must invent new artifice, new rhetoric. Imagination is the necessary but not sufficient condition for happiness, either as a human being or as a writer: the dreamer must transform himself or herself into a doer, at least to the extent of becoming a writer.[99] Having come that far, the 'dreamer' realizes he or she must please, but, as we just saw, does not want to cater to the socially corrupted pleasures of shared approbation. Therefore he or she can

only tap the erotic sources of pleasure, the one presumably uncorrupted fount of satisfaction left in each individual.[100]

Chateaubriand went one step further. This stylist undertook to write on public affairs and sought a public role. Something of the same romantic style invaded this other territory. As the *Mémoires* reach 1815, Chateaubriand, about to narrate his years as a public figure, warns us that the reader who has seen him in his dreams will now see him in his realities.[101] There is irony in both keywords: we are not allowed to feel that the dreams were hollow and the realities full, but neither should we feel that the dreams were real and the realities empty. The author who reconstructed poetry for private lives tries to do the same thing for the religious and political spheres.[102] He spread a vision first of an austere and compassionate Christianity, and then of a progressive one, both ever responsive to the needs of suffering humanity. His Christianity became more social, not by virtue of a second conversion, but because of the reflection that ripened in the process of writing the *Mémoires*.[103] To tantalize readers with the prospects of large-scale civilized association, his pen flirted with the political side that promises freedom. The legend of just, agreeable, democratic society must be nurtured.

There was, of course, a fatal risk in this move into the territory of politics: literature could get caught in power games. Instead of being the amusement of the idle and evaporating in futility, the writer might become the fellowtraveller of the new mighty.[104] Will the writer become squeezed by power interests? Distanciation is again the answer. There are Renés in any political regime. Romantic literature keeps nurturing the potential for antagonism to politics. Chateaubriand could credibly coin a proud boast: 'I dared to say everything to those who dared to undertake everything.'[105]

My contention thus is that Chateaubriand's style in religious (and political) writing invites the reader ultimately to break from all truth as imperative wisdom transmitted by authorities to submissive readers. More positively, it invites one both to a self-structuring of the self through an autonomous poetic voice,[106] and to the public assertion of individual rights made ringing through a democratic rhetoric.[107] Thus his very aesthetics creates the moral value of his writings and their political significance; we witness in them the rise of a new conception of morality, a modern democratic one, where virtues can stem only from individual freedom. The invasion of this style into the exposition of Christian truth broke with the past; it also laid the basis for new Christian solidarities. It restored pride and meaning in being a Christian in the new circumstances, when opinion was divided between those who had concluded (with sadness or joy) that the Christian faith had become spent as a cultural force, and those who refused to acknowledge that anything had changed and thought they thereby upheld the faith.

Things of course had changed and nowhere more radically than in France. In the world of traditional Christianity, religion did not just hold sway by virtue of the word. There was also Christian power: the anointing of the king, the placing of crucifixes behind judges, and the public execution of blasphemers. After the Revolution, Christian belief had to learn to survive without the support of such power.[108] It was, I claim, the new 'romantic' style, the aestheticization of religious discourse, that both released and ordered all the motivation and energy for the necessary redefinition of human identity, civilized intercourse, and Christian associational objectives. The erotic vibrations in the margins, the 'feminine harmonies' of Christianity, must be evaluated as ingredients in such a move for redefinition.[109] Thus descendents of Rousseau's chimaeras provided the nineteenth century with sources of a reformulation of the existence of human beings, a new basis that could be substituted for a nature that was providing only wooden formulations.[110]

Chateaubriand's works can be said to have religious significance because they are a powerful achievement in symbol-formation: autobiographical times and places are united and crystallized in a sentiment of existence that found an appropriate literary expression. Furthermore these times and places were linked by association to the centuries of Christian history and to the continents where the faith was spreading. And a doctrinal affirmation was ventured that linked Christianity with political freedom. A page had to be turned in European and world history; he turned it. Admittedly what he gave voice to is a human view of religion in general and of Christianity in particular. Still, riches were spread out and depths evoked before the eyes and ears of contemporaries who had lost contact with such religious worlds. At the hinge between the two centuries, he wrote this prayer: 'If we were unfortunate enough to ignore you in the century that comes to an end, you did not roll in vain a new century on our heads. It rang for us like the flash of your lightning. We awoke from our slumber.'[111] Such confessions are not numerous: most of the time, he prefers, like Montesquieu before him, to hold a magisterium on religion and civilization; the shoes he feels most comfortable in are those of the ambassador giving advice to the cardinals, not those of a penitent obeying his confessor. But, unlike Montesquieu, he states his belief. The 1826 Preface to the reprinting of the *Essai sur les Révolutions*[112] makes four careful points and their testimony must be allowed to stand. His faith is sincere. He belongs to the communion of all who, since creation, have prayed to God. He interprets the Gospel not in the service of despots but to serve those who are miserable. And he conforms to the exalted and compassionate spirit of the Gospel. The continuity with Rousseau's sincerity and natural religion is obvious. But there is a new commitment to put Christians on the side of the politics of freedom and charity.

At a time when the sentiments of modernity took shape, when legend and honour had to be recreated, Chateaubriand, who had an ego matching that of Napoleon ('I made history; I could also write it')[113], offered his alternative to the emperor's inventions (labelled 'the empire of ribbons' by Stendhal). His exploration of inner aesthetic spaces led to the invention of a personal style. Buffon wrote in the eighteenth century that the style was the man; style then was like good clothes worn with grace by a self who knew what he was and where he was. In Chateaubriand's time the self no longer knew that; man had to become style.[114] As Chateaubriand forged his unique voice, the chimaeras became civilized; they helped to create a social self that could communicate and act under the new conditions. His style is thus more important than the doctrines he helped formulate. In an era when certainties were gone and history was poeticized in a move to absorb all passions in historical struggles, or when prose furthered the ends of the economic betterment of a few in the midst of political injustice, the poeticizing of Christianity with all its apparent excesses or flaws of taste kept alive a sense of the continuities of Western civilisation and an *eros* for the suprahistorical. By historicizing Christianity, he led some to relativize it; he led others to an admiration of the faith that did not include belief in it. But more important, this poeticizing conveyed the sense that Christianity in history had a plastic quality, and that such interior matters as one's spiritual freedom or one's relationship to God were more important than one's opinion of a religion or of religion in general. The ongoing voice initiated by *René* enabled Chateaubriand to confess his God without becoming the tool of any of the conservative powers of his day. 'Only literary writing can prevent the reactionary coopting of religion' writes Barbéris.[115]

In an age when Christian dogma and mores were secure and defined realities, Milton, mourning the death of the Reverend Edward King, named him Lycidas and surrounded his death with the conventions and fictions of pastoral poetry and classical mourning, 'to interpose a little ease.'[116] But his realities remained defined by Christian eschatology, with glory awaiting the righteous and doom catching up with unworthy clerics. In Chateaubriand's time, the dominant realities are defined by the virtuosos of the battlefield and the stock exchange. The aesthetics of Christianity interpose a little ease, for comfort, for evasion, but also for refreshment, and the redefining of action. In the space gained in this manner, a little tune can strive for expression; and 'he who does not have this melody within himself, will ask it in vain of the Universe.'[117]

3

A Different Economy for Belief: Nodier

Most of the responses to the French Revolution known in the English-speaking world are responses from afar. There was no tunnel under the Channel when Burke wrote his *Reflections*. Kant reacted to newspaper reports in distant Koenigsberg. Hegel saw Napoleon riding in the streets of Jena, but kept away from the battlefield – he clearly did not believe in citizens' armies – and thus lived to digest more historical events and enlighten us on the meaning of them all. The French responses usually do not have the advantages of such distance. French men and women were inevitably caught up in the quick succession of events and were often actively politically involved.

Most of the specifically theological responses were also shaped at some geographical and temporal distance; usually those directly involved had already narrated the events (in mutually exclusive narratives) before theologians elaborated further views. Here again things are very different in France: very quickly clergy and believers were split between those who accepted and those who rejected the Civil Constitution of the Clergy. Such polarization of opinion was not conducive to theological reflection. Responses remained partisan for a long time.[1]

By drawing attention to the writings of Charles Nodier (1780–1844) I wish to offer an opportunity for some fresh thinking on the perspectives individual minds can gain on the rapid and chaotic successions of events they are subjected to. Nodier appears in French literary histories as the Catholic and royalist librarian of the Arsenal; there, in the late 1820s, he received and encouraged the young men who were to become the great Romantics (Hugo, Lamartine, Vigny) and some of the minor ones (including Nerval). His role in this *salon littéraire* somewhat eclipsed his own writing. But a recent edition of his *Portraits de la Révolution et de l'Empire*[2] draws attention to precisely the issues that are of interest to us: how does an eyewitness remember the events of the Revolution? What impact do the memories of a participant have on his subsequent life? What do they do to his imaginative and religious life? Nodier consciously faced the issues as he asked himself, both as a man profoundly aware he had gone through a major cultural earthquake and as an author involved in the innovations of the romantic movement, how he was to narrate his life and tell his tales. This also led him to think about the place books had occupied in human history and about their significance in the new society. His attention to books as *objects* made him the founder (in 1834) of the *Bulletin du bibliophile*.[3]

What Nodier had to remember was momentous enough: he was nine when the Revolution began, and ten when his father became head of the local revolutionary tribunal; at twelve, as a Latin scholar and member of the Besançon Jacobin club, he pronounced orations on republican virtue; at thirteen, his father sent him to Strasbourg to learn Greek, but he found his potential teacher to be an ardent republican embroiled in fearsome events, accused by none less than Saint-Just, tried, found guilty, and sent to Paris to be guillotined. Nodier witnessed executions that year and wants us to believe that he once attended a dinner and found out shortly afterward that all the other guests had been stretched out on the guillotine.[4] His father managed to disengage him from too-dangerous involvements. Nodier then dabbled in entomology, fraternal and secret societies, esotericism, futile conspiracies against Napoleon, jails, journalism, literary attempts, and unhappy love affairs. At twenty-eight, he married and found some stability.

The facts of his youth are not well known and certainty often eludes us.[5] What is clear is that he dipped into what we would now call alternate religions and what literary historians call *illuminisme*.[6] Illuminism is an offshoot of the eigthteenth-century masonic movement. At the end of the century, tenets found in, for instance, *The Magic Flute* came to be promoted by teachers-writers who appear to us to be entirely private persons spreading their 'revelations' to a few initiates.[7] Nodier most probably assimilated the teachings of one such person, Louis-Claude de Saint-Martin, author of *L'homme de désir* (1790), a volume of gnostic teachings inviting one to a fraternal utopia based on a new man to be born of a purely internal regeneration.[8] In Nodier's time the intellectual challenge inherent in all religious deviants ceased being offered mainly by enthusiasts, mystics, or *convulsionnaires* who lived on the fringe of the churches; what began forcing the attention of all students of human nature was rather a flowering of individual oddities, eccentrics, or crackpots in charge of a revelation they alone expounded.[9]

Nodier thus belonged to a very specific and troubled generation. Unlike Chateaubriand, born in 1768, who was a man of twenty-one when the Revolution began, and unlike Vigny, born in 1797, who as a boy (and from a safe position) had Napoleon's campaigns to get excited about, Nodier was hit by the glorious and gruesome facts as an eagerly participating and very young adolescent. As he put it himself, he witnessed 'a complete history.'[10] He saw the reformist enthusiasm, the republican fervour, the embattled Republic, the Terror, the military stabilization, the Empire, the conquest of Europe, the collapse, and the invasion of France. In 1815, at thirty-five, he found a Bourbon back on the throne. Historical cycles moved faster in those days than anything Herodotus or Thucydides (or the Bible for that matter) had written about.

In 1815 Nodier wrote a first account of some of the events he had been involved in. *Les Philadelphes: Histoire des sociétés secrètes de l'armée*[11] tells of unknown secret associations that nurtured visions of liberty and conspired against the emperor. As one advances in one's reading, one realizes that, for a subordinate who had only few contacts, writing the history of a secret society after the events is pretty much like writing a novel: little said is ever likely to be disproved, especially if all the leaders have been arrested and shot. What becomes very clear is *why* Nodier writes his account in the first days of the Restoration: he says that he wants the memory of these brave men to be kept for posterity; clearly he is also out to prove to the returned king and his followers that, while he had been an ardent and sincere republican, he never made his peace with the tyrant and usurper, and is now chastened and mature enough to understand that virtuous citizens will best prosper under the legitimate (and constitutional) monarch. This piece of writing did its job: in 1824, the Count of Artois, later Charles X, appointed him as his librarian at l'Arsenal.

With his secure position, Nodier dug back into his memories and came out with a more significant (and courageous) piece. *Recherches sur l'éloquence révolutionnaire* (1829) attributes literary merit to speeches made in the heat of the Revolution. 'Revolutionary literature produced a new form of society and a new form of literature.'[12] The Jacobins (Robespierre, Saint-Just) were the greatest speakers: their authority did not rest on

eighteenth-century (aristocratic) canons of wit and taste: they were elo-
quent because they gave expression to the thoughts and passions that
dominated the period.[13] No one had dared to make such points: praising Robespierre – even if only as an orator and writer – was not in fashion during the Restoration, when it was expected that the noble epithet
of 'literary' would be attributed only to works of 'good taste' and in the
classical mode. (The few Romantics around Hugo and Nodier were an
embattled minority and what they were praising then was the Middle
Ages.)

The pieces gathered in 1831 under the simple title *Souvenirs*[14] show
Nodier in full and conscious grasp of a few basic historiographical
issues involved in his narrative attempts. First, he notes that the Revolution disturbed more interests, stirred more passions, and involved
more actors than any previous event. 'Since everybody took part, everybody has the right to narrate.' Danger being omnipresent, everyone
had to navigate between a Scylla and a Charybdis. Every human being is thus the hero of an odyssey he or she alone can tell.[15] The time is
gone when histories were only memoirs written by dukes and generals,
or chronicles commissioned by monarchs. Second, theatrical metaphors keep recurring under his pen to describe the new excitement of
shared action. He evokes the great evening in Kehl when the National
Guard repelled a sudden enemy attack in the midst of a performance of
Brutus: the leading actor played his part in the fight and returned,
wounded, to finish the play. Tirades on liberty in the theatre were
punctuated by gunshots finishing the job with the enemies at the bridge.
Spectators no longer knew whether they were on the banks of the Rhine
or the Tiber.[16] Thinking of his own, more modest role, Nodier says he
was only a supernumerary in the Revolution. (He narrates his days in
jail in a light vein; it was a pleasant experience – he was not deemed
dangerous, he made new friends, and he gained invaluable perspective.) 'Everybody is in the secret of a tragedy, except the protagonists.'[17]
The minor actors understand the play better than the major ones, who
are absorbed in their role.[18] Saint-Just was such a fiery presence because
his life had become a role.[19] Third, Nodier notes that what he remembers at the time of writing are personal sensations. What he offers are
'naïve souvenirs.' 'Half-erased perceptions do not become truths by
virtue of being written.' Hence much diffidence and self-deprecation:
'I may err on the facts that move me most.' His narrative, he realizes,
is lengthy: it could have been short with just the facts, but he took

pleasure in conveying personal emotions. And yet there is assurance in his voice: Nodier knows he may err, but, like Rousseau, he certainly does not wish to lead anybody into error.[20]

Memories of the Revolution thus become an opportunity to ask questions about the boundaries between reality and imagination. What he saw *was* like theatre. What people experienced then was an invasion, by means of language and enthusiastic scenarios, of imaginary worlds into the real one. It follows that memory has to be preserved in a new style; narratives must include the record of what the participants (even minor ones) believed was taking place. The discourses of 'legitimate history' must also acknowledge the place from which they are written.[21]

The gaining of such a standpoint gave Nodier some literary boldness: in 1833 he published 'Le dernier banquet des Girondins.'[22] History has it that twenty-one Girondin leaders spent the time between their sentencing and their execution, a short night, having a meal that achieved a festive quality. Nodier presents the twenty-one protagonists, and has them converse in a platonic sort of dialogue. He had enough information about the Girondins to gain a good grasp of the character of each, and he has his protagonists utter sentiments their real-life counterparts had expressed, but clearly this piece will never pass for history. Are we to say it is only literature? No, because the dialogue contains a claim to be a high-minded sort of history, not very different from the history we have of the Peloponnesian war. (It is Thucydides who composed Pericles' famous oration.) Writing this text provides Nodier with an opportunity to state as historical truth a moral truth which to him is more valuable than the listing of facts. Referring to some disagreement among the witnesses as to the order in which the Girondins were executed, Nodier writes, 'History has enough work to do counting our dead, to worry much about the order in which they were hit.'[23] Easy and emotional moralizing? To be sure. But any history writing must achieve some *style*, lend tone to a narrative. We cannot be satisfied with historians who count the hair on the Sphinx's tail and never face her look.

There is also, of course, a fairly transparent personal agenda in the writing of the piece memorializing the Girondins. Forty years later Nodier wanted to protect the innocence of *his* revolution. He wanted to exorcise bad memories and create a moment of repose, of noble recollection. His Girondins are lucid (by then they probably were): 'The deity,' they say, 'that presides over social creations is the poet's nymph'; 'The miracle of a creation obeying the laws of the word will not happen ever again'; 'The intelligence of nations goes through dark nights that destroy the work of its days'; 'We legislators agreed only one day and on only one word – to which we all gave a different meaning' (the word is 'Republic,' of course).[24] Nodier thus recaptures, puts on the stage, and immortalizes a purity of republican intention that did exist, that must have existed, before the fatal contamination.[25]

As a writer of fiction Nodier owes his greatest success to a dark story of love and brigandry. *Jean Sbogar*, published anonymously in 1818, was so successful that public opinion was at first convinced it was a translation from an English or German 'gothic' author. (After this initial success, the genre became acclimatized in France and became known as the 'roman frénétique,' a label Nodier coined for it.) *Jean Sbogar* contains all the key elements of black romanticism: a remote, wild location (Croatia), storms, menacing monks, gloomy castles, and, most important of all, a hero who professes himself incapable of love and a heroine who considers herself quite gifted for it and wants to save the hero (or reduce him to normalcy). The portrayal of estrangement has sharp religious and political configurations. In three long 'explanations' to the heroine, the hero recounts how he has lost the faith of his childhood, and has seen 'le néant'; how he believes societies inevitably die in chaos to be reborn in violence; and how the only happiness he has ever known came through his contact with nature in Montenegro. The novel contains an inserted text, 'Lothario's Tablets,' a series of nihilistic aphorisms, expressing an aristocratic brand of anarchism. The ten pages became a classic with disenchanted youths. (They also explained why Nodier published the book anonymously; he maintains a distance in a later preface, acknowledging his authorship of the novel but refusing responsibility for the 'theories' of his hero.) The following are a few examples from the text:

When politics becomes a science of words, all is lost. More vile than the slave of a tyrant is the dupe of a sophist.

Of all governments, the one against which my heart least revolts, the one that least degrades mankind, is the despotism of the Orient; the debasement of the people is at least explained by superstition. I can understand a tyrant who is descended from prophets and allied with the stars. In Tibet, he is invisible, immortal, sacred. This is how it should be. Tyranny and slavery are two conditions that presuppose two species. The most debased of men are slaves who obey tyrants cast in their own image.

There lie at the heart of man three mysteries that induce him to live: God, love and freedom. – And society would have ceased to exist two thousand years ago if a few Galilean beggars had not chosen to create a religion from these very mysteries.

I know of only one profession left to discredit, that of *God*.

If my heart could give itself faith … if I had to *invent* a god, I would want him to be born on stable straw; to escape from assassins in the arms of a poor artisan thought to be his father; to spend his childood in poverty and exile; to be outcast all his life, despised by the powerful, ignored by kings, persecuted by priests, forsworn by his friends, sold by one of his disciples, abandoned by the most honourable of his judges, chosen for torture over the most ignoble of the villains, beaten with rods, crowned with thorns, vilified by executioners; and to perish between two thieves, one of whom would follow him to heaven.[26]

Nodier's fiction includes bizarre pieces, probably very puzzling to readers accustomed to classical norms. Much of his work is experimental; it casts doubts on the merits of narratives: they rarely convey any truth, and have, at best, only entertainment value.

In 1830, for instance, he published *Histoire du roi de Bohême et de ses sept châteaux*: the book promises to tell the story announced by Corporal Trim in *Tristram Shandy* (1760–7); Nodier, however, like Sterne, never gets to start the story, let alone finish it; his reader, like Uncle Toby, remains frustrated. This book is the culmination of his interest in 'eccentric narratives' (which he defined as books which do not adhere to ordinary rules of composition, and in which the reader cannot discern the author's purpose – if he had any – in writing it.)[27] This interest had started early: already in 1800 *Moi-même*[28] is brief autobiographical babbling by a narrator who proves incapable of finding a thread – for his story? for his life? The *Histoire du roi de Bohême* is a full-length disconnected series of procedural fireworks: three personages share the idea of getting to Bohemia, in the hope of getting the story started; they never get there; we do get, in bits, two stories that apparently have little to do with the main object and, in between all the digressions, we get plenty of lists and derision for scholarly academies and erudite authors (Rabelais is as much in the background as Sterne; Nodier always expressed contempt for erudite authors who, as he put it once 'take time to know everything but not to choose').[29] The reader is systematically frustrated of any completed emplotment, and deprived of any opportunity to identify with something going on or someone doing something.[30] In ultimate derision, the book is compared with what some hack would produce by letting luck determine which words get drawn from the 'inexhaustible lottery of dictionaries.'[31] The book is the work of a sad clown, writes Hubert Juin.[32] It is also the work, argues Pierre Barbéris, of an artist who has come to the disheartening conclusion that language is polluted by politicians and statesmen – the 1830 Revolution was verbose and had seemed to achieve a lot with words. Parody, Nodier seems to conclude, is the only form of verbal honesty left.[33]

Histoire du roi de Bohême is the farthest Nodier ever went in the direction of literary innovation: the book has been (justly) described as the first synaesthetic book.[34] Like an opera, the finished product integrates the input of various arts: text, illustrations, and typography were planned together to make a beautiful object – and the publisher went bankrupt over it. After this 'success' Nodier remained with what he clearly excelled in, namely, the more conventional type of romantic tale.[35]

La fée aux miettes (1832) is probably his most noteworthy achievement along this line. In the preface the author informs us that he dislikes any reference to truth in the arts and has come to the conclusion that stories are only for entertainment – clearly they cannot instruct and improve – and that 'in an age without beliefs' a good and truly fantastic story is most fittingly narrated by a happy madman totally absorbed in the combinations of some strange tale, provided some other madman, less happy but more reasonable, stands as an intermediary between the original madman and the reading public.[36]

In the text itself, we begin by meeting such an intermediate narrator, who also has some prefatory comments to make. We hear him express his dislike of Livy, 'a liar' not worth spending any time on, especially when there are first-rate works of fantasy available; he then adds that, in his view, the author of *Puss'n Boots* is as reliable and trustworthy an author as can be found. He goes on to say that lunatics are in touch with minds in another world unknown to us and that he met such a person in a Glasgow asylum. His head was full of chimaeras: he believed himself to be the carpenter who worked for Adoniram, Solomon's architect, and to be married to a woman three thousand years old. The narrator stayed in the asylum to enter somewhat into his folly, and thus became 'a voluntary lunatic,' to hear the carpenter tell the story of his life.

The body of the tale is the narration of his own life by Michel, the mad carpenter found in the asylum. Born in Normandy, Michel was raised by an uncle, and formed an acquaintance with an old begging woman who usually stayed under the church porch. She is mysterious; no one recalls ever having seen her young. Known as 'la fée aux miettes,' she is very clever, knows all languages, and entrances the young man with her conversation. Since the uncle sermonizes the young man on the need to acquire a trade, and since there is much high-minded talk about carpentry (the trade Michel chooses), the reader gains the impression he or she is embarking upon some form of *Bildungsroman*. The 'fée aux miettes,' in the midst of some joking banter, suggests Michel might want to marry her; earnest as always, he says he must wait three years, until he is twenty-one. She takes a larger and larger place in his imagination; as he rescues her from the quicksands near Mont Saint Michel, he learns from her that she is Belkiss, or the Queen of Sheba, Belkiss being her Arabic name. She gives him a magic medallion on which has been painted a portrait of her when she was young and beautiful. This portrait, with its mysterious attractive smile, brings bliss to the hero; he finds the woman in the medallion alive. At this point the young man, argues Jean-Luc Steinmetz, takes the fateful turn to insanity. The border line between representation and reality becomes erased. Instead of remaining outside the frame looking at the picture, the young man enters the frame to live in the picture. The signifier no longer points to the signified but lives a life of its own.[37]

What we call 'real' life nevertheless goes on. A long and incoherent series of events seems to test the virtue, patience, and benevolence of the young man. The demands of the 'fée aux miettes' are somewhat erratic; she has no character whereby her expectations might be said to be in character. She asks for money to reach a house she has in Scotland; he gives it. As the three-year deadline approaches, Michel himself goes to Scotland, only to become embroiled in terrible events, in which we may see further manifestations of the bizarre sequence of events to which we are submitted. Accused of having murdered a magistrate – who is a dog – he suffers a nightmarish (literally?) trial and is condemned to death. At the scaffold a most attractive young lass offers to become his wife and thus save his life. He refuses, since the old 'fée aux miettes' has his promise. Not unexpectedly the old woman appears and he marries her. At this point the virtue of the young man may begin to lose some plausibility in the minds of most readers: he professes to prefer the beauty of an old woman who never ages to that of a young one who will be admired for only a few springs. So Michel settles down to a happy life with his old wife, in her house, which turns out to be the size of a doll's house – mysteriously he shrinks to feel comfortable in it. The house contains a marvellous library and a magnificent Oriental garden. They live chastely; she has for him a mother's love. Life in this house looks a lot like that of a prisoner in a cell; the conditions are hard but they are redeemed by the possession of a good book.[38] Outside the house, Michel maintains an economic sort of existence. Modest successes in carpentering enable him to help his friends become rich, but he admits that none of his wife's instructions are of any use to him. Civilization has ceased to be 'the mutual and universal practice of benevolence'; he cannot understand what it has become, nor make himself useful in it.[39] The plot thickens when at night (in a dream?) the beautiful young Belkiss comes to him; what his marriage offers him at this point is wisdom and the study of languages with the old woman during the day, and love (real? imagined?) with Belkiss at night. A crisis occurs when the old woman informs him that she must die unless he finds for her a singing mandrake. He agrees to leave on this quest; then for the first time she lets him into her bedroom, where he falls asleep next to her and relives a night like the first one (whatever that was) with Belkiss.

Readers must have asked themselves more than once before reaching this point what, in fact, they are reading. The text insensibly shifts from one sub-genre to another. Readers cease to know what implicit conventions govern their relationship to the text. How are they to read it? as an edifying tale? a fairy tale? a fantastic one? or as a piece fraught with irony? Is *La fée aux miettes* a story of resignation climaxing with the message that married life is a mixture of drab, confining realities and pleasant illusions? Or is it a sobering novel of virtuous masonic initiation? Clearly Michel is being tested, and possibly initiated, but he shows little desire, and takes no initiative, certainly no erotic initiative; he is even less sexed than the already very tame Tamino. And is not masonic wisdom supposed to lead to some less confining, more expansive, climax or fulfilment? Are we not rather reading the story of a descent into a harmless and happy form of madness? Is not Michel being slowly degraded to a life in which the only communication with his fellow human beings occurs magically? Does this 'roman de formation' turn out to be a 'roman de déformation'?[40]

The tale ends in an equally inconclusive way. The narrator meets a 'philanthropic' doctor who gives a lengthy, learned diagnosis about lunatics in search of singing mandrakes and plans a barbarous treatment for Michel. Later the narrator learns that the young man has es-

caped from the asylum to search for his singing mandrake. This interrupts the tale; the 'voluntary lunatic' cannot share in the search. No
clue is given to help readers decide on one of two possible interpreta-
tions. Perhaps the young man has a diseased imagination and must be
kept in an asylum for his own self-protection. (That he will be treated
unwisely and cruelly is only the sort of misfortune that is common to
all humankind.) Or, perhaps, he is as sane as the rest of us, in spite of
his fantasies about Belkiss, and able to live free, outside the asylum (far
from the torturing alienists), as safely as the rest of us.

Nodier's text is carefully crafted to keep both views plausible. 'In an
age without belief,' all clues about what is really going on are missing,
or confused. As Steinmetz puts it, Nodier's writings keep wrestling
with inner demons (and their deceptions); can some grasp of reality
emerge triumphant?[41] Clearly Nodier wants to put in a word for the
'lunatics.'[42] Fictions keep resonating in all of us – Rousseau and
Chateaubriand made that clear enough – and always cloud such clear
conscience as we strive to attain. Nodier's art manages to elicit some
sense of complicity between the most prosaic reader and his more 'fantastic' heroes. As he puts it, we find in such heroes 'the tunes of our
own unreason.'[43] We also have bees in our bonnets. We also drift away
from a firm grasp of reality. Maybe all men dream at times of women
they do not have to reach out to. (The singing mandrake is an emblem
of apersonal erotic bliss, of sexual lyricism without encounter with a
partner.)[44]

As the thirties 'progressed' under the bourgeois king, Nodier felt
more than ever lost in the civilization that surrounded him. Clearly a
political system that limited the franchise to wealth (and to a large
amount of it) lacked in his eyes both the elegance of the ancien régime
and the panache of the Revolution. The alliance between throne and
altar was relaxed, if not broken, by a more pragmatic regime. In those
circumstances, Nodier became increasingly aware of what he needed to
write – and needed to believe. He thus became more affirmative in his
praise of the merits of dreaming and fantasizing. His personal, intimate
religious bent also expressed itself more openly. (The fact that the court
had ceased to be visibly devout may have helped here.)

Nodier's 1830 article, 'Du fantastique en littérature' reflects on the
then-current taste for fantastic tales.[45] The author starts with a distinction between religious and purely poetic fancy. Since the former must
make a 'serious impression' and have an impact on 'positive life,' it is
'necessarily solemn and somber'; the latter presents everything in an

agreeable light. The author, however, promptly obliterates the distinction: religion nowadays has no impact on the imagination, or brings it only confused notions'; imagination, therefore, is nourished by poetry alone.[46] Nodier's clearest definition of the fantastic, something that 'stirs the heart profoundly' without imposing sacrifices to reason, is found in an 1832 tale.[47] This definition fits his own earlier tales, such as *Smarra* and *Trilby*. They are not mainly characterized by suspense, and thus are quite unlike those of Edgar Allan Poe. Neither are they magical like those of Hoffmann. What is typical of them is a sort of epistemological unease rooted in the perplexities caused by human interaction; readers are bound to ask themselves with some anxiety, What is really going on among these people? What remains implausible is nevertheless attractive.

Focusing on what is implausible becomes widespread in the modern age because, Nodier thinks, poetry is exhausted and religions are shaken. 'Two things are essential to poetry, he writes, the poet who believes what he writes and the listener who believes the poet. Their meeting has become very rare and so has poetry.'[48] In periods of disappointment and despair, when 'life' is dominated by 'positive' realities, writers and readers alike look for compensation and the ability to produce what is fantastic runs along vulgar channels. Thus the belief of the religious man and the imagination of the poet become the only sanctuaries freedom can find. (And the folly of the madman is not far behind.) In a world dominated by positive, utilitarian, and allegedly progressive minds, religious faith and poetic illusion tie their fate. Nodier seems to have some hopes mainly because of whatever fragile beliefs poets have to give; our inclination for what is marvellous is the only truly providential compensation left. As he was to put it, 'Religion no longer lives up to our dreams.'[49] The religion he refers to of course is French Catholicism, which had been riding high politically (or seemed to) from 1815 until 1830 and had seemed aesthetically renovated. But the newly romanticized religiousness of Chateaubriand and his admirers does not impress Nodier. He has more distant dreams. We know that as a young man he had toyed with illuminist beliefs. But these did not make miracles either; he does not seem to have derived any lasting satisfaction from them and no stable beliefs settled in his mind.[50]

But his interest in the esoteric left him with a constant sense of the enormous amount of odd stuff that can be found in rare books and that needs to be conserved by dedicated bibliophiles. Hence his fascination with *grimoires*, books of magic with mysterious, incomprehensible formulas, unknown alphabets, and hieroglyphs.[51] As a collector he was proud of his copy of the *first edition* (Venice 1499) of *Hypnerotomachia*. This book on Aphrodite and the erotic mysticism of antiquity was the work of Franciscus Columna, a Dominican who wrote in a macaronic hybrid of vulgar Italian and Latin with a sprinkling of Oriental languages; the book also contains, acrostically, the name of the friar's secret love, Polla. (Previous commentators thought Polla was an allegory for antiquity but Nodier preferred to think she was a lady of noble birth.)[52] All alternative views of life deserve to be preserved. Nodier, although very fond of butterflies, might not have shed many tears over the disappearance of the dodo, but he was, I think, utterly serious when he wrote that there is no greater crime than killing the tongue of a nation.[53]

Published in 1831, 'De l'amour et de son influence' seems completely disenchanted with worldly affairs.[54] (Earlier, in 1827, Nodier's review of Hugo's *Odes et ballades* had argued that politics had disenchanted society.)[55] Revolutionaries, Nodier recalls from his youth, did not apply teachings; they followed their spontaneous inspirations. Forty years later, the heirs still discuss the theories but have lost the enthusiasms. Now that God is dead, humankind has only poetry left. Even that, however, is small comfort; Nodier multiplies self-deprecating comments about his words and their weight.[56] (It takes vanity to write a preface, he once stated.)[57]

Thus in his last years Nodier seems increasingly to detach himself from worldly realities. His last two tales (1839, 1844) are labelled 'mystical' by their editor, Castex; they clearly manifest a disposition to believe in the reality of the world one gains access to in dreams.[58] This time, a set of ideas, or a system of beliefs, comes to buttress (or try to buttress) the fleeting magic of the texts. He gives more and more credence to spiritual notions of immortality which, in his view, are in fact believed everywhere and are expressed particularly clearly in the poetry which appears at the birth of a nation. He adds that these notions are still echoed in legends circulating in the countryside.[59] (This praise of simple folkways brings water to the mill of political conservatives.) Henceforth he seems to let 'civilization' go its way. 'I closed my eyes on society.'[60] Nodier, had discovered that the Revolution, for a while, was like theatre, in that the actors could create reality; now that reality is prosaic, dull, and even dismal, he seems simply to have decided that it is a bad play. His last 'souvenir' (1834) narrates his youthful escape from 'gendarmes' with a warrant in his name, *Suites d'un mandat d'arrêt*.[61] This text is heavily 'romanced,' as the cliché has it, and includes fantastic features. Nodier confesses at the outset that his early years had an unmatched charm, and are more important to him than the Revolution. What he enjoys writing is an account of the past that takes him away from the present, into his youth, running in the Jura mountains in spring-time, when he was strong and had vivid feelings.[62] A line has been crossed: we have the old man not as sage or witness, surrounded by young people and talking about what he saw in his youth, but as soli-tary dreamer-writer recapturing for himself the emotions of his youth.[63]

When Jean-Jacques Rousseau wrote to Christophe de Beaumont, 'In their eyes, I live in a country of chimaeras; in mine, they live in a country of prejudices,' he wanted to jolt his reader and hoped for a dialogue of minds.[64] Nodier seems to have resigned himself to the exist-ence of an abyss between his modes of mental operation and those of most of his contemporaries. He has thereby crossed a line, somewhat pitifully at times; he admits his writing is compensatory. The story Rousseau narrated could be labelled a myth because its author could not live without it; it became part of his identity and the backbone of the discourse he held with others. The fantasies of Nodier are just pass-ing ones. Contented with his little wife, Michel professes this piece of wisdom, 'I am in this world to enjoy my life and my imagination, and ignore its mysteries ... I take my life as it is.'[65] Nodier's Christian alle-giance, when affirmed, is likewise fleeting. 'Each time unhappiness weighed heavily upon me, or solitude gave me back to myself, I found myself again as sincerely Christian as in my mother's arms.'[66] His faith comes to him in puffs. With Nodier what is beautiful is not really ex-pected to enchant permanently any more. He has also moved beyond the position exemplified by Chateaubriand: no exchange is expected to take place between the dreams of the self and the historical processes which construct the new society.[67]

There is something extreme about Nodier; Heinrich Heine put his finger on it when he quipped, 'Nodier was so often guillotined during the Revolution, that it is no surprise he has somewhat lost his head.'[68] The word Nodier put in on behalf of the lunatic stayed. His way of posing the question of individual insanity versus dominant rationality was timely. Doctors and lawyers paid attention in those years to the fate of mentally unfit people, and began to reform both hospitals and law. Philippe Pinel was reputed to have broken the chains holding the insane at Bicêtre, riding the wave of revolutionary emancipatory practices.[69] In 1832 the law accepted the notion of temporary insanity (*aliénation mentale*) as a cause of irresponsibility. But Nodier's way of raising the issue was also somewhat academic: it was a further exploration of the themes of marginality and of social alienation. 'We are today too much preoccupied with serious follies, which are the shame of mankind, when they are not its terror.'[70] His treatment of the theme of 'folly' was not clouded by severe mental suffering. While it is true that he was uncommonly depressed after the marriage (1830) of Marie, his only child, this does not suffice to put him in company with Rousseau, who occasionally suffered from personality disorders and accusations of madness. There was no malice in Heine's quip, while some of the insinuations about Rousseau by the 'enlightened' camp were malicious and proceeded from an overconfident rationality. It is also true that Nodier discussed Piranesi's etchings with deep feeling and wrote that these labyrinths are too dangerous to live in, that madness and suicide lie in wait there.[71] But, unlike Nerval, who had to be hospitalized, Nodier never was entirely swallowed by the labyrinth. Nodier placed quite a few mad people in his fictions; they are all harmless and happy. While Nodier made many apt observations on the way the insane speak, he did not make his insane characters speak that way. As has been suggested, he made a compromise with what was then readable.[72] In other words, his lunatics are literary. They serve to portray innocent lives that remain unaffected by the insanity prevailing in the public world. Such portrayals started a literary convention. Who is not prepared today to entertain the idea that sometimes the physicians doing the locking up are more dangerous than the lunatics locked in? And who in our age is not tantalized by the rapprochement between religion, literature, and madness, and not in search of some clear demarcating principle?

Such musings over insanity also put us on the track of a radical consequence of the French Revolution. Everyone knows that the Revolution destroyed the traditional social order and that the church afterwards had to redefine and regain its place in society. What Nodier's memorializing, autobiographical, and fictional attempts show, is that the Revolution also destroyed the order of time.[73] This of course was felt particularly keenly by someone who entered the disruptions as a young adolescent. Nodier experienced a complete historical cycle (and therefore felt he could survey the rise and fall of civilizations) and found himself incapable of holding this cycle within a narrative of events that had the traditional features of beginning, middle, and (cathartic) end.[74] Perhaps, he suggests, all accounts of such events are inevitably delirious; there is something wistful in his concluding, after an evocation of the exalted talk *of* the Revolution and *about* the Revolution, that 'behind all these metaphors, there is a history.'[75] Nodier's autobiographical writings thus deserve to be placed next to those of Chateaubriand, the thirty-two-year-old aristocrat who wrote *René*, the story of a young aristocrat incapable of joining the new public history. Nodier also anticipates the art that Chateaubriand brought to perfection in *Mémoires d'outre-tombe*, namely the art of relativizing the meaning of grandiose events by writing next to the record of them the memory of deeply felt private feelings. He also anticipates Proust and his discovery of the art of narrative structure that hinges on the personal becoming that leads to the decision to write. When sincere, do we tell what we are or become what we narrate?

Nodier's 'historical' writings thus illustrate what appears in all early attempts to write about the Revolution: a breakdown of narrative technique. The widespread violence and the rapid rise and fall from power of individuals and groups cause emotions to be unsettled and make the hands that hold the pens tremble. Aristocratic novelists mention 'atrocities' and repeat some clichés: they want us to believe that, in their indignation, words fail them. (Later, authors of *romans noirs* cash in with the accounts of stereotyped but apolitical horrors.) Rétif de la Bretonne tries to narrate what he sees daily in the streets during the nineties in Paris. His *Nuits révolutionnaires* is predicated upon his belief that every incident can become a novel; he mixes the account of things seen with the outpouring of his phantasms.[76] Thus, memoirs and confessions, previously quite distinct, merge. To sum up, the narration of time is forced into new paths and a new ordering of temporal existence seems to be in the making.

The breakdown of old narrative technique makes room for a new one: the French fantastic tale works because social as well as supernatural beliefs have been shaken and discredited. All of the suspense – such as it is – hinges on whether the lunatic (or the curse, or the apparition) is 'true' or not, on whether there is a rational explanation for the disturbing occurrences. (Nodier's tales, like most, hint in the end at a rationalist explanation; meanwhile, the story successfully toys with readers' beliefs. And readers begin to feel the hand of the writer turning the screw.)[77]

His 'fiction' thus admits it is playful, it can afford openly to admit to being fiction, and it can claim that its worth rests on this alone. Nodier can formulate an explicitly new aesthetics: 'Nothing is true but what is false.'[78] Daily reality appears in art only to be abolished and yield to another, poetic, reality.[79]

The new aesthetics comes with a high degree of self-consciousness about what a book really is. One side renews and extends the mythical stature of books: a book shelters prodigious secrets; it magically gets hold of a person; it becomes an asylum, and creates a better world for a wounded being. A bibliophile, Nodier dreams about a perfect book;[80] a bibliographer, he also plays with the idea of a complete science of books (including that most elusive achievement, a proper and thorough classification!) that would offer, finally, a *complete* science of the world. He envisions, furthermore, a complete religious library that would gather *all* sacred books (from ancient Scriptures to recent esoterica); the feeling of coming thereby to the threshold (but only the threshold) of some complete revelation is cultivated.[81] But another series of discordant associations heaps derision and contempt on printed matter: humankind has books only in its current infralapsarian state, when human beings are incapable of reading the Great Book of Nature. The low cost of printing multiplies worthless – and cheap, ugly – books. Pseudo-scholars pile up useless erudition (hence the derision of the lists). The literary and publishing world keeps sordid associations with commerce and politics.[82] When commercialized in this manner, the book, far from being liberating and healing, only serves further to rivet authors and readers to the mechanisms of an imperfect world.

Nodier's bibliophilic activities enable him to find some sort of reconciliation between these contradictory evaluations. Made into a beautiful object, the book becomes a stepping-stone for dreaming. The quality of the book as object helps the imagination of the reader as much as the text. The 'physical' appearance of the book (paper, type, ink, design, binding) becomes an end in itself and may even displace such interest as the content may have. The text is not allowed to take up all the mental space.[83] Here Nodier did us a service: he helped us notice the realities, the ethics and aesthetics of book production and use. For instance, he drew attention to the fact that alphabets contain numerous irrationalities; why should we keep inflicting on young children the notion that capital G, lower case g, and italicized *g* are the same letter even though they differ so much in design? He answers that such imperfect alphabets, consecrated by usage, function very well and that our age, progressive though it wants to be, would err in trying to change them.[84] Nodier was also a meticulous (if not obsessive) proofreader.[85]

He deplored the lowering of standards in printers' shops. He bemoaned the appearance of lithographic printing, which has the ink drool onto the page instead of being impressed on it. That he shows little confidence in the ability of our codes to capture reality does not prevent him from paying considerable attention to these codes and urging great respect for them.

Nodier's literary aesthetics is coupled with a specific vision of post-revolutionary society. 'The long disenchantment of social life has reduced us to a state of narrow rationalism.' 'Material principles prevail over imaginative ones.'[86] Balzac invented the label 'école du désenchantement' for five works published in 1830 and 1831: his own *Physiologie du mariage*, Janin's *La confession*, Stendhal's *Le rouge et le noir*, and Nodier's *Histoire du roi de Bohême*, all in 1830, and his own *La peau de chagrin* in 1831.[87] Nine years later, Sainte-Beuve wrote an article on 'industrial literature' describing the degradation of literature resulting from the new methods of mass communication.[88] (Many writers joined the businessmen to produce commercial 'popular' literature. Under the new conditions of the bourgeois monarchy, the writers had the excuse of needing the pay for their physical survival.) Nodier's disenchantment was probably among the most extreme. He stayed disenchanted and did not compromise. (He had an ancien régime sinecure.) His conviction as to the impossibility of any common and steady historical discourse (or narrative) explains his diffidence as to the public value of the accounts he gives of what he remembers. It explains also his belief that society is now held together only by crude interests, and not by any ennobling vision.

On one point, however, Nodier makes a constant, public stand: he is opposed to any form of the death penalty.[89] (Victor Hugo picked up the theme and gave it masterly orchestration.)[90] The basis for such commitment is clear: no account can be given of human affairs and no narration made that can credibly include the planning and inflicting of death. The age of Homeric, Virgilian, or Miltonian epic is dead. All Nodier can write is the story of his own escape from death, a 'bourgeois epic,' as he puts it somewhat derisively.[91] Such an epic tells of individual survival, not of wars or massacres originating in some divine purpose or made good by some providential mission.

Nodier offers also a new construction of the continuing place of belief in human life. By linking the life of religion to that of the imagination, he utters a romantic commonplace. But he gives it his own twist: the imagination for him is asocial, and creates a fleeting poetic reality –

fleeting beliefs – that remains private. Most important, he conveys to us the inevitability of this kind of imaginative life and of ensuing literature, by linking them to his experience of the Revolution. The consequences for theology of such a personal evolution seem clear. The very framework for traditional acts of believing disappears as social experience is theatricalized, as belief is derealized. The very forging of loyalties in the course of a life becomes next to impossible. The providential sort of narrative that narrates decisive interpersonal and social fidelities becomes hard to believe. Believers henceforth seem incapable of constructing for themselves the faith in their own history which plays such a crucial role in H.R. Niebuhr's argument on the meaning of revelation.[92]

The challenges flung by Nodier's writing to the feasibility of narrative thus reach much farther than just the target of historical exactitude. Whether or not Nodier sat at table with future victims of the guillotine is irrelevant; everyone knows that such things were in the atmosphere in 1793 and that they mark a person for ever. Whether or not *Suites d'un mandat d'arrêt* presents a version of events that Nodier and the gendarmes would agree on is also irrelevant. Every one knows – or should know – that closeness to nature provides comfort to historically uncomfortable people. We will readily allow that the writing of history must henceforth include an account of what people felt and must open up subjective worlds, even if this disrupts the attempt to provide a common, intellectually satisfying, and general narrative of what 'really' happened. In a similar manner, theological writing has commonly abandoned its ancient alliance with the writing of epic and developed greater kinship with the art exhibited in the writing of autobiographies and novels.

But as autobiographies and novels became the literary genres that provided the decisive framework for accounts of human living, these frameworks were challenged by the very writers who used them. As the novel, which has been labelled 'the epic of men without God,' embarked upon its brilliant nineteenth-century career, the anti-novel made a simultaneous appearance. *Histoire du roi de Bohême* radicalized the challenges flung in the eighteenth century to the novel as a form, and upset its rising prestige, just as Hugo's *Hernani* the same year challenged the traditions of French classical theatre. Hugo won the battle of *Hernani*; his play was not too eccentric.[93] *Histoire du roi de Bohême* challenged the value of the beliefs induced by reading a good story (along with the pleasure gained by it) only for the members of a small avant-garde, Gautier and Nerval among them.

Nodier dug up the old Spanish motto chosen by a seventeenth-century sceptic, La Mothe le Vayer: In the case of things most securely established, the most prudent course is to doubt.[94] The target of such scepticism is now secular, worldly, and overconfident narrativity. I believe that Nodier rejected narrative accounts (whether grand and solemn or lucid and realistic) because it was clear to him that, in an age of religio-political conspiracies in defence of the existing social and economic order, such accounts carry an invidious rhetoric that masks individual and this-worldly interests. He thus came to prefer the pleasure of telling a fantastic tale, or the more perverse pleasure of teasing readers who want tales; in any case, he renounced the self-indulgent habits of didactic teaching. Language cannot carry metaphysical views any more. But it can hold metaphorical views of the world.[95]

As Steinmetz put it, casting doubt on the truths found (or adumbrated) in one's own fiction is not a recipe for massive and lasting literary fame.[96] We should recall, however, that with Nodier the aesthetic quality of the book becomes the object of meticulous care; style becomes a matter of personal integrity. Here the very Nodier capable of finding everything implausible gains his plausibility. In one of his finest articles, Sainte-Beuve portrayed Nodier as the live embodiment of the 'littérateur indéfini.' The erudite librarian of l'Arsenal did not try to be or claim to be a specialist in anything; he did not undertake to instruct. But in his intellectual life he maintained an exacting taste for belles-lettres; thus he deserves a recognition that many specialists will not get.[97] In other words, what Nodier managed to encode is awareness of codes and careful workmanship in the use of them   the less stable and certain our hold upon realities, the more our codes deserve attention and respect.

4

Civility and Belief: Vigny

Reviewing in 1831 a collection of poems by Victor Hugo (*Feuilles d'automne*), Charles Nodier wrote, somewhat sententiously, that it is not poetry but experience that will decide what political hypothesis best serves human interests.[1] Such a contrast between poetry and experience puts Nodier outside what was then becoming (and would be for a while) a widespread liberal consensus. Most of the French Romantics believed that poets could distil the meaning of experience and chart the path to the future. (Thus Lamartine published in 1831 a long pamphlet entitled 'Sur la politique rationnelle,' and trumpeted his hopes again in 1834 with 'Des destinées de la poésie.') Nodier also wrote that modern political parties were devoid of enthusiasm and devotion. (He was among those who believed that moderns always calculate their interests strictly – and wisely – and are incapable of sacrifice.) Such universal 'absence of social sentiment' led him to speculate that the nineteenth century might well become the witness of 'wars of religion started without belief.'[2] This notion of a purely prosaic civilization also put him out of step with the 1820s and 1830s in France: the common notion was that society needed beliefs, was struggling to find them, and would find those it needed.

There was also a widespread confidence that by finding the appropriate set of beliefs modern minds would not stay in the critical rut of the eighteenth century and would not repeat the violent excesses of the Revolution. The task of the nineteenth century is 'to conclude,' proclaimed Balzac in *Les illusions perdues*; he meant that the century had to draw conclusions and settle things. All the work of François Guizot, as historian, writer, and statesman, as opposition liberal or establishment figure, was predicated on the view that, in France, the time had come, not to criticize, but to found.[3] In the 1820s, Guizot was only one of many new, talented, and much-applauded university teachers (or orators). A new level of competence was being reached in the handling of historical, social, and political issues.[4]

What, therefore, is perhaps most significant in France for the period 1802–48 is not so much the religious revival (there was some of that) or the revival of interest in the history of religions (this had already existed in the eighteenth century) but the outburst of energy spent in theorizing on the links between religion and society. The Revolution, after all, first attempted to reform the church, by giving it a *civil* constitution. This was meant to restore to the church its power as a civilizing force.[5] The Revolution then tried to destroy the church. As we know, it failed each time, but a link was commonly seen between political chaos, the rise of social violence, and the revolutionary failure in religious matters.[6] And all this was done under one heading; the problem of 'civilization,' ancient and modern, was constantly aired. The classic was Guizot's *Histoire de la civilisation en Europe* (1828).[7] Saint-Simon's socialist-type answers, spread through his *Le nouveau christianisme* (1825), were not widely accepted, but the questions he raised could not be left alone.[8] Radical questions were therefore frequently asked. Faith thus was not seen as a narrowly religious problem (as was the case in the eighteenth century), but as a broad civilizational one.

Handling these issues had, of necessity, a strong literary component. A new vocabulary had to be forged. *Salons, cénacles,* and *ateliers* saw to that; fashion spread the new terminology. New rhetoric was in the air, thanks to public lectures, parliamentary debates, and opposition or government newspapers.[9] Nodier was in full command of the new language of historical despair and political nihilism – and held himself at a distance from it. He also turned sententious as he gave opinions gravely on grave subjects. (Stendhal complained that one of the least endearing features of the democratic age was that everybody felt called upon to give a serious opinion on all serious topics.)[10]

The works of Alfred de Vigny (1797–1863) are an important witness to the treatment of these issues. He assimilates the new scholarship. The author of poems and prose works, he is one of those who believes that poets should and can lead humankind; what differentiates him is a tone of constant pessimism that accompanies his statements of brave belief.[11] And he is keenly aware of problems of civility. Again like most Romantics, he is for social progress and fears popular turmoil. But we do not meet here with the conflict common to all progressive liberals, torn between philanthropy and self-interest. As a nobleman, Vigny has first-hand experience of the old aristocratic politeness and still practises its manners; he also sees clearly that such models of civility cannot set the tone or dictate the mores of the new, democratic society. What new civility will then emerge among the citizens?

Vigny also saw that such questions cannot be handled dogmatically – and this, above all, makes him original. He thus experimented with prose forms, and came up with a sequence of three works, *Servitude et grandeur militaires*, *Stello*, and *Daphné*. These texts are important illustrations of the French romantic handling of issues of civilization in two ways: human problems are linked to problems inherent in religious believing; and an adequate literary form is being searched for, a form that will fully examine the problem and enable the reader to think about the issues, and think freely.

Vigny's probes into the problem of belief are rooted in personal quandaries; as he put it in his *Journal d'un poète*, 'I have charity and I have hope, but I do not have faith.'[12] He knew himself well. Courteous by upbringing, he became compassionate. Even though familiar with romantic melancholy, he struggled not to despair of humanity and kept wagering on a better future. Faith, however, eluded him, whether the deist sober faith of his mother, or the Catholic faith of his ancestors and many of his contemporaries. He wrote on religion, and did it with seriousness and care, that is, with art. In three of his prose writings, *Servitude et grandeur militaires* (published in volume form in 1835), *Stello* (1832), and *Daphné* (published posthumously in 1912), we find him involved in a steady work of demystification and renunciation of belief that nevertheless leaves a residue of commitment.[13] The life of the soldier is under scrutiny in the first, that of the poet in the second (contrasted with that of the wielder of power); the third ponders the lives of religions and religious reformers. In this last case, the literary and intellectual solution seemed to elude Vigny and the work was unfinished at the time of his death. All three works ponder the specific characteristics of modern society.

Most important, the sequence of works evidences a struggle in search of a form that will be adequate for the examination of religious belief in the modern context. (The first two will thus have to be examined closely before we can grasp what is attempted in the third.) The basic device Vigny experiments with is to insert in each work (or, in *Daphné*, to mean to insert) three narratives (stories, anecdotes) enclosed within a larger framework. What began with Rousseau's insertion of the 'Profession de foi du vicaire savoyard' inside *Emile* becomes now the setting up of a rich and complex structure.[14] The 'inside' pieces are presented as anecdotes from life. The larger framework provides a context that is more didactic in nature, and less stamped with the character of a 'story' or fiction. Compared with *Le génie du christianisme*, for instance, the inserted 'stories' gain much more space and more weight than was given to *René* and *Atala* in 1802. In *Servitude* the anecdotes are freely anchored in fact and echo events in the author's military career. Some anchoring in historical fact can be found for the stories in the other two writings, but the connections are more tenuous. In *Servitude* the architectonic 'didactic' part is a meditation and admonition from the author. In *Stello* and *Daphné* this part is itself a piece of fiction. The apparently clear distinctions between didactic prose expressing the author's true belief, narration of true occurrences, and fictitious story are being undermined in the very structure of these three works. As one of Vigny's characters puts it, 'My stories are half-truths, like all human words.'[15]

We shall examine each of these three works in turn, to observe what statements of belief each contains, and, more specifically, to see how the dynamic structure devised by the author causes all expressed beliefs to waver. Finally, we shall strive to see how the writer resolves the wavering, if at all.

Vigny had been a soldier. By birth, first: his aristocratic family had always served under the white flag of the Bourbons. By personal choice also: as an adolescent he had been captured by dreams of glory triggered by the Napoleonic feats. In 1814 he was just old enough to become an officer in the reconstituted royal guard. But disenchantment came quickly. His first long ride in uniform was the escape to Belgium, fleeing with his king before the returning Bonaparte.[16] The disenchantment went deep: By 1825 he clearly saw that the modern army could not keep the moral traditions of the old, noble one, and, more important, that it would increasingly be used against the nation, doing the work of police forces, attacking citizens to defend economic privileges.[17] His 1830 diary notes with admiration the behaviour of an officer in Paris who, incapable of disobeying orders, blew his brains out rather than shoot women and children in the street.[18]

There are three stories: that of an officer who regrets obeying a criminal order he received from his superiors and atones for it; that of a sergeant killed in an accidental explosion, the victim of overscrupulous duty; and that of an officer who had been totally devoted to Napoleon and who slowly disciplines himself to become a decent professional soldier who hates war. The overarching reflections ponder the submission of the modern army officer to bureaucrats and civil servants, and affirm the right of any soldier to disobey orders that run against his conscience and sense of honour. They also brood over the need human beings seem to have to stop doing their own thinking and become involved in some larger action (he thus unveils the psychological root of blind obedience). And they conclude that, after 1815, the age of feats of military glory is over: moral greatness henceforth will lie mostly in resistance and refusal. One belief is shaken in this work – the belief in the automatic, self-evident dignity of soldiering, traditionally one of the most honoured stations in life, and the one which had offered the author the lineaments of his identity as a youth.

The third and longest story is the most complex and sets the final mood. (It is clearly a story of military greatness, the other two being mainly of servitude.) In this tale of the sober officer, much more than the Napoleonic feats becomes demystified: we hear that the condition of the soldier in the nineteenth century is either excessively honoured or despised without measure.[19] Two contemporary rhetorical stances are exposed and denounced.[20] First, that of Joseph de Maistre, who professes to see a supernatural being in the man who carries the sword: he who sheds blood does God's work as he kills.[21] But Lamennais, who writes (after his condemnation in Rome) that soldiers are bloodthirsty hounds doing the job of cruel tyrants, is equally denounced; the soldier is neither a divine nor a beastly creature. He is a human being; his integrity, when he has any – and many do – is painfully earned. The introduction to the second story is a long meditation on the fact that every soldier will sooner or later receive criminal orders; should he obey them or not? Every commander may become another Moses, who, finding out that the people had worshipped the golden calf, ordered the sons of Levi to kill family (brother, son), friend, and neighbour. To Vigny, it is clear that the hand of a knight should never be that of a slave.[22] In Exodus 32 Moses' order was obeyed, in immediate and blind adherence, and the chapter ends with the statement that it was God who struck the people. Vigny knew the Bible well and chose a strong example – a civil massacre, meant to punish religious deviation.

In the end *Servitude et grandeur militaires* unveils a residue of humanity. It finds in the model officer of the third story a new kind of human integrity that restates under the new conditions of life the old noble independence of mind and judgment: Captain Renaud manages to be actively humane in the midst of the horrors he cannot stem. His integrity rests on a sense of honour, of which Vigny writes, on his last, didactic page, that 'in the current shipwreck of all beliefs' it is the universal, manly religion, a virtue that does not come from heaven but is innate in us, and rises with us toward heaven.[23] In these pages, Vigny's search for the implicit beliefs that remain (or can remain), now that the Christian system of stated beliefs has been shattered, comes to rest on an explicit conclusion. Honour is the one human virtue left that still commands in the individual a disposition to sacrifice. It is thus not just caste interest that causes Vigny to write about soldiers; in his opinion, the lot of military people has become of interest to all humankind since they have cultivated with their sense of honour a morality that receives nothing from God and owes nothing to him; in the name of honour a man may choose to die rather than see his image blemished, whether before his own eyes or those of others.[24]

Yet the style of *Servitude* prevents the work from becoming a simple declaration of faith. The alternation between narrative and reflection is made to foster conscious ambivalence. There is both emotional entrapment in the lot of the soldier and complete distanciation from all soldiering. Vigny informs the reader that he wrote the book ostensibly as a farewell to his military career and as a public commitment to a new identity and new lot, that of the writer: 'There is no officer left in me, but only the solitary and independent writer.'[25] But the work somewhat belies the confessions of the author. There lingers in it a strong positive feeling for one characteristic of the soldier – his word binds him for ever; men of notoriously few words, military men use words advisedly – unlike politicians, who waste them.[26] At this point, the soldier becomes a symbol of the human condition nobly lived. Vigny, who detests public eloquence and fears the depreciation of writing by the press, finds in his soldiers the most human use of words, the closest approach to silence.[27] It is ironic that the very writer who says his farewell to arms and takes up the pen finds paramount excellence with words in the social world he leaves behind. The book thus goes much beyond its ostensible subject. It is designed to shake all dangerous verbal assurances of the mind, the quiet or the vibrant ones. Fanatical soldiers who carry out orders blindly are not the only human beings with a captive conscience.

Stello refines the art of the literary creation of ambivalence that undermines acquired certainties or customary and readily expressed beliefs.[28]

The overarching story is a (fictitious) dialogue between Stello, a young romantic poet, who escapes reality thanks to his imagination, and Doctor Noir, an old physician who has seen a lot. Stello fits the romantic stereotype: he has 'spleen' and suffers from 'the blue devils.' The black doctor is a more original figure: although dressed in the anonymous black adopted by the bourgeois under the Monarchie de Juillet, he harks back to the eighteenth century and has all the ruthless rationality of the more audacious *philosophes*; his mental boldness even smacks of Mephistopheles. The discussion between the two is both a debate of ideas and a confrontation between disease and mental health, which ends with a therapeutic effect. The poet, a captive of his extraordinary sensitivity, is taken on by the physician, who practises distance and analysis (defined as a sort of philosophic optics) and looks into causes. The doctor helps the poet become sober by leading him to the inevitable conclusions. This doctor openly offers himself as an heir of the old priests; he has also, with reason, been seen as the harbinger of the future analyst.[29]

The three internal stories are reminiscences from his own life that the doctor tells Stello in order to broaden his outlook. The narration is frequently interrupted by exchanges between the two protagonists and by occasional reintroductions of the authorial voice. (*Stello* is thus more complex than *Servitude*: we see a process, a story being told to an active listener, and do not just read stories.) The stories tell of the fate of three poets who suffered at the hands of the mighty of the hour. In each case, the doctor was closely involved with the major participants: Gilbert under Louis XV, Chatterton under George III, and André Chénier in Year II of the Republic. Since the events take place in societies that cover a range of political regimes, the lesson is clear: the poet will never be at home in society.

The doctor makes his toughest points in his third story: there is a sinister foundation for any form of authority of man over man; the masses adore those who kill, as is illustrated by the power of Robespierre and Saint-Just, who did not hesitate to order the execution of Chénier. (In contrast, the monarchs only neglected the poets, or let them die.) Here, however, the doctor stops suddenly in his tracks: he admits being shocked at what he has just said, and is forced to articulate a sharp conflict inside himself between two contradictory thoughts.[30] In an interlude, he points to Joseph de Maistre, the arch-monarchist, who made an open apology for the merits of authority founded on the power to kill.[31] The doctor deeply recoils before such a system. He argues, with some heat, that both republicans and monarchists exhibit the same cast of mind: the spirit of synthesis, the violent passion to reduce everything to an encompassing truth from which everything in turn can be deduced, the frenzy for covering the unfathomable abyss with some doctrinal system. In the course of his tirade, the doctor imagines the words of the inventor presenting the guillotine to the ruler: 'Here is a machine with the help of which you will be obeyed by the whole nation: you only pull this and push that.'[32] The doctor in the end disallows any representation of society that makes it work by pulling here and pushing there; this of course is precisely what men of power want.[33]

But *Stello* is the story of the cure of a poet. After the second story, and during the third, it becomes apparent that the young man has been roused to moral indignation. Henceforth the doctor and he are in agreement. Stello has managed to expel his false belief, namely, the expectation that humankind feels in need of the poet's message and will eagerly receive it. Sensitive, sick soul and rationalist physician therefore reach a common standpoint; this, inevitably, tends to undermine the message of the stories with their repeated affirmations of duality and impassable gulfs.[34] The common standpoint earned in the process could be summarized by saying that life in society, being an artificial state, creates problems for human beings that only fictions can solve. Hence there is a common ground between the manipulation of power and the writing of poetry: both compete for the allegiance which the many grant when they believe what they are told. Hence also the basis of a conflict that cannot be reconciled, since the powerful, unlike the poets, derive great gains from their successful manipulation of beliefs. The poets appeal to belief, with a genuinely human appeal, only if they renounce all manipulative practice, and only if they break with – and emigrate from – a society that sees nothing beyond the daily operation of social power.[35]

Meanwhile those who wield power tend to believe that the arts are either useless to the social state (the first and second stories) or dangerous (the third story). And they do not hesitate to act upon this belief. They impose by force and violence a 'synthesis,' a view of existence, a practice, which is closed to the future. To govern is to act and this can be done only if at some point one does not listen and ceases to try to explain. The silent operations of the mechanics of power are terrifying. (So much I might say for the praise of silence.) Political and social action is determined to ignore any utterance that might postpone it or recall its imperfection.[36] While *Servitude* attacked the problem of blind obedience, *Stello* attacks the corresponding problem, the prosperity of those who exact it.[37]

To this presentation of an enduring dualism between thought and action, Vigny adds a dated judgment that fits the circumstances of his post-1830 world: in reality it is always the worst political fictions that succeed. Society is now openly committed to nothing but productivity and pragmatism. Visions of glory, of honour, and of justice are gone, apparently for ever.[38] As his *Journal d'un poète* puts it, he now feels immune to every political superstition.[39] The doctor's final prescription is clear: the poet must remain free and be concerned only with the demands of his own vocation. *Stello* was born of Vigny's second wave of doubt: after renouncing his identity as soldier, must he also renounce that of writer and poet? The book ends on an affirmation of stoic belief: the writer must remain true to his mission, in any circumstances.[40]

This is what is clearly said in the final section of *Stello*. But the very process of healing and the unity gained by the doctor and the poet suggest something else, namely, that in some circumstances poets can become part of society, and that they have something to contribute to society even as it is. Once again the literary procedure undermines the manifest message.[41] To the society that works like an inhuman machine is offered, shyly, tentatively, an alternative: a society where intellectual domination is based on 'infinite development of judgment and imagination,'[42] namely, one based on an open ideology. But can there ever be such a society, the reader might well ask?

Stello is a complex work, perhaps ultimately an unsuccessful one because of the constant shifting of standpoints. On the one hand, it may be construed as another of the author's apologies for silence.[43] On the other, it may be seen as the path toward a new, higher, poetic voice.[44] In support of this view, one can argue that the last, openly dualistic utterances about the constant war between poet and society (utterances on which Stello and the doctor agree) are in fact an effort to gang up on the reader. The two protagonists force the reader into the unthinking crowd or the group of crude profiteers; they thus sting his or her sense of honour and lead him or her to a distanciation from the social realities of the day.[45] *Stello*, as a work that wages war against closed ideologies, is, formally, an open work.[46] It is calculated to bring readers to the point where they are equipped to ask and answer their own questions about beliefs, their own initial beliefs, the beliefs articulated (attractively) by the protagonists, and, finally, beliefs which the writer (through his craft and his own voice) elicits from them as they read. This threefold attempt makes the work hard to classify. It is not an essay, in spite of the overt ideological content; it is not a platonic dialogue, since discussions are not aimed at finding the truth; it is not a personal epic, in spite of the fact that the protagonists mirror two sides of the author's personality. What it comes closest to in the end is the novel.[47] One might add that it contributes to the definition of that still-emerging genre in that it tends to make of the novel a work that annihilates itself. The text equips readers with everything they need to be able to distrust the message of the text.[48]

The version of *Daphné* that we have is a relatively complete whole, which was part of a larger project, frequently modified and in the end unfinished.[49] Vigny's intent was always to write a second consultation of Doctor Noir. In the completed text, the fiction is continued where *Stello* left it: Stello and the doctor are now a sort of dialectical team, and the narrative framework shows them moving through scenes of Parisian life, on a specific, eventful day. A new protagonist, Trivulce, introduces fresh intellectual tension. Drama is thus heightened by a richer overall narrative structure, and new heights are reached in the art of the simultaneous development of contradictory certainties.

Every stage of the *Daphné* project has its focus on religion and religions. Since Stello is cured and the stage urban, one can presume that the task is to find a compromise between unbelief and the desire to believe (or something that Stello can embrace and that the doctor will not rebut), and something that will be more than a personal answer, a collective, civilizational one.

Vigny comes to the task with a persistent unease with the God of Christianity. God is the hateful being behind all unjust power; like all wielders of power, he is cruel. Honour requires that his tyranny be denounced.[50] Furthermore, all religious belief is intrinsically dangerous when active on the social scale: the most beautiful doctrine becomes a cruel law, since believers unfailingly want to impose their views.[51] He also brings to the project a real competence in the history of religions. His generation, we must remember, witnessed a sudden, enormous expansion of the known religious world, in which the texts of Asian religions became available to the cultivated French. Vigny kept himself fully informed. The orientalist Pauthier de Censay was a corporal in his regiment; they became friends in 1823. From that time on, the corporal kept his lieutenant in touch with the new learning and the new translations. Moreover, a relative of his, Bruguière de Sorsum, was one of the founders (1832) of the Société Asiatique de Paris and translated *Saccountala*. Vigny, in their wake, undertook to write a précis of the teachings put forward by the world's religions.[52] *Daphné* thus reflects both his personal unease and his vast learning. As Raymond Schwab puts it, it is a 'novelistic transformation of the philosophy of religion.'[53]

The *Daphné* we have is a coherent whole, one narrative framework with our familiar protagonists and one 'internal' episode focusing on the life of Emperor Julian, known to Christians as the Apostate, and taking place in the fourth century A.D. in Daphné, a hellenistic pagan sanctuary on the outskirts of Antioch. In the opening scene Stello and the doctor walk the crowded streets of Paris on the last night of the 1832 carnival. Stello finds the crowd sullen on this festive day and feels sympathy and pity – he would like them to be happy and would like to show them how; the doctor of course smiles at him. At this point, they are met by a grey nun who summons them to the bedside of a sick young man. They follow her through the crowds. On their way they reach the banks of the Seine and see books and manuscripts floating on the dark waters. Riotous crowds have just stormed the archbishop's palace and pillaged its library. (This happened on 15 February, 1832.) They go on walking; their path takes them first through the street where Abelard lived and next through the one where Peter Ramus was killed on the day of the Saint Bartholomew's massacre. All this occasions conversation between the two protagonists. The Sister of Charity of course remains silent.

The young man sick in bed, Trivulce, is a voracious student who had the means to pursue his studies enthusiastically and has left the study of law for that of theology, in fact, 'of all theogonies, cosmogonies and mythologies of the world.' There was no exact terminology available then (nor is there now) to label this new sort of specialist: a theologian? a historian of religion? He is an erudite student of world religious history and of all theologies, a comparatist, but a passionately involved student who is completely distraught by what he reads.[54] Trivulce has been sick 'in the head' ever since he read a certain manuscript. He lies in bed under a large crucifix of 'the Expiator' that shows vivid marks of suffering.[55] But across the room, behind a curtain, the doctor finds a heroic statue of the dying Julian.

This second 'consultation' has thus a much vaster scope than the first one. We no longer have just an individual meeting his physician in private quarters, but two individuals witnessing mass behaviour, political breakdown. We also are made aware of thick layers of French history, of conflicting religious traditions, and of vast treasures of world literature. History as an ongoing reality storms onto the stage. And books are present besides people, defenceless, despised, destroyed, or potent disturbers of readers' minds. The crisis of civilization is made into a literary theme, and is linked to the death and birth of religious traditions.[56] Vigny's framing of the religious issues closely reflects the intellectual and social conditions of his day. He is up to date with the new learning produced by the historians of religion; the place of Christianity in world history has been relativized. His Orient however, unlike theirs, is limited to the biblical, Jewish, hellenistic, and Christian East. His philological abilities took him only that far, and he did not venture beyond the languages he knew.[57]

The text goes on with the anecdote: four letters written by a hellenistic Jewish merchant, telling of events at Daphné. Presumably we have here the text that so disturbed Trivulce.[58] The letters convey to an unknown correspondent events the merchant witnessed as well as long reports he heard on Julian before he actually saw him. This procedure of 'reversed telescope' increases the distance between modern readers and the ancient pagan emperor; it tends to separate readers from the core of the text and increase its sacred halo or its ultimate unintelligibility. The form here mirrors the theme of veils that will loom so large in the text.[59]

In focusing on Julian, Vigny is occupying well-ploughed ground. The main feature of his reign, the conflict between Hellenism in its noblest form and a newly muscular Christianity, had been examined at length by many concerned authors, Gibbon, Voltaire, Chateaubriand, and Benjamin Constant among them. Vigny has read them all, as well as the contemporary works (in the original Greek). His picture is very different from the one to which Chateaubriand had tried to give credit. He rather pointedly (and with good historical evidence) denies to Christians every mark of superiority that *Le génie du christianisme* had so generously ascribed to them: in *Daphné* they are indifferent to the fate of slaves, and divided among countless hostile sects; the women are emancipated and shameless; they all are generally uncouth and antisocial. Significantly, throughout the merchant's letters, it is those who convert to Christianity who are labelled apostates.[60]

In the first of his letters to his friend, our learned merchant describes his arrival in Antioch. The Christian city is feverish: the crowds are unruly and mindless, the monks fanatics and ruffians, the bishops petty chieftains. City life is about to collapse because of internal strains and the threat of external invasions. But the Christians, divided among themselves and incapable of political vision, do not seem to care.[61] Our merchant travels through this chaos to reach his philosophical friends in Daphné: there, beauty and peace still reign. He is welcomed by Libanius, the aging philosopher, and invited to a philosophical dinner, where the conversation turns to Julian and his policies. Julian had been connected as a young man with the circle in Daphné and the hope had been nurtured that he would be an emperor such as philosophers wish. But he seems to have been sucked in by the life of action, the military struggle against the Barbarians at the borders and the restoration of Hellenism. Julian, it is said at Daphné, has yielded to his mystical – or enthusiastic – propensities, and has lost his path. Libanius formulates a diagnostic: cults useful in elevating the masses carry away noble, exalted souls too far.

The mood changes, however, when Julian arrives; his heroism is self-authenticating. His dedication to action ceases to appear as a weakness and becomes a mark of the nobility of his soul. The reader is relieved finally to meet someone committed to the process of civilization and civilized government. But the mood changes sharply again when Libanius, with regret in his voice, informs Julian of his error: hellenistic religions are powerless among men of this age; Julian should have stayed a Christian, as he had been in his youth, but a political, not a mystical, Christian; he should have identified with the religion of the Barbarians. His hellenistic undertaking is failing, not because of some intrinsic flaw, but because of its very perfection. Libanius develops his views further. The treasure kept at Daphné in the circle of philosophical friends, namely, the morality which lifts men above violence, is about to die. To make his meaning clear, Libanius takes his guests to an inner sanctuary to show them a mummy enclosed in a crystal case. The mummy contains 'the treasure of mankind,' wise moral sayings from all cultures. The crystals of the case have a wide variety of symbols engraved on them. Those belonging to Hellenism are now too pale to be read by most; the Christian ones are more sharply edged.[62]

Letters 2, 3, and 4, much briefer, tell of the death of Julian on the battlefield at the hands of Christian barbarian invaders. We also learn how the merchant buys and buries the statue of Venus which was worshipped at the centre of the sanctuary.

As Frank Paul Bowman summarized it, *Daphné* is a commentary on four central romantic problems: the cyclical view of history, the nature of religious syncretism, the notion of myth or symbol as vehicle for truth, and the contrast between Platonism (or Neoplatonism) and Christianity.[63] The commentary is in the tragic vein. Julian's public religion was philosophically superior but historically impotent.[64] The 'veil' was 'too transparent.' The Christian symbols are visible to the many and capture their allegiance because they are written on far more opaque material. But, Libanius informs us, it will be a long time before the new symbolic system, or the new idolatry, gives rise to thoughts as noble and as beautiful as those created by the old system. Julian became inebriated on the poetry he created for the Empire, but, even in his enthusiasm, he did not have the sincere love for his symbols that the Barbarians have for theirs. (The more opaque ones, we are led to believe, are more readily taken for real.) A poetic religion is a contradiction in terms: one cannot believe that the gods are the creation of poets and at the same time hope that such gods will stem incredulity. Incredulity can be held at bay only if one believes that the gods are gods. But this belief cannot be commanded. In other words, enlightened religious reformers are always doomed to fail. In the manner of Victor Cousin and many others, Vigny acknowledges the need for a dynamic spontaneity that is found (or not found) on a plane totally separate from the plane of thought. (The theme will reappear in Renan. It is not a tragic one there, only mildly melancholic.)[65] Faith is a vital dynamism, quite alien to reason. One has it, or one does not. The only approaches to religion, more precisely, the only conscious stances one can develop religiously, are those of the poet and the Sister of Charity. The first one speaks but has no impact on the masses; the second one acts devotedly but is silent. Philosophers can win adherence to truth, but cannot inculcate belief or win allegiance to symbols. Statesmen can have a policy on religion, or about religion, but they cannot pursue a religious policy and hope to succeed.

A final fragmentary scene has Stello and the doctor again walking the streets of Paris, later in the night of the anti-clerical riot. They pick up an abandoned manuscript, which tells of the destruction of Alexandria's library by the invaders. The manuscript is incomplete; it has been torn by the nineteenth-century urban Barbarians.[66] In front of a pillaged church, the two men listen for a while to a new-style prophet, an ex-priest, who excites the people against kings and clergy and announces a book of revelation that will be a work of hatred.[67] The nineteenth century is not like the fourth: the Barbarians are not burning with the love of some Christ who will civilize them in the long run. *Daphné* thus represents Vigny's definitive farewell to all and any flirtation with the idea that a new religion (elitist Saint-Simon-like, or popular Lamennais-style) is about to be born. Henceforth, he will never see or attribute merit to any active enthusiasm.[68] God is for ever silent. No revelations are to be expected. In 1839, Vigny read Littré's translation of D.F. Strauss's *Life of Jesus* and was confirmed in his views on the silence of God.[69] One of his poems, *Le Mont des Oliviers* (1843), echoes Jean Paul Richter's poem on the death of God (made known in France by Madame de Stael). Jesus meets with God's impenetrable silence.

But this does not prevent the older Vigny from mellowing his stance toward Christianity. Starting in 1837, one can notice a public position of support for Christianity that has personal and moral roots. This poet will not further erase the already barely legible 'salvation'-bearing symbols. It is a matter of policy but a felt one.[70] At the same time Vigny remains as close as ever to his favourite Stoic writers, and he shows interest in Buddhism as its literature and doctrine become available to educated readers.

It is clear that at one level *Daphné* is unfinished because the subject kept raising new problems in Vigny's mind, calling for further reading and reflection.[71] (The Jewishness of the merchant is an obvious theme that is inadequately developed and remains unintegrated.) The root of the matter, it seems to me, is that Vigny could not find a controlling, overarching story, an adequate meta-story. We have already seen that Trivulce remains unhealed. In a sense this is unimportant since the central question asked is rather about the healing of modern crowds. But on this issue too, the succession of ideological dramas in the text is not adequately resolved. A tension remains between a final hint that art is superior to religion (the saved statue), a position taken by the author during his later, attic years, and the earlier, deeply felt indictment of the motivational inadequacies of poetic religion. Demystification reached new territory in *Daphné*, but when it came to religious history, no live residue could be found comparable to honour and literary vocation, the virtues of the first two books. It is significant that 'the treasure of mankind' consists of abstract moral teachings stored in a dessicated mummy. The life of religion is deemed, in the end, totally impenetrable to the mind.

Ronald Grimsley draws a parallel between Vigny and Kierkegaard: both were led to envisage a new kind of poetry that would overcome the usual 'aesthetic' limitations in order to serve a deeper existential purpose.[72] It should be added that it is through the medium of dramatic prose that both introduced a new element into the emotional, imaginative sphere in which writer and reader live. And both authors used the new element in order to dispel illusion and bring the self to the threshold of an act of will.[73] With the deftness of all the literary resources developed by the Romantics, the poet thus became more than a poet, something rather like a sage. Vigny himself makes some subtle and timely distinctions concerning the crafts of writers. Men of letters, he tells us, do their job in conformity with the spirit of society; poets, gifted with an extreme sensibility, are carried away by their imaginations and become strangers to their contemporaries; and great writers differ from both: they practise philosophical meditation *and* solitude, are ever mindful of their readers and their purpose, and lead those who believe in them.[74] (In their case, I might add, the act of writing is moralized, in contrast with time-serving careerism and pure romantic self-expression.) In *Servitude, Stello,* and *Daphné,* our 'great writer' does not lead those who believe in him in the manner of a persuasive ideologist: he rather awakens possibilities in his readers' mind, stirs them to autonomous thinking.[75] Poets seduce us easily, probably because of the alliance they strike in their imagination between youth, eros, and life. The 'great writer' cultivates a more consummate skill, one that helps readers live *with* their imagination, after living *in* it. *Stello* attributes to the thinker-writer an 'armed neutrality.'[76] Such a writer does not waste efforts of will on the immediate projects of practical life, or become the proponent of any ideology. Superior to all this, great writers are on the alert against any invasion of their own intellectual independence and that of their readers. They do not promote beliefs; by skilfully manipulating our beliefs through the attention their text's obtain from us, they get us to examine all our beliefs. And they do that as artists, aesthetically, literally 'out of nothing.' In art, Vigny writes, truth is nothing, probability everything. Marc Eigeldinger comments that the artist does not try to convey what is true, but what is probable, possible, once born in the world of the imagination.[77]

Vigny's literary devices thus effect a sharp break in a rhetorical tradition that made belief appear easy. As Chateaubriand wrote about it, Christian belief became attractive. Lamennais (1782–1854) wrote one fideistic apologetic book after another. We keep yielding to beliefs, he argues; belief is natural, language is impossible without it, society is based on it. Vigny does not join the Catholic chorus newly enamoured of the Middle Ages and singing the beauty of the 'age of faith'; nor does he join the accompanying Saint-Simonian hum praising the merits of 'organic periods' of widespread unanimity. He sees the complex nature of belief, and, for instance, makes the rather penetrating comment that religions usually have only been half-believed in.[78] He is open to the prospect that societies might function without stable belief: modern armies seem to do the job without any of the older moral and religious traditions. The Garde nationale, he wrote, is 'scepticism armed,'[79] a formula that deserves to be placed alongside Spinoza's armed prophet and Chateaubriand's armed poet. Yet he does not snap all the links between the poet-thinker-writer and society. In both 'consultations,' Stello and the doctor keep their link with their contemporaries, even though it is a constantly painful one. Thus, Vigny makes a novel point: belief is difficult.[80]

It should therefore not surprise us that in *Daphné*, his last and most ambitious work, the one that focuses on religious belief as the most explicitly systematized and far-reaching form of believing, the 'great writer' does not reach a positive conclusion. As Vigny moved from examining the symbols that were significant for him or his whole generation to examining the historical destiny of symbolic systems as such, he could not keep up active involvement in the issue: he left a text that encourages one to accept the position of an ultimately powerless, even though deeply moved, beholder. He did not come up with an ideal identity for the theologian or with a model that could be placed alongside his statements on the soldier and the writer. Any other text, I suggest, would have made belief appear easy.

Is this a defect that could be remedied, we may well ask, with the framing of an adequate meta-story, like that of Hegel for instance? Or could it be rather that, instead of lacking the insight and wit to devise a way to control his material, Vigny reached an absolute limit, and left us with the best that can be done under the circumstances? *Daphné*, may I stress, takes on the largest possible issue: it links unrest in religion with revolution in society and politics.[81] And it links ancient history with modern urban life.[82] When it comes to such issues, we may have to acknowledge that the mind can stop in the process of demystification only by just stopping, and without having found a proper 'credible' residue. *Incipere non discitur* goes the adage. Perhaps the thinker cannot learn to stop either – yet sometimes he stops. In other words, the discussion and evaluation of symbols necessarily come to an abrupt end when it is the symbolic function itself that is under scrutiny. One should not overlook the distinction between the symbols that issue from convention (honourable soldiering, for instance) and the symbols of the convention itself, that is, between the symbols that we use and examine in our social and intellectual existence, and the symbols that provide a basis for this existence.[83] The first ones issue from convention and can be modified, displaced, or replaced, by more or less conscious historical choices. The second ones are not conventional in the usual sense of the word, since they make conventions possible among human beings. Emile Durkheim and Marcel Mauss call them sacred.[84]

Those who look deeply into the issues involved in the confrontation between Hellenism and Christianity as *systems* of belief, or between Emperor Julian and the Barbarians, must acknowledge that they are looking at an area of historical life where the usual reasoning procedures are useless. There cannot be an apology for belief except through existing, functioning rhetorical fields. Discussing the place of the soldier or the poet in the modern world, Vigny could come up with an apology, albeit a muted one. Existing or emerging conventions with respect to a life that strives for integrity, or to the life of a moral will or even to civility, provided such an operational framework. But there is no operational framework to argue about operational frameworks. Either one uses one or one fosters a perplexing and inconclusive look at some of them. It is worth noting, however, that the literary treatment of these issues, the sort of treatment we find in Vigny, ensures a complexity of form that makes it impossible for the reader automatically to assimilate the meaning found in the content. Such treatment has the merit of lifting us above our usual, daily reasoning procedures, of helping us see beyond our entrenched ideological perplexities, and of keeping insoluble issues open.

5

Writing Words of Life: Nerval

The remarkable development of Nerval studies over the last thirty years and the importance of the issues addressed by critics make it possible to undertake an evaluation of Nerval's work from a religious and theological perspective.[1] It is not my intention, however, to argue that Gérard de Nerval (1808–55) was engaged on a 'religious quest' in the manner made familiar by the French series, Writers Facing God. I propose instead, as an author familiar with theological problems, to examine closely the experience evidenced in this author's work. Nerval is of particular interest to me because he is so clearly situated within his own unique space – as shown by his answer, one evening at Victor Hugo's, to the allegation that he had no religion: 'You think I don't have any religion? I have seventeen of them ... at least!'[2] Behind this facile quip we can discern Nerval's own distinct effort to appropriate a vision of origins and construct an identity for himself – an effort that was to prove particularly perilous. He channelled all his desire into this endeavour and his style reveals the process in all its complexity. The religious representations that constantly invaded his imaginary world were very much part of what he had to wrestle with.[3]

A brief review of Nerval's life may help clarify exactly what religion (and religions) meant to this Frenchman born in Paris in 1808. Four particular features of his life shed useful light on his condition as man and as writer.[4]

1 Nerval was the son of a doctor in Napoleon's army. As was often the case in those days, his mother followed her husband on his campaigns, so the child, immediately after birth, was sent away to a wet-nurse. Later, after his mother's death, when he was two, he went to live

with his great-uncle ('the Mortefontaine uncle') in the Valois country-side, northeast of Paris. From the age of seven he lived with his father in Paris, and spent the summer holidays in the Valois, where he was given the freedom of his uncle's extensive library. No one in his family gave Nerval any religious instruction. Instead, he absorbed the contents of this library of 'mystic' works – books on esotericism, freemasonry, and pythagorean thought – which his uncle had collected throughout the last years of the monarchy and during the Revolution (times when a great number of such works were published).[5] This uncle also introduced him to certain local antiquities which he believed to be Celtic in origin and to which he attributed esoteric meaning.[6] He seems to have encouraged his nephew to cultivate a disposition for immediate union with nature, based on a broad pantheism. The hunger for revelation from books seems crucial. Through his uncle Nerval also learned to endow the spirit world with a flavour of reality. The theosophic and esoteric authors wrote realistically about the spiritual world and gave a heavenly geography similar to the earthly one. From them, Nerval learned that the soul never dies and, in the words of Goethe's Faust, that the spirit world is an open world. Above all, he learned to believe entirely in the images spinning through his mind. (Everything that exists in the mind exists in nature.) He was also interested in theurgical writings and through them acquired the desire for proof particular to the eighteenth century: magic 'proves' the power of the spirit; esoteric experiences 'verify' religious beliefs.[7] The 'illuminism' that Nerval appropriated was neither a religion nor a philosophy;[8] it had no authority or common interpretation that might limit the enthusiasm of believers, who could easily believe everything they read and anything they wrote.

2 Once in Paris, Nerval lived a hand-to-mouth existence and witnessed urban poverty. After 1836, having invested his small inheritance in a literary journal and lost it, he was obliged to step up his production of newspaper copy and plays in order to earn his living; his articles appeared in approximately sixty magazines and journals. While he lived in the vain yet constant hope of theatrical success, his friends Alexandre Dumas and Théophile Gauthier prospered.[9] He allowed himself to be caught up in the new Parisian way of life. At a time when the old village ways were disappearing from the Parisian *quartiers*, Nerval lived in the chaotic centre of the capital, surrounded by small businessmen ever attentive to profit. (Because there was a considerable demand for copy it was possible to make a great deal of money; popular theatre, a cross between country fairs and more cultured entertainment, was flour-

ishing.) During his time in Paris Nerval lived in about thirty different lodgings, mostly in the new quarter of Notre-Dame de Lorette, where those aspiring to success in what we now call the 'media' lived along-side young women in search of the good life (the 'lorettes'). Surrounded by sandwich-men, shop windows, and posters, he savoured the colour and language of a new urban landscape. He delighted in the boul-evards and their atmosphere: the endless passers-by, the crowds, the chance encounters, the extravagance, the escape. He was also attracted by café night-life, and was arrested for disturbance of the peace in 1831 and picked up in a police raid in 1832. Nerval used his writing to 'poet-icize' the city.[10] Like others before and after him he stressed its labyrin-thine qualities.[11] Descending into the streets becomes an analogue to the literary descents into hell. He saw the formless mass, the indefinitely expandable space, the prison without walls as symbols both of the spir-it's capacity to sink into its own innermost depths and of the inevitabil-ity of this destiny. His interest in the ever-changing human spectacle was unflagging. While Nerval the jester appreciatively accentuated its fascinations, Nerval the moralist perceived it as a scene of perdition.[12] The Valois, the countryside, the landscape of his childhood emerged in his mind as an ideal elsewhere, promising salvation.[13]

3 Nerval's reflections on artistic matters, specifically his evolution from classicism to romanticism, provide powerful illustrations of the issues at stake in the romanticism of his generation. As a schoolboy in Lycée Charlemagne, son of a Napoleonic officer, he imbibed liberal political ideas and classical aesthetics. His first writings are satirical poems, anticlerical and egalitarian, ridiculing various Restoration poli-ticians and a sycophantic French Academy. He espouses the cause of nations struggling to be free: Spain invaded by Bourbon armies, Greece revolting under the Turkish yoke. After 1824, he is perplexed by the place of literature in society and doubts that indignant satire can do much to amend mores. He therefore becomes preoccupied (and remains so for the rest of his life) with aesthetic regeneration; new art forms must be invented to meet the problems inherent in modern civilization. Like his contemporaries, he was intrigued by foreign romantic exam-ples such as the historical novels of Sir Walter Scott and the fantastic tales of Hoffmann. Both interests remained with him all his life. He tried his hand at historical drama for the stage and translated both parts of Goethe's *Faust*. (The job earned him the author's praise and the trans-lation is still in print.) But Nerval was concerned to renew the French

literary tradition and root his aesthetic experimentation in national precedent. He thus left aside the model offered by Hoffmann and strove to
find art forms that did not effect such a complete break from dominant and public thought processes.[14] As Michel Carle puts it, Nerval
sought a path to the true emancipation of thought elsewhere than in
direct criticism of society; but he did not believe in art for art's sake
and wanted to find a solution that would be relevant to both art and
society.[15]

4 Nerval also suffered from periods of madness; as early as 1831 he
had fits of mythomania. He began to love only uncertain reality. His
nom de plume – the name of a meadow in Mortefontaine – marked the
beginning of secret fabrications about the 'true,' noble ancestry of his
mother. In 1841, after several bouts of mental illness, he was hospitalized. (Carnival masks in February had set off his first loss of identity.)[16]
By the end of the year he was better and attempted to prove he was
cured. The years 1849 and 1852 were witnesses to further attacks, which
were followed by a more serious one in 1853. (Nerval did not try botany
or collecting butterflies, but clearly this would not have been sufficient
to soothe his nerves.) His stays in the hospital were lengthening. His
delusions began to take the form of dreams of omnipotence and were
diagnosed as theomaniac delirium.[17]

Critics have demonstrated how closely writing and madness are related in his life and have sought to define the connection precisely. It is
obvious that 'madness takes refuge in mystery.' The mentally ill are
comfortable with esotericism; it provides all the answers.[18] Everything
becomes immediately clear, and social confirmation, which in any case
is rarely offered to those classed as mentally ill, is rendered unneces-
sary. Madness, writes Michel Jeanneret, supplies a substitute for temporary deficiencies. It permits the arrogant extension of the ego through
organized illusion. 'One then runs the risk of losing one's way among
the infinitely polyvalent signs: signs which indiscriminately refer to
meaning and suspend differentiation between true and false, between
reality and fiction.'[19] Every sign justifies itself, every discourse attains
infinite opulence, yet nothing refers to anything else. No meaning is
related to individual experience external to language. It is obvious that
Nerval did not happily accede to being dominated by signs. Unlike
Nodier, he resisted his dreams; they threatened to destroy him. Writing, capturing the role of narrator, gave Nerval the means he craved to
impose some order on signs that seemed to have a life of their own. He

thus perceived madness as an obscure speech, as a discourse to be first accepted and then deciphered by the narrator. In writing he sought salvation.[20]

Did madness lead Nerval to a more profound approach to truth and a better grasp of it? Some have ventured to think so. But should we not rather see madness as an object of fear impossible to describe, and a source of irreparable suffering? (The madness Nerval suffered was not something literary, written up in a piece of fiction. He was, at times, stark raving mad.)[21] Could the so-called truths discovered through madness simply turn out to be more of the futile utterances that never prevented anyone from going mad? In *Nerval, le charme de la répétition*, Sarah Kofman points out the danger of concentrating on psychoanalytical and philosophical readings that would replace literary charm with some version of 'truth.' She sees Nerval as bewitching the reader and, at the same time, curing himself of his delusions (more or less). In finding more than this in his texts, she argues, we run the risk of joining the 'repressive forces, psychiatrists, police commissioners and fathers,' and of allying ourselves with those eager to lead Nerval back to the fold of 'Louis-Philippian' normality.[22] Kofman recognizes that Nerval clearly aims at repossession of control through recourse to the pen, but she prefers not to pass judgment on how therapeutic the practice of writing turned out to be. In the end she favours a mimetic and critical approach similar to that of Jeanneret, who chooses not to assess what Nerval's writing accomplished for his own life, but forces readers to reconstitute the frightening strangeness of the discourse of madness and face the unexpected, and thus leaves it up to them to reclaim, for themselves, the rigour of rational discourse.[23]

In October 1854, Nerval left the hospital for the last time. In 1855, during the night of 25–6 January, he committed suicide; he was found at dawn hanging in the rue de la Vieille Lanterne, near the Tour Saint-Jacques. *Aurélia*, his last work, was still at the printer's.[24] Several months later the neighbourhood was torn down to make way for the boulevards that were part of the city's new urbanization policy.

Some of Nerval's works may lead one to the impression that he spent his life as a 'private' person, working towards his own personal salvation. But this impression should not be allowed to stand. The demonstration of Michel Carle confirms views expressed earlier by Gabrielle Malandain. She showed that Nerval reflected on existing social and political conditions throughout his life and thus played an active part in 'romanticism's vast rereading of history.' Nerval descried the fragility

of the individual yet criticized the individualism society offered.[25] Therefore, I do not think I am merely describing Nerval the individual when
I describe him as suffering from serious deficiencies in identity definition, or as living in a state of constant, vague tension between myth and
reality, or as gradually constructing a personal myth in order to establish the dimensions of his own destiny. I am addressing, in some way,
the problem of an entire generation of artists who, failing to find their
place in society after 1830, searched for solutions to an inimical situation. Surrounded by a world intent on pragmatism, many sought new
paths to knowledge and salvation.[26] They commonly saw bourgeois
society as hopeless and looked to poetry for escape or compensation.
But Nerval demanded more of poetry: it had to help reorganize individual and social lives. Problems of belief are for him practical problems.[27] Nerval found it difficult to distinguish between faith, belief,
intellectual play, and make-believe, and considered himself the child of
a 'skeptical rather than incredulous' century.[28] When he described himself as always 'more inclined to believe in everything than to deny it,'
he was also describing an age without landmarks, without beacons.
And he is astute enough to have one of his characters state, 'When one
believes in everything, one believes in nothing.'[29]

1 In December 1842, Nerval began his journey to the Orient. As well as
an attempt to prove to himself and others that he was cured, this voyage was in keeping with much in the mood of the period: leave a
pathogenic community and rediscover a taste for life under new skies;
break with a difficult social and personal scene; move towards the source
of light and perhaps rediscover the purity of revelations that have been
obscured by their translation and transfer to the Occident. On his return
to Paris in 1844 he began to write Le voyage en Orient, which was finally
published in its entirety in 1851. This work conformed to a contemporary literary mode. A travel narrative can be a sequence of disconnected
events.[30] The poet-traveller is more spectator than actor. Everything
unfolds before him: he has only to slacken or quicken his pace at will.
He can remain detached and invent a personal happiness for a momen-
tary need. His only task, which commits him to little, is to produce a
story. The creator can observe himself in his work, without fear of
losing himself.[31] The poet can try on various identities, and cultivate
one for public display.[32]

Through his travels, Nerval hoped to assimilate mythologies and create his own. He travelled to Egypt, Lebanon, and Istanbul, thus avoid-

ing the Holy Land, which had drawn Chateaubriand. Gascar claims that Nerval wanted to prove his hallucinations were descents into a 'collective unconscious,' and dismisses the voyage as a failure: in Egypt, he abruptly announces, Nerval discovered that Isis did not exist.[33] Perhaps. But the truth in this matter is likely to remain beyond our reach. We should rather concentrate, I suggest, on the one success Nerval owes to his journey to the East, namely, the text of *Le voyage en Orient*. It becomes clear from the finished product that he gained some knowledge that amounted to a sort of initiation.

In the introduction, 'Le songe de Polyphile,' Nerval embroiders on Nodier's story of the Renaissance Dominican author of the eccentric book; as Nerval tells the story, a poor fifteenth-century Italian artist loves and is loved by a noble heiress, yet they cannot hope to marry – 'the altar of Christ ... of the God of equality ... was forbidden them.' He becomes a monk and she a nun, 'spending their days studying ancient philosophies and religions and their nights dreaming of (their) future happiness, embellishing it with glorious details (they) discovered in the writings of ancient Greece.' Polyphile, the unfortunate lover, records his visions and finds his freedom in dreams and foreign mythologies, and in writing. Like Faust and Helen, also sublime lovers, these pure lovers meet in a book.[34] 'Polyphile knew Cithère (Cithaeron), because he had never been there, and true love for having shunned its mortal image.'[35] Nerval was less fortunate: the first thing he saw on setting foot on the famous island (then an English possession) was a gibbet. In his case, the 'other life,' discovered through dreams, poetry, and travel, also includes dissension. Here, too, he meets with conflict and finds no easy path towards mastery.

Throughout *Le voyage en Orient*, Nerval gradually built up a religious alternative: he articulated daring syncretist hypotheses that gave way to his inclination for promethean revolt.[36] Nerval's parallel revelation reduces Jehovah to the rank of one genius – and an inferior one – among many. This jealous and petty God hates women (in differentiating itself from polytheism, monotheism stripped itself of the female element) and any authority other than his own. He burdens humanity with endless, exhausting dissociation. He grants earthly power to the mediocre. Some rebel against him in vain; others, the sons of Cain, or Cainites, succeed. These superior creatures, the masters and daughters of fire, know the secrets of metallurgy, magic, and art. They are able to create beauty. In this alternative religion, scholars, artisans, artists, labourers, and true women are opposed to tyrants, kings, and priests.[37]

Nerval did not, however, intend *Le voyage en Orient* as a doctrinal text.[38] His own state of mind, half-way through the book, is indicated by his conversation with the scholar from Berlin at Gizeh. The Prussian was a learned guide ('No one has mastered the mysteries of Antiquity better than the Germans'), yet for him the meeting between East and West induced no dreams, set off no creative sparks. The prospect of staging a performance of *The Magic Flute* in the Great Pyramid left him indifferent. He merely pointed out the technical difficulties involved and continued on with his explanation of Egyptian initiations. Nerval humoured him: 'This system ... could essentially explain all religions.[39] But what have we to gain?' Nothing, replied the positivist scholar. It is clear that Nerval, a passionate pilgrim, was more interested in the stories of the illiterate sheik he had met on the Isle of Roddah, who had told him the pyramids were built by a pre-Adamite king.[40] The legend, especially of interest because it had come to him by word of mouth, fanned his desire to rewrite the sacred pages of the origins of humanity.

The revelation he designed as an alternative to biblical text was finally developed in three major stories inserted in the tale of his adventures. The first, related by his learned friend from Berlin, is the story of Orpheus' Egyptian initiation, at which Isis was revealed to him. The second, told in Lebanon by a Druse sheik, recounts the adventures of Caliph Hakem. The third, heard in a café in Istanbul, tells the tale of the Queen of Sheba, named 'Queen of the Morning,' of Soliman (i.e., Solomon), of the Prince of the Genii, and of Adoniram, the Temple architect who showed himself a more fitting husband for the Queen of Sheba than the unworthy Soliman.[41] All three stories include the image of a majestic woman and tell of an initiation – unsuccessful in the first two cases, since Orpheus lost Eurydice by failing the simple test, and the Caliph Hakem was unable to rise from the underworld because of his excessive faith in the supposed virtues of hashish. As Schaeffer has shown, each story contributes to the development of a perfect model of a true poet. Only Adoniram, however, managed to give direction and shape to his dream, to convert nature to his own purpose, and to defeat God on his home ground.[42] Through the progression of the stories, we realize that Nerval, the poet travelling to the Orient to conquer the absolute, was also being gradually initiated and slowly transformed. Only in Istanbul did his myths and his reality finally merge. There, finally, the son of Voltaire and the disciple of the dervish mastered and achieved his art. In Istanbul he embraced the tolerance practised in Turkey, where Jews and Christians live in peace under Koranic law.

Nerval, the Westerner steeped in the Orient, moved from passive to affirmative tolerance. He adopted a conciliatory, universal faith and returned to Paris to work at regenerating the Occident on his newly gained principle.[43]

The story of Nerval's travels thus reconstitutes the elements of a disturbing adventure that begins with the 'ethereal dissipation of the self.' To an infinitely pliable self, the world is transformed into a theatre: Cairo is the playhouse and the European traveller the audience. (He can buy a ticket to the performance and, if the fleeting mental images it nurtures no longer serve, he may leave at his leisure.)[44] But the adventure ended with a self committed in the real world. Once the poet finished writing *Le voyage en Orient*, he was back in the real world of the West, with an exalted but real task. He had arrived at some settled identity and belief. As Max Milner puts it, in a world no longer sacred, only tolerance, or a kind of syncretism, can perpetuate the essence of a religious experience which keeps humankind from sinking into the sterile and solitary longing for a lost unity.[45] Nerval was thus able to orchestrate his fantasies and find his own mythology. He reformulated his dream, transforming it into his destiny.[46]

2 In 1852, Nerval published *Les illuminés*, a collection of articles devoted to various eccentric personalities. These articles had previously been published individually, the earliest dating from 1839. Except for Spifame, a gentle crackpot who lived under Henri II and thought he was the king, and the Abbé de Bucquoy, a seventeenth-century adventurer, these eccentrics – Restif de la Bretonne, Cazotte, Cagliostro, and Quintus Aucler – all lived in the eighteenth century, just before or during the Revolution. The tone varies from story to story; their value is uneven. In all the stories Nerval adopts a historical approach; through them he also gives a broad outline of a religious history of the West seen from the pre-Christian point of view. He thus claims that the 'apostasy' of Clovis was able to rout 'a creed as old as the world' for only 'a mere fifteen centuries,' and that Apollo will reappear.[47] He also maintains that many pagan cults survived in spite of the triumph of Catholicism. Polytheism allied itself with philosophy, united with the cabbala, and resurfaced in the Renaissance to be propagated by the doctrines of freemasonry. Nerval also refers to the French illuminati, Saint-Germain and Saint-Martin, and seeks to discover their sources.[48] His information is good: his 1844 articles include results of inquiries into the many strange sects common in Paris at the time.[49] These sections of his work

are steeped in esotericism. But his comments on how the writers in question kept their beliefs alive in chaotic times also echo some of the stock formulas of his day. After citing Aucler's professions of pagan faith, Nerval takes on the tone of a moralizing liberal: Aucler restored sincere feeling to religion; it took courage to suggest the restoration of paganism during the Revolution. Finally, Nerval makes it clear that he considers any religion diluted the moment poets touch it. He thus claims that Christianity, in spite of its worthiness of love, is in great peril of imminent demise.[50]

But these stories go beyond the voicing of such opinions. They articulate the drama of a protean 'I,' excluded from social reality, committed to the powers of the imaginary and of signs. The text invites us to prick up our ears and perhaps pick up unusual 'truths.'[51] Nerval identifies in particular with Restif de la Bretonne. He is fascinated by Restif's ambiguous attachment to pagan spiritualism, which seems to take the form of a materialistic pantheism conciliating naturalism and spiritualism. Yet it is difficult to decide how deep his attachment is to such piety. (Nerval refers to a 'half sceptical, half credulous' initiate of Isis in Apuleius' *Golden Ass*, a classic he was most fond of.)[52] Nerval's statements on literary history are clear and firm; he correctly situates Restif in the tradition of autobiographical writers, utopians, and inventors of literary forms. In Restif's pathos he seems to discern something of his own destiny. 'We don't live life!' he has Restif say. 'We analyze it ... To earn our bread we have to turn our loves into books.'[53]

Nerval also relates these eccentricities to the social and political crisis of the time. Their study is thus relevant to 'the appreciation of the moral causes of our revolutions.'[54] The collection is subtitled 'The Precursors of Socialism.' (It should not be forgotten that between Babeuf and Marx who were anti-religious, French socialism was religious in orientation and sought to bring about a return of 'soul' as well as justice to the daily world.) The section devoted to Cazotte is especially striking. In it, a royalist clairvoyant forewarns a salon of philosophers, blithely awaiting a favourable future, of the coming of the scaffold and the Reign of Terror.[55] Nerval then proffers his own analysis: 'Our century has not yet encountered a man, superior in spirit and heart, who, understanding the true relationship of things, can calm the clashing forces and restore peace to troubled imaginations.'[56]

He is hopeful but hardly enthusiastic. He keeps trying to accommodate both reason and unreason. For him, 'reason wonders at and curiosity feeds on' the combinations of monstrous, aborted ideas that flourish in troubled times, and these very ideas contain the seeds of a new world.[57]

3 *Octavie*, a narrative of eight pages, leads us into the magic kingdom of Nervalian story-telling. Raymond Jean describes *Octavie* as having the 'extraordinary ability to appropriate the most varied realms of the real and the imaginary, of experience and of memory.'[58] As we will see, the various stages in the writing of this work are most revealing.

We find its first traces in a letter Nerval drafted, apparently to be sent to a lady-love in Paris, describing a strange experience he had had one night in Naples.[59] In this letter, a man attempts to tell a lady of his uneasiness about the uncertainty of her feelings. The man is haunted by the idea of death; he had felt its powerful attraction three years earlier, when he had spent the night with a Neapolitan woman who earned her living by embroidering church vestments with gold. He describes her room in 'mystic' terms. Her speech was barely comprehensible to him. Bedecked with the sacerdotal ornaments crowding her room, she was strangely beautiful. 'With her curious manner, royally arrayed, proud and capricious, she seemed to me like one of the sorceresses of Thessaly who seized one's soul in exchange for a dream.'[60] Nerval related this encounter to reassure his love: because the embroiderer resembled her, he explains, she kept reigning supreme in his heart throughout the entire adventure. He was in the end to tear himself away from this seductive yet frightening spectre, and wander through the city, refusing to believe himself created for eternal suffering, thinking of suicide.

As Marie-Jeanne Durry sees it, this 'letter' (which probably never was sent to an actual correspondent) marks Nerval's first decisive step 'into the kingdom.' An incident from real life moves into the world of magic distortion; Nerval attempts to introduce personal anecdote into myth. 'These pages bring us to the junction of the ordinary world and that other strange, exalting world where Nerval would henceforth live his truest life; his imaginary life would hereafter be indistinguishable from his literary life.'[61] This then is the beginning of 'the infiltration of dream into reality.'[62]

In 1853 the 'letter' was inserted in a longer fiction entitled *Octavie*.[63] Here again the narrator begins with an affirmation of his unhappiness. Since his love has been rejected, he has decided to make a trip to Italy to take his mind off his problems. On the beach at Marseille, or more exactly, in the sea, he meets a young English woman, an excellent swimmer. He later meets her again by chance at Civita Vecchia, travelling with her invalid father. On the boat to Naples she asks him to meet her at Portici the following day. He spends his first evening in Naples at the opera, and later with friends. It is on leaving their palace that he meets his embroiderer. Here the narrator introduces the 'letter' written to his lady in Paris describing his strange adventure.

At dawn, anticipation of his rendezvous with the young English woman banishes his depressing thoughts: they are to visit Pompei. Throughout the trip her father remains unobtrusive, giving the narrator the opportunity to see that Octavie is no rustic provincial. In the temple of Isis, Nerval writes, 'I was pleased to explain to her the features of the cult and the ceremonies that I had read about in Apuleius. She wanted to play the role of the goddess and I found myself in the role of Osiris, explaining his divine mysteries.'[64]

On their return, 'struck by the grandeur of the ideas we had just discussed, I dared not speak to her of love.'[65] When she comments on his pensive mood, he tells her of his nocturnal adventure and his love for the lady in Paris. And so ends the romance. Ten years later the narrator and the English woman meet again. She is now married to a famous painter stricken with paralysis who, in spite of his wife's devoted care, is extremely jealous. The narrator is left with only the memory of a brief and cherished apparition.

The narrator's daytime outdoor romance with his blond Nordic naiad ends no better than his nighttime sojourn in the den of his chthonic Mediterranean sorceress. He thus admits to failed attempts with three different women. Octavie is the most immediately seductive of all Nerval's heroines; her openness to flirtation is simply an indication of her greater generosity. However, the interior drama the narrator is enacting for himself – his 'betrayal' of his Parisian lady-love whom he adores with a pure and boundless love – interrupts the story he weaves with his new encounters. I would like to suggest that the narrator perceives still another failure, another desecration: the temple of Isis has been used as a setting for a 'vulgar' seduction.

Perhaps too, the narrator, unable to lay hold of his prey, prefers to see them as shadows. It seems to me that the women the narrator flees, women whom he dishonours or fails to honour, are avenged in *Isis*, the story that follows *Octavie* in the collection *Daughters of Fire*. *Isis* also tells the tale of a voyage. This time, however, the narrator describes Pompei, the temple of Isis, and a 'rather ingenious' party given by an ambassador in Naples, where costumed guests attempted to revive the customs of the ancient Roman colony. The narrator dwells at length on this 'effort at resurrection' and its Isiac rites, often doggedly translating from a scholarly German source. Suddenly there is a change of tone. When alone at the Naples Museum of Archaeology and again at the temple, the narrator is invaded by an intense awareness: all cults are destined to perish as did the cult of Isis.[66] The initiate who had thought to attain eternal life by lifting the sacred veil of Isis appears at last to have come 'face to face with the image of Death.' Nevertheless, the narrator confesses that he is still captivated by the seductive 'illusions of the past.' In the days of the Roman Empire, paganism, rejuvenated by the cult of Isis, managed to bring unity back to mythology. This pure concept of divinity still retains some of its power. The goddess, the Holy Mother, has not totally disappeared: Catholicism increasingly emphasizes the Virgin Mary. Nevertheless, he concludes that, while the religion of Isis is designed for happy people, humanity prefers to surrender to 'the religions of despair.'

In *Isis*, Nerval reveals his nostalgia for a religion that glorified the female element: the Great Goddess crowns his syncretist theories. The narrator, who was unable to bring happiness to the actual women he met, finds compensation in extolling Woman in his religious philosophy. In *Octavie*, he confesses his bewilderment: he feels threatened and acknowledges the fact; he admits he is on the verge of suicide. In *Isis*, he is able to recover a certain amount of control, contrasting the jocular tone of the reporter with the detached, judicious, critical tone of the scholar.[67] But in this particular text, the death that lay in wait for the initiate of Isis is only a genteel expression picked up in the sceptical *salons* that chatter about the deaths of civilizations. It was not the concrete death that haunted the lover of the lady in Paris. (And woman, in this text, is no real person but only a sublime element.) In both stories, the reality of the myth turns into a mythology. In *Octavie*, the mythology is subjective, delirious, and literary: reality sinks and drowns in the quicksands of the interior monologue. The mythology in *Isis* is objective, literate, and learned: here reality slumbers and dies away in archaeological tomes or in a professor's remarks on historical cycles. In both cases life stops, scatters, and takes flight.

4 The narrator of *Sylvie* is in love with an actress. In the theatre, he lives for her and she seems to live for him alone. But, as he fears disturbing the 'magic mirror,' he never attempts to meet her. The theatre thus leads him into a dream world to which he can constantly return. By accident he catches a glimpse of her with a group of friends. Reality approaches: she is escorted by someone else.[68] He then leaves Paris for

the Valois, drawn by the memory of happy childhood games, dances, and festivities. Yet even here dreams disturb reality. The narrator, flashing back to the time of his youth, tells how he had faithfully loved a childhood sweetheart, the dark-haired, black-eyed Sylvie; but when the blond Adrienne came to upset their dance, he forgot his early love. Adrienne, who was of noble birth, attracted him; she came from afar and lived in a castle. He later learned that she had become a nun. So even then illusion had replaced reality. Now, in his adulthood, the narrator's heart has been captured by another illusion, the actress in Paris, a blonde who resembles Adrienne. Fleeing this actress to the Valois countryside, the narrator once again meets his dark-haired peasant girl, now grown into a charming young woman. The narrator too has grown: he has become a poet. He speaks to her of *La Nouvelle Héloïse*, but she remains indifferent. Their reunion is of short duration, for Sylvie no longer resembles her former image. She has a simple, hard-working young suitor; pragmatic and unsentimental, she knows the limits of poetry. There is to be no repetition of their childhood happiness and their reunion scene is simply pleasant theatre. The narrator then falls back on culture: he drifts to Ermenonville, to rediscover the haunts of his dear Rousseau. But the tomb of the Ile aux Peupliers is empty. He realizes that life in the castle gardens was also transient theatre. Back in Paris, he returns to the real theatre and begins to pay court to the actress Aurélie. Although he takes her out and they travel together, she eventually leaves him. In the last section the narrator soberly sums up the situation: 'Illusions crumble, one after the other.' Having attained the stature of a narrator who embraces life in its entirety, Nerval recovers a certain well-being; distance provides protection.[69]

Throughout the story, the narrator remains caught in the same fatal circle: he confuses phantasmagoria and reality.[70] He sees the other only in his fantasies, never recognizing difference. The ideal other – the actress on the stage *repeating* the same magic every evening – triggers the same dreams. In leaving the theatre for the countryside of his childhood, leaving the city for the country, the narrator expects to regain a community that will allow him to communicate and participate – in short, a community where he understands the code and where he in turn can be understood.[71] But he cannot repeat the joys of childhood: Sylvie and the narrator have become adults for whom work and sexuality count. The quest for repetition prevents the integration of the changes time has wrought. Reality therefore becomes theatre; the magic ritual of reunion and regeneration leads only to destructive repetition. Even the wisdom and beauty amassed at Ermenonville have been altered by time. Here the narrator encounters change that destroys dreams. There is no repetition without difference; nor is there life without death. The narrator, however, conceals this discovery from himself. According to Sarah Kofman's psychoanalytic reading, the narrator's return to the Valois is motivated by fear. He refuses to see the connection between love and death. He seeks an eternally youthful mother who will ensure his immortality rather than the embrace of a mortal woman who at best could only give him a child.[72]

Although the story ends with admirable resignation (the sort of commmon-sense advice found in proverbs or offered by well-intentioned parents and psychologists), this resignation is contradicted by the text in its entirety. To quote Gabrielle Malandain, 'The object of desire is *by definition* a mutable and impenetrable vanishing point, because it touches on realms inaccessible to the conscience "in transit".'[73] Adrienne, Sylvie, and Aurélie are not real women with whom the narrator really tries to share pleasure – that 'verification of accomplished desire'[74] – they are lures on which he hooks his obscure desire, thus making sure that it never attains its end. Although the faintly moralizing tone at the beginning hints at a story of initiation and gives the impression that the narrator, a captive soul, is leaving the iniquitous city in search of a lost innocence, it remains that his initial desire as he starts out is vague and confused. The rest of the story makes it clear that the narrator seeks to return to childhood rather than learn about life.[75]

His confrontation with time is thus a failure. Desire remains spasmodic.[76] The narrator is not involved in any work or labour. He is subjugated by repetitive scenes (at best, the actress who repeats her role every evening) which, although they engender and revive his desire, prevent him from attaining it. The dreamer refuses to become a man. He wanders in search of situations that bring back, if only for an instant, the emotions and images that inflame his ideal.

5 *Sylvie* has long been considered the pinnacle of Nerval's art. Today the place of honour might perhaps instead go to *Aurélia*.[77] Léon Cellier has stressed the broad range of this unusual text, showing its three dimensions: a methodical examination of the phenomena of sleep and madness, a stylized autobiography, and a story of a soul in search of peace.[78] The writing of *Aurélia* comes at the end of a long process. After 1840 Nerval worked on a variety of autobiographical pieces; he published fragmentary, or veiled, indirect accounts of his life. When he was hospitalized in 1853, his doctor, Emile Blanche, encouraged him to write

down his dreams. This same year, his insanity having become public knowledge and threatening his literary reputation, Nerval undertook to save his name by describing his affliction.[79] Started during his second major onslaught of madness, *Aurélia* was finished just before his death in 1855.[80]

'Dreams are a second life,' announces the introduction. They take us beyond the gates of ivory and horn 'that separate us from the invisible world.' The narrator obtains access to this second life in two stages.

In the first section, the narrator informs us that he has decided to travel abroad because he has 'lost' the woman he loved. Sleeping dreams and waking delusions then take over: 'I lost the meaning of the images that came to me, and the connection between them.'[81] The narrator is hospitalized. He relates what happened then, and besides the narration of actual facts, we find on the page obviously 'literary' dreams and delusions, written (or rewritten) after they occurred. These 'dreams' are erudite: extensive knowledge (mythological and religious) and oneirism contaminate each other. They are also structured: what the sick person writes on the page is transmittable.[82] These voyages 'beyond' lead to peace at first. The glimpse of 'the mystic fatherland' and of the loved ones living there after death resolves any doubt about the immortality of the soul. 'No more death, no more sadness, no more anxiety.'[83] He is given paper and attempts to write 'a sort of history of the world mixing memories from books and fragments of dreams.'[84] The system is borrowed from 'Oriental' traditions. History begins with the happy agreement of the forces of nature; an elite, pre-Adamite race lives at the centre of the earth. (They are sinister this time, however, and far from the prestige of the honoured Cainites in *Le voyage en Orient*.) When peace enters his spirit, he is able to leave the asylum.

A few years later he has a relapse. He begins to fear that he is unworthy of rejoining Aurélia and is driven to despair by his feelings of guilt. But he wants to resist. 'We must fight against this fatal spirit, and even against this god, with the weapons of tradition and science.'[85] But the theurgical effort ('I used all the strength of my will') fails. As the recurring dreams turn to nightmares, his feelings of guilt become explicit: 'I was perhaps cursed for having tried to penetrate a formidable mystery by offending divine law.'[86]

The narrator begins the second half of the story exclaiming, 'Lost a second time!' When he turns to religious teachings for solace, he finds it difficult to 'reconstruct the mystic structure.' He therefore suffers still another defeat: the letter is lost, the sign erased.[87] He begins then to think of the misfortunes of others. He pays a visit to a sick friend who seems to have found God, and in doing so, he forms a new diagnosis: 'I have preferred the creature to the Creator.' This echo of one Christian text leads to another: 'If this religion speaks the truth, God can forgive me once more.'[88] The moment this new element – the God of the Christian religion – enters the picture, the entire text changes its focus. As Malandain has pointed out, this God speaks to a subject different from that of the God in the first half of the story. He is not the God of dreamers or of thinkers who 'isolated within their own system are resigned to the hope of achievement elsewhere.' He is the God of a 'subject confronted with the difficulty of action in a real world and of real communication with the other.'[89] Even though the narrator suffers at not having been able to share his friend's faith, he has at last been able to make the biblical gesture of visiting the sick. He then renounces his cult of the dead and becomes invaded by feelings of guilt towards his live family and friends. After visiting his father, whose servant is sick, he reproaches himself for not having brought in the firewood.[90] The next passage describes his wanderings through Paris, under a black sun in a barren sky as he entertains thoughts of suicide.[91] Once more he is picked up in the streets and brought back to the clinic.

In the asylum he is again submerged in delusion. 'At first, I imagined that all the people in the garden had some influence on the stars, and that the person endlessly rotating in the same circle was directing the path of the sun. It seemed to be my task to reestablish universal harmony through Cabalistic art and find answers in the occult forces of various religions.'[92]

Once more the doctor intervenes; this time, he introduces the narrator to a young man, a soldier wounded in North Africa, who can neither see nor speak, and refuses all nourishment. 'I began to love him because of his misfortune and his helplessness.'[93] He calls him Saturnin and looks after him, singing him songs from his childhood. And Saturnin awakes. The following section is entitled 'Mémorables.' In a tone of sustained lyricism, these pages announce universal pardon, amicable duality, victory over death, the reconciliation of the gods proclaimed by Christ, and, returning to the factual story, Saturnin's relative improvement (he has opened his eyes and asked for something to drink) and the definitive solution to the Oriental question.[94]

In *Aurélia*, something which had never been described before is revealed, namely, the suffering, the subjective delusions of the person who, at birth, was named Gérard Labrunie. This delirium, always on the edge of the indescribable, comes to fill a mould, the established genre of autobiographical writing. (At the beginning of his text, Nerval places himself in the company of Swedenborg, Apuleius, and Dante and situates *Aurélia* well within their 'poetic models' of 'studies of the human soul.')[95] He reshapes the genre and thus contributes to literature something that had never been said *in this way*. Finally, the initation story, an established genre, becomes closely related to the story of conversion familiar to Christian theologians. (Under this aspect, the text shows a didactic intent.) Briefly put, for the first time under Nerval's pen, the public person, the author, and the narrator are one. As J.P. Richard puts it, the power of *'Mémorables'* lies in the fact that for once words have a single stable meaning; there are no unfathomable depths, no hovering halo of plural syncretistic meanings.[96] One can also say that Nerval's usual distanciation, as he writes out of the mess of images that crowd his mind and denounces them, gives way to a tentative progression towards an organized narrative.[97]

Milner makes a further, cautious, point. Beside the abyss of unreason, *Aurélia* opens up 'luminous perspectives of reintegration which, if they do not have a therapeutic virtue, at least have a cathartic power of which any reader may feel the effects.'[98] The text in fact does 'flow.' Not only does Nerval lead readers back and forth through his usual, imperceptible shifts, he also takes them firmly around crucial corners. The story makes choices: it moves forward rather than wanders. This writing allows the past truly to become the past and die away. The sensations and myths in 'Mémorables' automatically arouse other sensations and myths that draw the reader on to the end of the narrative. The story seems to impose its own order.[99] In spite of the common insistence on the primacy of the text and on the need to view each text as an autonomous work,[100] I would like to suggest that *Aurélia* should be read as the culmination of the author's life. (I believe this to be true despite the inevitable confusion caused by the close relationship between the writing of this text and the author's suicide.) Besides reading the text structurally we may also read it hermeneutically, and venture beyond the life of the text to discuss the life of the man. The writer who allowed himself to be invaded by myth, the 'sick person' for whom 'a thousand details took on the power of hieroglyphs and the force of revelation,'[101] finally completed a narrative that could well pass for the story of his life. Conscience is no longer 'in transit.' The text now confirms the reality of an ego free from the indefinite and unending sway of commonplace myths; we now encounter a self capable of constructing a complete and firmly founded personal mythology.[102] The Nerval who had thought to find a second life in dreams and tended to think ideologically of both the dreaming and the waking state, ceased looking elsewhere for lost truth and was finally able to come to terms with his life.[103]

There is implicit here a very large claim. It is that Nerval came very close to writing the ideal book, the truly salutary book. Such a claim is already hidden in *Le voyage en Orient*. Much erudite baggage about Oriental religions is included: ignorance cannot be learned; the science we have acquired, we must keep. But science is not life. Are then the private phantasms life? the dreams and fears? Not either. But they too must be included. Sciences of religion and personal growth merge to enable the author to write a book that both cures his irresolution and shows the path to the reconciliation between Eastern and Western peoples.[104] *Aurélia* takes on an even more superhuman task – to bring harmony back to all religious conflicts, all conflicting cosmogonies, and all disturbed imaginations, including those wracked by mental sickness. Should a writer indeed ever take on such a task?

To return to more mundane, historical considerations, we must note that, when the narrative attempts to recount life, the entire symbolic world abandons esotericism and moves toward biblical notions. Where the example of Adoniram served as an identity for the artist, the biblical example serves as an identity for the man.[105] With Saturnin, Nerval plays neither the role of the Caliph Hakim nor that of the mason Adoniram. He is renouncing esotericism exactly as, in the text, he had renouced theurgy when he admitted having lost Aurélia. The 'dream' Saturnin is the same as the invincibly pitiful 'real' Saturnin. Image and meaning are now superposed. His actual neighbour in the asylum is also his neighbour in the biblical sense. This myth leads to something tangible; rather than simply referring back to other myths, it mediates a reality. Nerval has finally found an imaginary world that does more than simply feed on itself. He has found a world that explicates the meaning of the subject's relation to the world and detheatricalizes the relation between the self and the other.[106]

In spite of its obvious uniqueness, Nerval's literary journey illustrates at length and in various ways how hard it was for religious consciousness to achieve some stability in the early nineteenth century. It was perhaps particularly difficult for those who had never received any religious training from their families (which would have given them a faith they could later have accepted, rejected, or changed), and who were led by their reading into a cosmopolitan but shattered world, rich in scattered religious symbols. In Nerval's case the problem was compounded by the fact that he never had the famous lost childhood that so many feel nostalgic about.[107] His texts thus point out with unique force the problems inherent in attempting to determine the power of some or all of these symbols and in discussing the grounds of belief in them with some authority.[108] Versed in German literature as he was, Nerval insisted on his attachment to the French literary tradition, which to him meant writing both morally and politically.[109] A writer's mission is 'to analyse sincerely what he feels in the serious moments of life.'[110] In the voice of a confidently healthy moralist, he then articulates the experience of his entire generation. 'For those of us born during revolution and tumult, times in which all beliefs were destroyed ... it is very difficult to reconstruct a mystic edifice when we feel the need to do so.'[111]

Some critics may attribute the despondent passages, in which the narrator fears that 'the lost letter,' 'the obliterated sign,' and the 'discordant scale' are beyond recovery and reconstitution, to mental illness. It would perhaps be more accurate to say that Nerval, in order to relate the meanderings of a mind determined to conquer its relationship to truth, dared to attempt an intricate and complex literary mode. Describing his autobiographical project, he said he was attempting something like *Les rêveries du promeneur solitaire*[112] but clearly his undertaking was without precedent: none of his rêverie could be allowed to stand. *Aurélia* is undoubtedly the most complex of the structures assembled by the five authors in this study. The writer is always impaled on dilemmas, revealing fragments of himself and trying to get at the whole, telling the truth about himself and denying the adequacy of what he has just said.[113]

Four stages in Nerval's journey shed light on the workings of a religious conscience that cannot be easily situated within one particular realm of belief.

1 Nerval begins by distinguishing between dreams, the waking state, and erudition.[114] He allows himself to be seduced by both dreams and learning in such a way that one invigorates the other. Writers have no need to be reminded of the force of dreams, but historians of religion would do well to remember the Prussian scholar in Egypt: the history he writes is quite useless to him, for it inspires no dreams. What his history brings to others is also suspect. Like many later orientalists, he

visits only monuments and inscriptions and, unlike Nerval, has no interest whatsoever in meeting Egyptians.[115] The reader of *Le voyage en Orient* learns to see that the accumulation of 'religious knowledge' may be just as compensational as rampant oneirism. It is simply another form of compensation, one, however, which is more appreciated by university scholars. Nerval's dreams of the Orient are also a form of escape: the sacred is not to be found in spatial journeys any more than in scholarly ones. The language of initiation which concludes *Le voyage en Orient* is the language of a better-informed Frenchman, desiring to bridge two cultures that had previously remained closed to one another.[116] *Le voyage en Orient* is the work of an author who wishes to participate in the history of relations between East and West. In Nerval's version of the Orphic myth, the poet who descends into art's hell comes back with life.

2 The free examination of myths and symbols can set off a whirlwind of images – an elating phantasmagoria – which in the end reveals nothing other than the games of a narcissistic ego. Nerval symbolizes the fate common to Jean-Jacques Rousseau and his followers: in withdrawing into an intimate self, the conscience is constantly attempting to decipher freely symbols which are ultimately indecipherable. It is an intoxicating venture that leads only to conflict between the limpid pool of the conscience and the murky world. No univocal expression can bridge the gap between the two. The disconnected, non-referential symbols enter into a frenetic dance that leads to madness. As Georges Poulet has observed, it is not so much the belief in divinity that then dies, as the form which makes this belief possible.[117] The decipherer endlessly and vainly peers beneath the veils. The phantasmic world that appears to restore life to religion, the customary institutions and abodes of which have died, eventually depletes the sacramental signs of all their referential value.[118] The quest for transcendence must then take refuge in the fantastic, which can only compensate for inadequacy in the presence of the real.[119]

3 At a decisive moment, Nerval feels something akin to the reawakening of a Christian heart. In *Aurélia*, the I of the author 'undertakes to express its story and its fantasies, confronting the problem of their reciprocal dependence.'[120] He discusses his parents, his uncle, and the others who taught him and gave him a history. He also attests to a conversion to the Bible and its version of spiritual development. In this text, the literary ego gives way to the religious ego; the desire to write mingles with the desire to be.[121] The author's pagan imagination, which

had been aroused on contact with the polytheism of antiquity and the Orient is, in a manner of speaking, baptized: it is set to serve a heart which, when it finally declares itself, declares itself Christian. In an ambiguous note in *Aurélia*, Nerval observes that 'we are born under biblical law';[122] the reader of *Le voyage en Orient* is tempted to read this as the proclamation of a curse. In the second part of the text, however, biblical law turns into a blessed gospel: it imposes duties towards neighbours and mediates their presence. Polytheistic oneirism was unable to fix desire. Dreams were appealed to in vain; they could guarantee no transcendent foundation. The narcissistic ego deified itself and remained alone. Faced with the biblical God and the law of this 'solitary kingship' (which had at first been an object of dread),[123] the narcissistic ego sacrificed itself and discovered the other. This God finally legitimizes signs. Saturnin *is* a brother. The commonplaces of conversion narratives are thus incorporated into the text to validate rather than to deceive or to lie; they represent the reality of what has actually taken place.[124]

Why this change of direction? Has the solemn, wise, and generous Sarastro simply triumphed once again over the radiant, seductive, and unreliable Queen of the Night? Why has Nerval suddenly granted exclusive authority to biblical text? *Aurélia* informs us (following a passage on his deistic, pagan uncle) that a passing Englishman taught him the Sermon on the Mount and gave him a copy of the New Testament.[125] Are we witnessing the resurgence of a Christian cultural atavism?[126] This may well be the case, but a psychoanalytic reading would view this change of direction as the return of the Father and his symbolic law, which would thrust the ego into the reality of the world, forbid it to seek repetition (and the accompanying loss of self through its fusion with it), and finally transform the descending vortex into hell into an upward salutary spiral.[127] In other words, with the discovery of a transcendent God comes recognition of the transcendence of the other. If we accept as religious a conviction that comes to terms with an abiding reality, then *Aurélia* is a genuine religious document.

4 Nerval finally allows us to glimpse some issues at stake in the feminization of religion that invaded the West, and Catholicism in particular, from the first half of the nineteenth century. Some of Nodier's texts have already given us some clues: now that the pompous rationalism of Sarastro is denounced and King Solomon is exposed for the oriental despot and petty macho that he was, it is not at all clear what males have to offer to such impressive females as the Queen of the Night or the Queen of Sheba – or what they have to oppose to them.

Nodier surrendered to the pleasures of regression and of devotion to maternal figures. Nerval kept doggedly showing interest in the daughters but does not seem to have found his way with them. 'Oh Mother Héva – my heart was ensnared in your daughters' blond hair!'[128] Like many of his contemporaries, Nerval pushed his idealization of women beyond all limits, only to find that his Ideal Woman had grown to such proportions as to incarnate all the problems of the universe. While 'Woman' became the supreme metaphor, she never mediated relationship with a real person. Reading and rereading Nerval's metaphor of 'Woman,' we see an endless relocation of discourse.[129] Certainly he strove to accept, and even praise, female nature, and yet he always idealized it in relationship to male desires. According to Sarah Kofman, the psychological truth beneath the illusion is revealed in the similarity of his ideal women: he is unable to love a woman in her difference. For Nerval, the principle of evil is always extrinsic to woman. His aesthetic gaze 'derealizes' individual woman – and keeps him from marriage.[130]

The most consummate expression of the cult of the Great Goddess appears in *Aurélia*: 'I am the same as Mary, the same as your mother, the same as all the other figures you have always loved. At each of your trials I have removed one of the masks that hid my features, and soon you will see me as I am.'[131]

He has reached the summit of delusion for, throughout the rest of the narrative, the goddess reneges on her promise. A benevolent female vision reappears, however, just before the end of the story, after the doctor's intervention and the encounter with Saturnin, after the author has renounced the futile and depressing memory of Aurélia. A star takes the form of a woman to tell him that the simple soul of Saturnin has communicated his wish to the Virgin Mary (Mary is no longer ranked with the 'other goddesses'). From here on this benevolent female vision is allowed to comfort the author.[132] The 'divinity of his dream(s)' is brought down a notch or two and becomes a messenger (the station granted by the Christian heaven), the Beatrice of the *Divine Comedy*.

Poetic delusions reveal instant meaning, as do the Scriptures read by believers in literal inspiration. The theopneusts, when they receive the divine message, reproduce, in their own particular way, the act of the visionary who perfectly and completely assimilated the Scriptures by eating them (Ezekiel 3:1 and Revelation 10:10). At the end of 'Mémorables', the 'healthy' narrator feels obliged to explain, 'I tried to discover the meaning of my dreams and this effort influenced all my waking observations.'[133] For readers of religious texts, Nerval's work carries a basic warning: they too must strive to discover meaning. They must work at reading books without 'humiliating' their reason.[134] And today, they should strive to understand the disconcerting literary texts that attempt to reveal the presence and absence of God.[135]

Nerval is not an orthodox believer, in any religion or in any heresy.[136] He described himself as 'a comedian with religion'[137] and it is in this role that he speaks to us all, because, as we now know, we are all, except for a few artists, comedians. He articulated with great precision 'a melancholy experience of man's symbolic resources.'[138] His method is the 'mise en abîme' within a text of the concrete, painful conditions of producing that very text.[139] Readers of *Aurélia* must learn to distinguish between its delirious tone, its 'healthy, ordinary' tone, and all the half-tones and quartertones in between. In fact, *Aurélia*, by expressing the extremely perilous conditions of the gestation of the text, points to the difference between repetitive, empty religious statements and those which may bring the reader closer to what they claim to attest.

Conclusion:

Beyond Any Greater Code

The picture emerging from our sequence of five writers is a composite one. Yet they form a sequence; the last four read those who wrote before them. Some lines of development may therefore be sketched and some contrasts drawn.

Reviewing first their use of the Bible makes manifest the width of the spectrum their works span, and adumbrates something of their divergent attitudes to the writer's craft.

Rousseau's Protestant upbringing in Geneva did not seem to include much study of the Bible; at least, no reminiscence of it found its way into book 1 of the *Confessions*. Around 1750, as he returns to his Genevan roots, he starts reading the Bible, especially what he calls 'the Gospel.'[1] In book 11, telling us about his insomnia, he adds that he used to read the Bible in bed and thus read it five or six times from cover to cover.[2] His writings reveal familiarity with its contents.[3] He admires Moses as legislator. The good priest from Savoy, however, marshalls arguments against any idea of a revelation made at some special place to some special people; yet his profession of faith takes a sudden new turn at the end: 'The majesty of the Scriptures amazes me and the sanctity of the Gospel speaks to my heart ... If the life and death of Socrates are those of a wise man, the life and death of Jesus are those of a God.'[4] The *Lettres écrites de la montagne* (the high-water mark of his self-affirmation as Christian and Protestant) speak of 'l'Evangile' as a 'sacred book,' as the 'rule of the Master'; his own books are only those of a pupil.[5] An ill-informed reader might gather from it that the 'Gospel' is one book; nowhere do we find Rousseau stating he has read Matthew, Mark, Luke, or John. He has formed for himself a version of the teaching of

Jesus and that suffices.[6] His sources are not made explicit. In his discussion of miracles the priest from Savoy alludes to the fact that he finds them in Scripture; he adds that he suspends his judgment and that his salvation does not hinge on his decision on this point.[7] Thus one gets the impression that Rousseau's discussion of the Bible is frequently second-hand: he reviews topics commonly discussed, especially in the rationalist controversy, and he sees the Bible as containing teachings rather than narratives.[8]

Chateaubriand, in contrast, is highly aware of the narrative power of the Bible as a whole and he conveys a sense of it to his readers. The preface to *Atala* (1801) advertises that for many years now he has been reading 'only Homer and the Bible.'[9] Such a pose is of course an essential element of the romantic revolution in taste. Book 5 in the second part of *Le génie du christianisme* (26 pages) contrasts the Bible and Homer. He even amused himself rewriting part of the story of Ruth in homeric style: in his view, the charm and colour are all gone.[10] A full comparison between the Bible and Homer touches upon six specific points: simplicity, antiquity of mores, narration, description, similes or images, and sublimity. The views are balanced but the Bible is the clear literary winner.[11] Simplicity is the Bible's major trump card. This writer has done his homework. His reader learns that the Bible begins with Genesis and ends with Revelation, and that it has numerous authors spread across centuries. Three styles are found in it, historical, poetic, and evangelical. The Gospels (there are four, and some of their distinctive features are mentioned) speak of divine love: here the Word truly becomes flesh. The pages on the life of Jesus cite the Church Fathers at length and, briefly, the New Testament.[12]

Arriving in Paris in 1800, Nodier joined a group of young men, Les Méditateurs de l'Antique. These artists (poets and painters) aimed at recapturing ancient beauty and virtue and formed (between 1797 and 1803) a sort of pythagorean group, which practised vegetarianism and experimented with an Oriental lifestyle. 'We sat in a circle, on a carpet, and smoked Oriental tobaccos in bamboo pipes; we then ate oranges and dried figs, and read Ecclesiastes and the Book of Revelation.'[13] In these circles romanticism travels with illuminism and theosophy. Nodier often includes the Bible in a list of ancient poetic and religious scriptures worthy of reverence.[14] Later on (1831), he affirms that the Bible is the 'only book one is obligated to believe,' but adds the odd (illuminist) view that some of its most precious traditions rest on revelations made in dreams.[15]

With Vigny we leave such vagueness. The Bible is a constant presence throughout his life. Quite a few of his poems are on biblical topics;
the best-known are *Moïse, Samson,* and *Le Mont des Oliviers.* Being somewhat like short epics, they contain a great deal of narrative content;
Vigny also read up on the geography and history of the Biblical world.
Vera Summers writes that he approaches the Bible as an orientalist.[16]
He has read and appropriated the new emerging scholarship on biblical
topics. (This included German scholarship; he read Strauss's *Life of
Jesus.*) For him Israel and Palestine are completely integrated in the world
of the East. He appreciates Hebrew poetry and his poems spread this
appreciation. What used to be called 'sacred history' is very much
present, but has completely lost any privileged relationship to Truth.
He feels free to rewrite Genesis; in *La maison du berger* woman is created
after man's fall.[17] Clearly Vigny does not even feel the need to deny that
the Bible has any special authority. As Bénichou puts it, his silence on
the subject is simply a response to the silence of God (made most manifest in Gethsemane).[18] No one reading him can mistake the return of
Eden for the return to Eden.

With Nerval we find a confusing range of attitudes. His journey to
the East ignores the biblical world (both in his travel and in his text), or
sets up a rival, superior, more ancient revelation, in the illuminist manner. His poems juxtapose the gods of all scriptures. Clearly his preoccupation with the nature and authority of religious scriptures, his obsession with the symbols they contain, his toying with esoteric meanings,
and his apparent openness to them preclude what we would consider
to be the disciplined (or historical) study of any of them.

To conclude: None of these writers works with the Bible as a Great
Code[19] already assimilated, directly or indirectly. Neither do we find in
France writers anguished by the Bible's loss of authority, or obsessive
about the translation to be used. But the Bible was read, more frequently, I think, than is commonly believed. As our writers find a place
for this book, even an important place, it clearly is a place within something else. And those who view it most purely in literary terms
(Chateaubriand, Vigny) are those who know it best. Those who view it
religiously interpose the haze of their own wavering beliefs between
the text and their eyes.

A second thread can guide us through the changes and continuities
among the five writers. With the exception of Rousseau, who comes
before the Great Divide, all were aware of the new economy surround-

ing the elaboration and diffusion of literature. They did not just see the change in the material and spiritual conditions of writers, but also felt a necessity to change the very nature of texts themselves. They did their work in a manner that acknowledged the breakdown of the old persuasive styles.

Rousseau, I said, is the exception. As a Swiss in France, he quickly positioned himself as a member of a minority. With *Emile* burned in Paris and condemned in Geneva, he found himself a persecuted member of a minority. He did not doubt that his ideas were better than those of his persecutors and that he should try to persuade his readers (if not his persecutors) of that. His innovations in style can be traced back, in his mind, to the moral abyss that separates his own sincere and lonely self from his powerful, hypocritical, and incorrigible adversaries.[20] He thus settles in the role of sensitive victim. He creates in the process a new literary myth: books used to be about people; now people put themselves in books and people become books as they write and express themselves. He gives a brand-new tone to the old persuasive prose.

But from Chateaubriand on, all our writers are on the other side of a great divide; our last four writers know the political turmoil and bloody violence into which words (even well-meaning words) can precipitate human beings. Self-expression is not enough. They have thus lost any innocence about the power of language and the beauty (or usefulness) of books. They have seen censorship, imprisonment, and ostracism of writers. They have felt the chilling weight of the conventions upheld by official art. The Republic, the emperor, and the returning Bourbons disagreed on many things, but all maintained the classical canons of literary taste and believed that such canons were necessary to the safety of the state and the purity of morals. (Napoléon added a further wrinkle to state control: he openly despised writers.) Being a Romantic meant groaning under such an establishment. Moreover, unlike the *philosophes*, the Romantics could not assume that it was just a matter of time before common sense would prevail. So, with them, the art of writing was faced with a very large challenge and had to resort to a subtle array of wiles in its contest with entrenched social and political power. 'Literature' became a problematic reality. Its instability as object, and the fact that it could be or become a variety of things, became manifest. Such matters received explicit treatment in *Stello* but were omnipresent.[21]

Chateaubriand, Nodier, Vigny, and Nerval met the problematic nature of writing head on in their prose. Brutally instructed by the social and political dynamics of human oral and written interaction, they took on a larger problem than that of the self-justification and self-possession faced by Rousseau (whom they admired). And what their prose sets in motion must be clearly distinguished from the mainstream of French romantic poetic production. The poets too undertook something very large. In France, as elsewhere in Europe, romantic epics took up the soteriological myth and wrote of the trials and travails of humankind on its way to its final destination.[22] Ballanche (*La vision d'Hébal*) presented Orpheus as the poet-priest who gave what Lévi-Strauss has since called the 'arts of civilization,' namely, the cultural innovations introduced by the neolithic revolution. Verses by Lamartine and Vigny (and others) envisioned a universal salvation, with Satan himself converted. In Quinet's prose epic *Ahasvérus*, the Wandering Jew was redeemed. Victor Hugo was confident poets could hasten the ripening process and help bring a better future. These poets did not feel they had to choose between perpetuating the older Christian myth and becoming priests and prophets of a new one; they expanded the soteriological myth, which they found too restricted, and undertook to write a Greater Code, with universal salvation and a more exalted place for women. Renan echoed in 1848 the widespread belief that civilization dawned with the songs of a poetic priesthood.[23] Some of the romantic poets did not hesitate to put on the mantle and prepare or even usher in the next stage.

Chateaubriand came close to this role of herald of a dawning civilization. He forged a style that was collectively persuasive about the value of Christianity in world history. But many features even in *Le génie du christianisme* break with the attempt simply to take up the myth. First, he writes of civilization, not of salvation. And second, his persuasive style rests on departures from the grand rhetorical and learned style and on a fresh appeal to private subjectivity. (He keeps *seeing* something that interrupts the train of words flowing from his pen.) The fragility of common beliefs is always acknowledged, and even produced by the disruptions in the text. His last work, *La vie de Rancé*, perfects the art of making interruptions, breaks, that establish an impassable distance between the self and what he just wrote, between the 1845 writer and the seventeenth-century convert and ascetic. Chateaubriand includes his troubled subjectivity in his statements; the actual text undermines the system of the language marshalled for the (pious) biographical effort.[24] Thus nothing that he writes can be used for purposes of propaganda. And when he writes his *Mémoires*, he avoids the temptation of trying to please (and silences all suspicions he might be trying to please) by arranging to have them published posthumously. His biggest shove to history was saved for after his history was over. (He arranged to collect the royalties before.)

Nodier formulated the clearest diagnostic: 'It was not surprising that the childish bondage to which writers were held by the rules of rhetoric be relaxed when the vast unity of the social world broke from every side.'[25] He judged that the era of books as people had known them was over, and broke boldly into new, even eccentric paths. The part of his production that was most successful was the short stories fit for solitary and escapist reading.

Nerval exhibits the greatest virtuosity in striving for a new art of prose writing. *Les illuminés* surveys a number of oddly enchanted people: the poet who believes in his own fable, the narrator who believes in the legend he tells, the inventor who takes seriously the dream that hatched in his brain.[26] The tone of the book is anecdotal: the narrator marks his distance from all these amusing, sincere eccentrics. Yet a weighty matter is being raised, and a serious judgment, if not ventured outright, at least sketched: religious energies are always latent in the human heart. Even in the century of the *philosophes*, the presumably soberly classical and coldly rational age, religious imagination prospered and undertook to fancy new shapes for the world and for society. All these visionaries (save one, Cazotte) were also tinged with the madness of utopia or busied themselves with plans for social reform.[27] (Nerval's subtitle, we may recall, indicates that the book is also about precursors of socialism.) Nerval also writes cryptically. *Le voyage en Orient* requires careful reading. It is very different from Chateaubriand's *L'itinéraire de Paris à Jerusalem*, which was apparently a grandiose journey in history, soaking up the past and foreign scenery, and drawing an impressive panorama. Nerval's journey is rather one through the lies of history.[28] The reader must pierce veils to arrive at the truth that the traveller rose up to.[29] Finally, in 1850, Nerval has to dodge the new censorship laws of the Second Empire, which were aimed against *feuilletons*; he writes what starts as a historical chronicle (and thus can be serialized in a paper) but becomes the story of a search for an unattainable book. The first part of Nerval's *feuilleton*, the one of interest to us, became 'Angélique,' in *Les filles du feu*.[30] The narrator sees a rare book on the abbé de Bucquoy at the Frankfurt book fair; later, back in France, he decides to write a chronicle on the abbé but cannot locate the indispensable book, the only reliable source, the one authority that would make his *feuilleton* a genuine historical report and thus legal. Gendarmes stop and search wandering intellectuals; bookstalls never have what scholars look for; bibliophiles do not admit to what books they have; librarians refuse to let books circulate. At the end of the text, we have not learned anything about the abbé de Bucquoy, but the book, as the printed object impossible to find, has become a metaphor for all the books writers would like to write but cannot. (We also guess that the censorship laws are only emblems of larger obstacles.)[31]

Thus the four writers who came after Rousseau fail to take up the great myth act of the visionary writer, and eschew the style of the autobiographical writer who spreads his sincere soul. They create a new image of the fragile, solitary writer who creates his book out of his personal (non-visionary) experiences, and includes frustrating experiences with books in his accounts. So, unlike Rousseau, they do not let their book take on a mythical dimension. Myths are already inside their book, embodied in books as objects – objects of loving veneration, objects of anxious search, objects of popular contempt, objects of disillusioned irony, objects, finally, of an aesthetic admiration that pays little attention to the text they contain. All the ambient myths thus become visible as texts shaping experiences described and assessed, and distance is gained from them. Hence the complicated form, the frequent recourse to insertions, and the willingness to publish only fragments.[32] Hence also the eccentricities, the textual jolts shaking up the readers and toying with them. And hence the sudden, unexpected windows into the very genesis of the book, the assaults upon the reader of pieces from the life of the author, giving a sense of the vulnerability of the one who undertakes to write. Not allowed to take up for good any of the writer's myths, forced to acquire distance from all of them, readers must forge their own, or learn to live in the absence of commonly shared myth. So what our prose writers attempt to convey is quite beyond any idea of a greater code.

Such literary practices invading the handling of religious issues should cause us dissatisfaction with simple classifications of nineteenth-century religious writers as conservatives and progressives, orthodox and illuminists or gnostics. A more significant break is between those who remain with old, traditionally persuasive prose styles, using hard or soft rhetoric to influence, it is hoped, attentive readers, and those who try to obtain a new type of relationship between reader and writer. Vigny, stepping into the shoes of the *moraliste*, offers the clearest denunciation of the totalitarian implications of any hope for obedient readers. As Walter Moser puts it, even the sober, rational prose of the *philosophes* is suspect among the Romantics since it has lost any emancipatory force and has become pure 'utilitarian delirium.'[33] But we have to turn to Kierkegaard to find what I take to be the new principles of emancipatory writing formulated with exemplary clarity. Commenting on the essay *Du socialisme en son principe*, published in 1846[34] by Alexandre Vinet, an author in whom he placed great hope for a while, Kierkegaard writes: 'He is a brilliant author who writes something about the single individual, but is not in character, does not operate in character, is not existentially higher than all discussion – no, no, he writes something which he then submits to public opinion; he palavers with the public in the usual author fashion.'[35]

A more reflective state is to be induced in readers' minds: they must do some work to figure out the meaning of what they read; they must become responsible for what they believe when they have completed their reading.

This being said, a contrast may be drawn that places the three commoners, Rousseau, Nodier, and Nerval on one side, and the two aristocrats, Chateaubriand and Vigny, on the other. Rousseau, Nodier, and Nerval theorized about language and were prone to see it as 'fallen' and in need of some cure. Rousseau's theories on 'primitive' language were ventured at a time when pretty much everything Westerners said on the subject was speculative. Nodier was most expansive as he advanced his theories on the birth and life of languages; unfortunately for him the field was beginning to be occupied in a genuinely scientific manner and Eckstein had to write a review informing the public that investigations were not done in this way any more.[36] Still, with his singing mandrake, he created a vision of a lost, perhaps inaccessible, 'natural' language, erotic and poetic, innocent and spontaneous. Nerval, more prudent, or better informed, did not court ridicule with pseudo-scientific theories but he did dream, and lent fresh life to the myth of an original language (or to that of an ideal language). With all three, the breakdown (or debasement) of normal communicative processes led to some form of utopia about the unique gift of writers as restorers of language.[37] As one moves, however, from Rousseau to Nerval one must admit that the utopia becomes less and less buoyant. (It seems that the magic of Rousseau's writing did not quite work ever again.) In contrast, Chateaubriand and Vigny did not let their sense of ruin and decay interfere with their brave (too confident?) attempt to do their best with the language (and literary tradition) they found. They renew but do not leave the mainstream. Their way of opening new perspectives is less radical but their achievements should not be underestimated. They managed to put religion again at the centre of intelligent conversation. As Paul Valéry puts it, 'No mental operation is more important than the one which metamorphoses what is boring into what is interesting.'[38]

The sequence of our prose texts also enables us to spot a slow but clear shift in aesthetics. Literature in the eighteenth century was conceived in the traditional terms as aiming to please and instruct; writing was inseparable from the attempt to persuade.[39] But the revolutionary orgy of potent, activist persuasions, the brutal invasion of new moral and political beliefs, has made all rhetoric suspect; at the very least, writers feel challenged to invent a new, higher, less disruptive rhetoric and start practising it. Unifying myths are seen as either jejune or dangerous, either sentimentalist-escapist or doctrinaire incitements to political terror. Beliefs thus cease being discussed by the better writers, unless the discussion includes a look at the way in which they are held.[40] And the tone of literature shifts, to a lower profile: just aiming to please seems enough.

From belief to pleasure: in his very fine and thorough book *L'enchantement littéraire: Ecriture et magie de Chateaubriand à Rimbaud*, Yves Vadé points out that in the ancien régime, an enchantment was a captivity, a constraint against which the person always resisted; with romantic literature, being enchanted becomes a much-sought-after state.[41] Magic used to be forbidden by state and church; it becomes legal (although exploitation of credulity can be a crime) as it ceases to be believed in; but the demise of traditional magic only makes room for the expansion of the new literary one. All writers, whether they believe in 'real' magic or not, or vacillate somewhere in between, have recourse to its vocabulary.[42] Romantics at first tend to believe that such re-enchantment will conspire to produce nobler human beings and bring about a better world. But with the collapse of what Vadé calls 'romantic individualism,' the ability of even extraordinarily gifted individuals to set history in motion, or make it swerve, with their words, becomes doubtful. (The hinge is placed by Vadé in 1844–5; the events of 1848–50 force the many to round the corner.) After that, it becomes apparent that poets are not spiritual beings who can exercise a mastery over language and thereby a power over human affairs; it rather becomes accepted that *poems* are remarkable rather than poets, that no artist can control the magic of language to the end, and thus that language knows more about the spirit than the spirit itself.[43] A whole new generation of writers shifts to the notion that rhetoric misleads its user: it presents itself too easily as an instrument the self might use for power over others.[44]

Using the distinction elaborated by Roland Barthes, we might then conclude that our series of prose texts shows the wielder of the pen becoming less and less an 'écrivant' to become more and more an 'écrivain.' The former writes within existing cultural conventions to achieve some practical end; the latter works on language, and his or her writing is an end in itself.[45] The former works within the constellation of beliefs that mediate the common coping with reality, and repairs it or modifies it. The latter looks elsewhere and ventures an alternative to that constellation that becomes a source of pleasure to the reader. Chateaubriand discovered very early that the pleasure of writing is entirely distinct from the satisfaction one derives from persuading others of something. Nodier took for granted that his readers knew the difference between the pleasure of reading and the satisfaction there is in becoming persuaded of something.

Nerval is, on this point, the pivotal figure. He writes entertainments that enchant readers. He half-heartedly tries to initiate them into some higher wisdom, of practical import. Matters come to a head with the enchantment he tries to exercise over himself: it all happens as if the text enchants him, but then enchantment works only on the text, in the text. Unlike Merlin's or Orpheus's formulas, those of the writer do not change the forest and its wild beasts. This insight leads Nerval to his greatest poetry: Les chimères gives up trying to enchant the world; crowded with mythical and feminine imagery, the poems give up trying to find 'the lost letter.' To wish to find a mother figure and to hope for the Return of the Gods stem from the same desire for happiness; neither will come to pass in a thoroughly disenchanted world, but both do come to pass in the magic of the text.[46] Now at last, the chimaeras of Rousseau and of Chateaubriand come of age in a literary way: their life becomes independent of that of the dreamers who invented them. Aurélia, Nerval's most ambitious prose text, seems to prove, however, that the author cannot transform himself by writing alone. The self narrated on the paper (and healed) cannot jump off the page and start walking along the streets healthy again.

But the dichotomy set up by Barthes in the twentieth century should not be too uncritically applied to our authors. True, they erase or blur the old firm boundaries between myth, poetry, and language;[47] the most awesome authoritative statements thus enter into the flow of pleasurable text. But the desire to instruct is still there. It is commonly said that after 1800 authors cannot just be 'hommes de lettres' and leave it at that; they must choose between the scholarly and the literary career.[48] Books like Voltaire's *Essai sur les moeurs* (1756), in which world history is narrated in easy, flowing style, seem no longer possible. On this view, *Le génie du christianisme* might count as the last great attempt; it is clear that the emulsion of erudition and literature was not entirely successful, and each component occasionally appeared in its pure state. But it would be a mistake to expect in France the split between the *wissenschaftlich* and the *literarisch* which became characteristic of Germany.[49] Vigny's *Daphné* and Nerval's *Le voyage en Orient* are notable instances of success in the art of conveying much updated historical knowledge inside a literary structure. (Clearly only Vigny could be deemed successful from a scholar's point of view.) The art of pleasing is thus not entirely divorced from the art of instructing. Or readers also seem to expect an intellectual (and modern) sort of pleasure, the pleasure of knowing that they are gaining some grasp of social and historical realities.

Such considerations of literary theory and history take us apparently very far from the Bible and its contents. But there is one connection, I think: the idea of The Book. At the beginning of the seventeenth century *Don Quixote* showed that the future for books lay in demonstrating that the world does not resemble what books say it is. It seems moderns have to learn to go through life finding not a series of analogies but one differentiation after another. At this stage, some early moderns discerned in the Bible an interesting promise: this book can hold chance in check; it contains *The* narrative of the beginning and the end. (The story was of course read in the Middle Ages but it became, as story, a promise of great moment in the early modern era.) 'Becoming' then happens – sigh of relief! – according to a pattern. And readers of this book can be illumined by the Holy Spirit: they then get its meaning properly and certitude fills their hearts. The rift that was opening wide between things and words becomes healed again. The discerning of such promise in Scripture lies behind Blake, I think, and his statement about the Great Code.

The French mind, however, could never see that as the most important aspect of the Bible; the Renaissance view of history (cyclical, and based on pagan Greek and Roman sources) had planted deep roots.[50] Before Bossuet's *Discours sur l'histoire universelle*, there was Jean Bodin, and after him Voltaire; both had little patience with Christian prophetic views of history; we also saw Chateaubriand voice his firm dissent. Furthermore, the promises religion made in France were usually sacramental in nature; and the doctrinal and moral content of the Bible always successfully discredited the promise inherent in its narrativity. (The French never had the ability to overlook or forget the offensive passages which the British ignore.) Thus in France one should not speak of a real decline of the biblical narrative since there never was a proper rise, at least not the sort of rise evidenced in the English Puritan revolution, when the battles of the civil war were seen to reduplicate those of ancient Israel.

There is, however, in early nineteenth-century France evidence of the decline of confidence in books. Rousseau is evidence enough that each 'definitive' sincere account must be followed by further accounts. The illuminist search for the ultimate anthology (which we saw surface in Nodier) became quickly discredited by the historical study of all sacred scriptures. Nerval wrote texts that alluded to the impossibility of books; this did not prevent him from hoping to write some 'ideal' book, even, perhaps, some text that would heal him. But he kept sandwiching texts within texts, and adding new parts. The patch of (sometimes wildly) heterogeneous documents reminds us, in the end, of the inevitable heterogeneity between books and experience. In any case, the very formula for the perfect book remained for ever elusive: Was it going to be something like an encyclopaedia, perfect because complete? Or was it going to be like the pithy oracle of a sybil, perfect because just right?

So we have to turn to German romanticism, to which both Nodier and Nerval were attuned, to find a full-blown aesthetic theory focusing on ideals of absolute knowledge and perfect books. With Novalis, the plan for the 'complete' book abandoned the (much-travelled) road of encyclopaedias to take refuge in literature.[51] Absolute knowledge then is absolute, not because it is boundless, but because it knows what it knows. The *Atheneum* group and Hegel are one on this point.[52] 'Truth,' writes Hegel in the *Logic*, 'can be only where it makes itself its own result.'[53] Those who assimilated the process that produces such results have in themselves the germ of all books. Thus closure is achieved on the process of knowledge. To find such a project taking shape in France, we have to wait for the second half of the nineteenth century; only then did the hope of educating humankind through useful and persuasive books wane sufficiently in the minds of some poets. Mallarmé effected a break from what we might call the philanthropic approach to book-writing; he undertook to write the 'perfect' book, the one to which everything in the world leads.[54] His project climaxed with the notion that the book holds chance in check for a while. The throw of the dice renders a decision, but does not abolish the need for future decisions, further throws.[55] His ideal, ultimate book got written in the end. 'Un coup de dé' resists being placed in a larger framework of available knowledge but generates, by itself, the knowledge that is at the basis of all knowledge. (It is the French analogue to Hegel's system, specifically to its claim to generate absolute knowledge.) Literature then appeared as the only rival (or is it a parallel?) to money, that abstract calculable precision that *can* order all our transactions; literature became, in fact, in the nineteenth century and with the monetarization of the economy, the most powerful agent of transformation of the world. In literary texts we exchange another currency, a radiant light which ignites dreams, the treasure we need.[56] Narcissists as we remain, we stay glued to statements other than those that banks issue. Thus both currency and books change the world – but it is not the same world. As Nodier puts it, we live in two societies, one ruled by the imaginative principle, the other by the material principle of life.[57] In books, an attenuated theological order survives: a text with a plot has a beginning and an end, or at least an entrance and an exit.[58] And the ideal books cogitated by such literary theory come with some secular equivalent of the inner testimony of the Holy Spirit. 'This tale,' writes Mallarmé, 'is addressed to the intelligence of the reader that itself arranges the meaning.'[59]. Misreading is impossible: either readers get it right or they do not get it at all.

To return to the literary world of Chateaubriand, Vigny, and most of Nerval, it seems clear that with these Romantics books and life (even prosaic life) cannot be viewed in completely antithetical terms. Chateaubriand coined a much-quoted formula that seemed to speak for all Romantics as he described 'le vague des passions': the self 'still has desires, but has no illusions left.'[60] But in fact, are not desires (as contrasted with needs) and illusions indissolubly bound together? Can we in the modern age reserve the word 'belief' only for those vast collective wagers, those unproved but shared objectified affirmations that entrance the many? Must we not use the word also for those individual wagers born of more or less secret desire? And can we really see the self as complete master of what he or she chooses to believe, with as much freedom of choice in that area as in, say, what to buy, or what books to read? Can we have pleasure without involvement in some illusion?

While allowing that the magic of a book and the suspension of disbelief it effects last only while one reads, while conceding that the worlds created on paper move nothing except human desire, must we accept the aesthetic theories that start with phrases about art being for art's sake and erect impassable barriers between art and life?

The same questions arise when one examines the textual procedures which surround statements of belief in the works of our five authors. It is well known that in the modern age affirmations of belief, especially religious belief, lack social indicators (church attendance, adherence to moral norms) to validate them. The beliefs affirmed by an individual thus become inaccessible to others, or accessible only through the verbal statement the believer makes. What, for instance, are we to make of Rousseau's statement that he is the only man in France to believe in God?[61] Judge him crazy? or prone to paradoxical statements? or show some sympathy to the enunciator, and work to find out what there is about Rousseau's way of believing in God that might make it entirely singular in its time and place? Consider also the scene in Chateaubriand's *Les martyrs* of the first meeting between hero and heroine. The young man, a Christian, walks the young woman home; she is a priestess dedicated to the Muses. On their way the conversation establishes quite a few contrasts in their attitudes; a climax is reached when she sees him bend over and give his coat to a naked, abandoned slave. 'You must have believed that this slave was some hidden god,' she says; 'No, I believed I saw a human being,' he answers.[62] The textual jolt evokes the overthrowing of expectations that makes human existence reflective, and free not to be overpowered by the presence of the divine. And what shall we do with Nodier's statement that Christian beliefs come to him in flushes? pity him? smile on him? or recognize the self-deprecating tone and ask ourselves questions about the way beliefs are held? And finally how shall we handle the practically inevitable question about Nerval's cast of mind on the last evening of his life? The facts have been submitted to minute investigation; the texts went again and again through fine-tooth combs. The inaccessiblity is, I think, absolutely final. We must accept it on faith that *Aurélia* is the only and the last word we shall have from him. Besides our persistent curiosity about the beliefs of our fellow human beings, even when we know that such beliefs can be, on good grounds, declared improbable, unverifiable, or bizarre, we have in us an equally persistent trust that our fellow human beings give us something when they formulate their beliefs, vague and changeable though they may be. The forms they give to their lives, and with which they enchant themselves, hold an enchantment for us too, a distant sort of enchantment, but nevertheless perceptible. We might call this a reflective sympathy. It is in our reflectiveness that we hold what they make with their reflectiveness.

Possunt quia posse videntur. Reflective sympathy and imaginative assent draw possible paths in minds and hearts and thereby prepare rearrangements of real assents. The sharp edges of appearances are not always determined by the hard facts of life, but sometimes by the entrenched habits of perception. John Coulson contrasted the response to primary metaphors with that to secondary metaphors; the primary metaphor remains obscure and the response to it alone is performative.[63] Thus a convinced British Protestant does not see the historical practices of slavery behind the word 'redemption'; he rather becomes personally involved in the biblical story of redemption. In contrast, the secondary metaphor is acknowledged as such, and the response to it is informative, or merely aesthetic (which does not exclude sympathy). Thus the one who sees 'redemption' as a secondary metaphor can state that those who believe in redemption compare their religious destiny to that of freed slaves. The distinction is very helpful but it would be a mistake, I think, to create tight categorial compartments between responses to primary metaphors (labelled religious) and responses to secondary metaphors (labelled literary). Our sequence of prose texts shows a process going on that is, in fact, an enormous rearrangement of responses to metaphors. Moderns are highly aware of the 'volatility of imaginative assent' and tend to despair that any of that can grow into certitude, or into a working basis for action,[64] but in France this 'modern' awareness did not start with a process of erosion of biblical metaphors as primary metaphors.

Our sketched contrast between France and Britain therefore needs some elaboration. Differences rest first on numerous and ancient differences between French and English cultural history. In France, the volatility of assent became a stock theme in the midst of the sixteenth-century civil wars (see Montaigne). The powerful dogmas of seventeenth-century classicism further erased whatever traces were left of biblical narrativity. In England, as Coulson puts it, seventeenth-century religion and literature held a common grammar and rested on a common culture.[65] Biblical metaphors therefore were not much of a straight-jacket to French romantic imaginations. And romantic public religiousness, which apparently granted a new lease of life for Catholics, was too mixed with Restoration politics to impress our post-revolutionary writers very much. (As we saw, that is true even of Chateaubriand, who helped start it.) As for the poetic religions, the numerous subsequent hybrids, they were either too apolitical or too inept politically to be of greater interest. In the midst of all these uncertainties,[66] responses to secondary metaphors could in France become culturally formative more quickly; the aesthetic response could more easily become a real response. In any case, in spite of Rousseau, artfulness was never seen as antithetical to naturalness.[67] With human beings, naturalness is artful; the antidote to bad theatre is good theatre, not some utopian untheatrical sincerity. One does not have to wait for the twentieth century to learn that sexuality and religion have to do with real separation and artistic union.

I find confirmation of such views in the notions of nationhood that found expression in post-revolutionary Europe. The unity of *Volk* is theorized as resting on a racial or biological basis. The English credit their unity to their history: centuries of common life on their island made them what they are. The French, even though their royalists repeated slogans about the thirty kings that made France, made a new experiment: they viewed the nation as an aesthetic form.[68] They spent energy and political talent creating new, modern, urban, public art forms. (Heinrich Heine had a pithy formula that well conveys the achievement, and marks the decisive break with *L'embarquement pour Cythère* and other pastoral views of human fulfilment: Delacroix's *La liberté sur les barricades* is the 'Venus of the streets.')[69] The nation has to be always represented to the people. But the forms do not convey content inherited from the past; they are rather containers that hold contemporary public attitudes.[70] As a receptacle for the people's aspirations and of the procedures for a good public life, the nation - as coherent fiction - manages to elicit every day the imaginative assent of those who live in the Hexagon and are citizens of the French state.[71] Social assent rests on assent theorized as free, rather than habitual.

Vigny's work provides the clearest illustration of this characteristically French cultural context. Libanius, the wise man in Daphné, informs Emperor Julian that, as he pursued his ideal of hellenistic reform, he mistakenly 'believed he was acting on the multitude, but was in fact acting only on himself' ... 'his own feet got caught in the net he prepared for others.'[72] But is this 'true opinion'? Is this the 'message' of the text? Are we to accept the fact that moral reforming intent is never effective in history? or that we never get caught in unintended consequences? Certainly not: These are only beliefs voiced in a dramatic sequence of voicing. And we are provided with enough context to be suspicious of Libanius: he chose withdrawal long before Julian started his effort; and he also committed himself to the view that the philosopher's mind can have a clear and pure grasp of essences and that such a grasp is humankind's chief end. Not surprisingly, therefore, the end of Julian's life, his failure, comes only to confirm the philosopher's earlier beliefs. In the end, what we readers 'really' see in this text is of a much more reflexive nature: human beings form beliefs, these beliefs sometimes shape history, many individuals reassess their belief in the light of experience, and most individuals end up having beliefs that make them uneasy with the collective beliefs that manage to move the mountains. In the aftermath of the French Revolution, people in France live in an age when no primary metaphor coming out of the past can shape their responses automatically. They become responsible for their response. In their freedom to respond, virtue may rise. In free civility, core social practices leave it to the voters to show their virtue, if any; and texts also let the readers decide. In this context, it is clear that each act of faith is only the prelude to further acts of faith (unless one surrenders one's judgment to a properly incredible church with outrageous claims to authority).

'Romantic religiousness,' as found in our writers, is thus an attitude, or a stance toward historical religion; it is not primarily a creative impulse richly creating new religious forms and directly affecting public religious life. Frank Paul Bowman established that preaching, for instance, was not much influenced by the new romantic outlook.[73] On this point too, there is a clear contrast with Britain, where theological thinking and church life were richly transformed under the influence of the romantic poets.[74] Romantic religion, as we find it in our prose writers, is rather a romantic handling of religious themes that acknowledges the fact that all human beings have an impulse to create forms. It must be seen as a *literary* movement. Its contribution is inseparable from the craft of the writers who strove to establish communication among individuals endowed with a volatile impulse to create (and accept) forms.[75] Christianity thus becomes *discourse*. Bits (or chunks) of its narratives and theologies enter into the cultural forms human beings create and use in their historical dialogue with each other.[76] (It remains an open question whether the discourse still obeys, more or less, the norms Christian theologians and preachers had elaborated for the guidance of life.)

The prose work of our four Romantics takes for granted that human interaction is political in nature. F.P. Bowman states in his work *Le Christ des barricades: 1789–1848* that France, for better or worse, singularizes itself in the early nineteenth-century discussions of the historical Jesus by always including the political element.[77] Historical scholarship clearly made more rapid progress among German scholars, who tended to ignore political implications. Bowman also argued for the profound kinship between the romantic aesthetic renewal and 'mystical socialism.'[78] This is true, provided one differentiates properly between the mystical socialists and the doctrinaire ones. The former address themselves to the imagination; their writing verges on the utopian. The doctrinaire ones write as if they were laying down the law, or laws.[79] The aesthetics of communication which the French Romantics practise includes constant warnings against the 'esprit de système.' Ballanche in 1819 attacked the 'fabricateurs de système' who wanted to show the path to happiness on the grounds that human beings should never be expected to agree on what constitutes happiness.[80] In 1848, and in a lighter vein, Victor Hugo declared, after reading the works of the leading socialist authors, that he never thought there were so many would-be founders of convents in France.[81] The dogmatically inclined Buchez clearly recognized the enemy when he published in *Le Globe* (then a Saint-Simonian organ) a strong attack against *Stello*. There cannot be any solution, he proclaimed, along such 'individualistic' lines![82] At the end of the *Mémoires d'outre-tombe* Chateaubriand reviews all the new social theories, including those of Saint-Simon, of course, but quickly shifts to a new voice. He describes the visits he paid in 1841 to Lamennais, who was then serving a one-year sentence in Sainte-Pélagie jail for subversive writing. The 73-year-old ex-peer of the realm climbs three flights of stairs to meet the 59-year-old ex-priest in his cell; then, just below a roof he could touch (Chateaubriand was not tall), we see 'two imbeciles, believers in liberty, talk of serious things.'[83] We are not given any transcript of their conversations. The portrayal of the conditions under which social theorizing is made is deemed worth more than ten pages of social theory. The reader's urge to assemble (or assimilate) theoretical systems must occasionally receive a jolt. Thinking about society is always done by individuals.

Chateaubriand, Vigny, and Nerval may be 'individualistic,' but certainly not in the German romantic way. The sort of 'mystical' closure found in the statement by Novalis to the effect that each person's story should become a Bible cannot be imagined under any of their pens.[84] In other words, saying that each person is a tale does not make of every one a scripture. Neither should one attribute to the French Romantics any strong 'spiritualizing' tendencies. With the possible exception of Vigny's last poem (entitled *L'esprit pur*, appropriately!), they do not offer a 'higher' reading of religion. Neither do they yield to a complete aestheticization of religion. That they find liturgies beautiful and moving does not prevent them from assessing the moral and political influence of the clergy. (Military uniforms are beautiful – and should be; but they do not make war beautiful.) In his *Shapes of Philosophical History*, Frank E. Manuel contrasted the subject of 'Taming the Future: The French Idea of Perfectibility' with that of 'Leaps into Free Consciousness: Resonances from the German Academy.'[85] The study of our literary prosaists adds a paragraph to his fine analyses. Saint-Simon and Comte do not corner the discourse on perfectibility. Our authors invented a discourse on it that challenged individual minds, potentially perfectible, to draw their own conclusions, and, possibly, act, in free resolve, toward an ever-insecure greater perfection. Under their pen, literature is not just a repository of views of life but a way of confronting life, and a way which readers are invited to emulate. Such authors can still be said to aim at changing life, but their way of doing it is through invitations extended to reflective consciousness. (Such was already the way of the *moralistes*.) Our authors can thus be deemed to have succeeded where the doctrinaire socialists failed, since they articulated a style of discourse appropriate to the new political era.

Among Rousseau's political fragments, we meet with a formula that succinctly summarizes the crucial point in his *Social Contract*: 'The moral condition of a nation results less from the absolute state of its members than from their relationships to each other.'[86] A group of unhappy, dissenting people accepting laws that will enable them to resolve their existing and future differences democratically is in a moral condition superior to that of a unanimous group of contented slaves, or to that of a cohesive group of creatures of habit who are happy to anticipate more of the same. In the post-revolutionary societies, time is inside society; every agent in it is cognizant of transitoriness and of possibility. Agents have moved from a 'lived society' (with time outside it) to a 'conceived society,' one where human beings articulate their views of their private and public future and strive to organize themselves for it.[87] Their formal procedures for mediating their relationships become more important than the substance of their shared (transitory) beliefs. What really matters under the new conditions is the continued existence of a realm of free communication.

Therefore, Vigny was also insightful, it seems to me, when in *Stello* he called for a simultaneous development of (social) judgment and (poetic) imagination.[88] The form of his writing served the new formal morality. Belief became a historical individual act; writing was calculated to uncover the fact that the only source of genuine belief is in the self. Thus a genuinely vertical transcendence was restored, and all oblique forms of it, all those that deviate to serve current social constellations of interest, set aside. He (and Chateaubriand, and even to some extent Nerval) did not entirely despair of finding fictions that would be useful to individual lives and to public life in democracy. Much closer to us, Valéry (who was Mallarmé's heir), wrote that the task of poets is to stimulate the life of the affections and the intellectual sensitivity.[89] These internal, subjective realities are the cultural realities that may still be shaped by books. And they are often decisive on the social and political scenes. Writing and reading keep doing their work at the juncture between 'material' and 'imaginative' principles. Such are the views already put forward by Madame de Stael in 1795. Her *Essai sur les fictions* commends the reading of novels, because they develop the inner movements of the soul, suspend the work of the passions, and replace them by independent enjoyments.[90] And, as Stendhal could credibly argue, such aesthetics are compatible with a strict commitment to human freedom: what is said invites but does not dictate interpretation; no conscience usurps the credulity of another.[91]

It thus seems more interesting to me if critics pay attention mainly to this cultural middle ground and to the changing occurrences of belief that fill it, and thus seek categories that prevent the erection of impassable barriers between 'art' and 'life.' For this study confirms, I think, that with the new frequent reading of fiction by numerous readers, something appeared in the modern world that might be called an institutionalized aesthetic realm (one of the subsystems that appeared in the newly fragmented social system). As Jay Caplan argued, during the second half of the eighteenth century the reading of novels became increasingly necessary to the lives of human beings, and served as a sort of proof that their bodies could communicate in the midst of the contingencies that shaped their individual lives.[92] Literary critics and social historians might then come to see, in their own fields of study, how fictions and realities interpenetrate. They might also come to agree with the insight conveyed by Clifford Geertz, for instance, who called *culture* an 'acted document.' (This of course applies also to religion.)[93] From this point of view the differentiation between 'life' and 'literature' loses its finality. In the final analysis, the writer is an acting document. The reader too. Thinkers step onto a stage, trusting they have something to say.[94] Magic, writes Vadé, creates forms that fascinate the other.[95] This is true of 'real' magic, of everyday social magic, and of literary magic. Such creation is never entirely innocent, since human beings tend to be starved for forms, and are frequently forced by their experience to turn to new ones – or to find shelter in old ones. Abandoning the mantle of the mythopoeic and priestly poet, our four post-revolutionary writers, who avoided Rousseau's narcissistic consolations, who created the new forms aiming at the stimulation of the reader's judgment, did not rest content with making formal points. They immersed themselves in the moral realities of their day – even Nodier, who cast a piercing look at the world of publishing and spoke his mind. Thus they all dealt openly and freely with some of the actually dominant contents of belief.

Their new aesthetics of communication also modified the theory of religion by including in religion a dimension of aesthetic attractiveness. While allowing for all the differences, their achievement may perhaps be usefully compared to that found in Balzac's great 'religious' (admittedly more catholic) novels: *Le curé de village*, *Le médecin de campagne*, and *Le lys dans la vallée*.[96] There, too, the discussion of religion is not made into an assault on the reader's conscience; nevertheless, aesthetically, its power is unashamedly and concretely portrayed.

Chateaubriand, Nodier, Vigny, and Nerval found themselves in front of an erased code. While they might disagree on the mix of causes that led to such a state of affairs, they would all impute it to the passage of time, to human weaknesses, and to the disruptions ensuing from the Revolution and the fresh energies released by it. They also did not want to do anything that might further erase it. Chateaubriand read it with greatest apparent ease. In *Le génie du christianisme*, he wrote what he read with much confidence, but interrupted his version with scenes from the life of a character, René, who, through no fault of his own, found himself excluded from life under any code. Later, in *Mémoires d'outre-tombe*, he used bits of the code to structure the story of his own life. Nodier was sure that the code had lost its power to shape the common life. As a matter of fact he did not think that any ennobling code would emerge that might shape the common life, so he retreated to free rêverie –

coupled with attention to codes as such and to a demanding craftsman-
ship in the use of them (even though he remained a sceptic and did not
think they could mediate the truth of any reality). Vigny wanted to read
the history of the Christian civilizational code, its rise to sharp definite-
ness, and the process of its erasure. He wondered whether mankind
could live without a clear, legible, and moral code. When Nerval tried
to read, so much was erased, and apparently irretrievably erased, that
the very attempt to decipher something involved him in constant mental pain. He put it clearly in *Aurélia*: 'I then saw plastic images slowly
taking shape, ancient images that seemed to be of symbols representing
ideas I could grasp only with difficulty. I only thought it all meant this:
all this was to teach you the secret of life, and you did not understand;
religions and myths, saints and poets, all agree in explaining the fatal
enigma, but you did not interpret it correctly; and now it is too late!'[97]
In such texts, the sacred enters the horizon of consciousness only through
a declaration of its loss or absence; and the absence is declared by
means of the narration of a failed attempt to decipher a code. Thus
Nerval brings to light the fact that codes normally make us forget that
what we see, read, and feel has been encoded. By its breakdown, the
useless code points to the artificiality of all codes.

Chateaubriand, Vigny, and Nerval wanted to *read* the code, and not
necessarily live under it. Their reading thus entailed an unreading. They
certainly did not want to reconstitute the system of religious power that
had been instituted in Europe. (In fact much of mainstream religion
was involved in a desperate attempt to shore up the old code: Roman
Catholic infallibilism and Protestant fundamentalist views of biblical
inerrancy are evidence enough of that.)[98] Neither did they want to reform the code and set up a new system. They did not want to *live* under
the code since this, practically, meant living under the authority of
those who interpret or reinterpret it. But they still wanted to keep the
code legible, or make it legible, as a meaning that can be conveyed in
writing and freely communicated, and thus help lives shape themselves.
The code they became interested in is therefore more like the codes
theorists of information talk about than what Hammurabi wrote.

As they wrote what they read, they were mindful that they were
wrestling as well as they could with a somewhat erased code – and not,
as it were, taking dictation from God. They wanted their readers to
remain aware of this condition so they wrote in a manner that made
clear how minimal their authorial authority was.

Something new happened to the code, since it got erased and was read in the senses I just outlined. But under the pen of Chateaubriand, Vigny, and Nerval much continuity was maintained, for the benefit of readers. The code remained a code of the biblical sort: it was about incarnate life, social and political.

Notes

1 See Stephen Prickett, *Romanticism and Religion: The Tradition of Coleridge and Wordsworth in the Victorian Church* (Cambridge University Press, 1976), 3, 11.

2 'Literature is but a branch of Religion, and always participates in its character; however in our time it is the only branch that still shows any greenness; and, as some think, must one day become the main stem.' (Carlyle, quoted and commented upon by David J. DeLaura in 'Religion, Poetry, and the Rise of Literary Humanism: The Nineteenth Century Matrix,' *Journal of the American Academy of Religion* 47/2, Supplement [June 1979].) Keats sees religion and poetry as sharing the same distress under the conditions of modernity. Matthew Arnold finds a basic contrast between scientific and literary language, and mourns the decline in the status of the imagination as an instrument of cognition (Nathan A. Scott, Jr, 'Arnold's Version of Transcendence - The Via Poetica,' *The Journal of Religion* 59/3 [July 1979].)

3 Bernard Reardon, who knows the French scene well (see his *Liberalism and Tradition: Aspects of Catholic Thought in Nineteenth-Century France* [Cambridge University Press, 1975]), gives it a rather skewed treatment in his *Religion in the Age of Romanticism* (Cambridge University Press, 1985) by limiting himself to three doctrinaire authors, Lamennais, Comte, and Renan, who are only peripherally related to the romantic movement. French romantic authors are conspicuously absent from the three volumes of *Nineteenth-Century Religious Thought in the West* ed. N. Smart, J. Clayton, P. Sherry, and S. Katz (Cambridge University Press, 1985). The two bibliographies on romantic religion most accessible to English readers,

found on pp 72–4 and 111–12, after the articles by D.G. Charlton and F.P. Bowman 'Religious and Political Thought' and 'Illuminism, Utopia, Mythology,' contain practically no titles in English. See vol. 1 of *The French Romantics*, ed. D.G. Charlton (Cambridge University Press, 1984). Fortunately Frank Paul Bowman recently translated some of his articles; see his *French Romanticism: Intertextual and Interdisciplinary Readings* (Baltimore & London: The Johns Hopkins University Press, 1990); the book adds a conclusion (201–14) clarifying methodological matters.

4 Paul Bénichou gave the title *Les temps des prophètes* (Paris: Gallimard, 1977) to his book on the social doctrines of the romantic era (e.g., Chateaubriand, Lamennais, Saint-Simon, Fourier, Quinet, Michelet, etc.), but his 'prophètes' have a more secular ring than prophets would have.

5 When it comes to Catholic fundamental theology, the balance, it seems to me, has been well struck in *Romance and the Rock: Nineteenth-Century Catholics on Faith and Reason*, ed. and intro. Joseph Fitzer (Minneapolis: Fortress Press, 1989).

6 Hans Frei, *The Eclipse of the Biblical Narrative: A Study in Eighteenth-and Nineteenth-Century Hermeneutics* (New Haven and London: Yale University Press, 1974), 51.

7 See Murray Roston, *Prophet and Poet: The Bible and the Growth of Romanticism* (London: Faber and Faber, 1965), passim, and Maurice Olender, *Les langues du paradis. Aryens et Sémites: un couple providentiel* (Paris: Gallimard/ Seuil, 1989), 48–51.

8 Olender, *Les langues du paradis*, 51–7.

9 Frie, *Eclipse of the Biblical Narrative*, 192.

10 *Pensées diverses*, 4th ed. (1704), vol. 2, 452–3, quoted in Patrick Riley, *The General Will before Rousseau: The Transformation of the Divine into the Civic* (Princeton University Press 1986), 51.

11 Hans Frei, 'The "Literal Reading" of Biblical Narrative in the Christian Tradition: Does It Stretch or Will It Break?' in *The Bible and the Narrative Tradition*, ed. Frank McConnel (New York: Oxford University Press, 1986), 36–77.

12 The Bible is omnipresent in sixteenth-century French literature: see the article by Michael A Screech, 'La littérature française et la Bible,' and Marguerite Soulié, 'Le théâtre et la Bible au XVIème siècle,' in Guy Bédouelle and Bernard Roussel, eds., *Les temps des réformes et la Bible* (Paris: Beauchesne, 1989). Biblical comedies and tragedies displaced the older mystery plays. But with the rise of classical norms, all of sixteenth-century literature was set aside in its turn.

Alain Michel, 'La grandeur et l'humilité: La Bible dans l'esthétique littéraire en France,' in Jean-Robert Armogathe, *Le grand siècle et la Bible*

(Paris: Beauchesne, 1989), 425–54 formulates appropriate nuances: discussion of the Bible remained central in the discussions of the aesthetics of the sublime. These, however, were erudite matters, and biblical topics disappeared from mainstream literature. The two biblical plays of Racine are thus exceptions. The minor authors who persisted with biblical poetry are reviewed by Anne Mantéro in the same collection: 'Récits bibliques et poésie religieuse en France,' 455–80.

One further fact: the Bible was subsequently made to appear more absent than it actually was. The literary historians who, in the second half of the nineteenth century, defined the 'canon' for use in schools accepted the classical standards of taste and had little sympathy for texts with biblical content. It is significant that the great biblical translation completed between 1657 and 1696 at Port-Royal has only recently become again available even though its place in the history of literature looms large. Pascal was involved in the translation; Stendhal gave it as the model of style; it was the Bible cited by Chateaubriand, read by Victor Hugo, and annotated by Rimbaud. Philippe Sellier only barely exaggerates when he compares its historical role to that of the Luther Bible and of the Authorized Version (Preface, p. xi, in *La Bible: Traduction de Lemaître de Sacy* [Paris: Laffont, Bouquins, 1990]). The original publication suffered a handicap: the preface affirmed that reading the Bible was a great support to eucharistic piety; this Jansenist tenet ran counter to the dominant 'mystical' school of spirituality. Subsequent versions deleted the offending passages, and in any case, this handicap should not have bothered literary historians. See Bernard Chédozeau, 'Les grandes étapes de la publication de la Bible catholique en français,' in Jean-Robert Armogathe, *Le grand siècle et la Bible* 341–60, esp. 346–54 and Claude Savart, 'Quelle Bible les catholiques français lisaient-ils?' in Claude Savart and Jean-Nöel Aletti, *Le monde contemporain et la Bible* (Paris: Beauchesne, 1985) 19–34, esp. 28.

13 See Despland, *La religion en Occident* (Montréal/Paris: Fides/Cerf, 1977), 408–10, 440–3.

14 See the preface by Jean-Jacques Courtine and Claudine Haroche in the 1987 edition (Paris: Jérôme Millon).

15 How strong this tradition was is shown by François Laplanche, *L'Ecriture, le sacré et l'histoire: Erudits et politiques protestants devant la Bible en France au XVIIème siècle* (Amsterdam: APA–Holland University Press, 1986).

16 Matthew Arnold, 'Equality,' in *Mixed Essays* (1879), reprinted in vol. 8 of *Complete Prose Works* (Ann Arbor: University of Michigan Press, 1972), 294.

17 See Stephen Bann, 'Romanticism in France,' in Roy Porter and Mikulas Teich, eds, *Romanticism in National Context* (Cambridge University Press, 1988), 240–59.

18 Marcel Gauchet, *La révolution des droits de l'homme* (Paris: Gallimard, 1989).

19 On the impact of the Revolution on public speaking and mass communication see Gérard Gengembre, *A vos plumes citoyens! Ecrivains, journalistes, orateurs et poètes de la Bastille à Waterloo* (Paris: Gallimard 1988). Analyses of the work of literary artists during the first ten years of the Revolution may be found in Béatrice Didier, *Ecrire la Révolution 1789–1799* (Paris: PUF, 1989).

20 Chateaubriand notes that during the Revolution political eloquence absorbs all other literature. See Gengembre, *A vos plumes citoyens!* 28.

21 Philippe Lejeune, *Le pacte autobiographique* (Paris: Seuil, 1975) 13–46. The 'pact' consists in promising that the narrator (the person the reader has the impression of meeting while reading, the one who says I in the text), the author (the one who writes the text), and the personage (the socially accountable person whose name is found on the cover of the book) are identical.

22 His family belonged to the minor nobility from Britanny but was connected with that of the great Malesherbes. As a youth, the boy from Saint-Malo was admitted into the best Parisian circles.

23 The metaphor of the palimpsest is frequent in the modern era. Freud sees in the unconscious a 'text' overlaid by the conscious, repressive one. The whole quest for the historical Jesus likewise believes the New Testament can be used to find an authentic teaching of Jesus that has become overlaid with the clutter of ecclesiastical tradition. In these cases, the true text, the valuable one, is the one overlaid. What is common to our sequence of literary figures is that to them the old text is an inadequate mess that needs to be rewritten. They do not model their work on that of archaeologists. Their views are thus perhaps closer to that of Derrida, who sees under all philosophies something like a hidden text – but does not canonize this substratum. See Jacques Derrida, 'La mythologie blanche: La métaphore dans le texte philosophique,' in *Marges de la philosophie* (Paris: Editions de Minuit, 1972), 247–324.

24 French romantic prose used to be divided between the texts of the public figures, the 'grands romantiques' (Chateaubriand, Lamartine, Hugo, Vigny), and those of the 'petits romantiques,' a line of younger authors who produced more bizarre texts, climaxing and closing with Nerval. My selection will ignore this distinction (fading now anyway). The distinction is still there in the two articles by D.G. Charlton and Max Milner, 'Prose Fiction' and 'Romantics on the Fringe,' in *The French Romantics*, ed. D.G. Charlton, vol. 1, 163–203, and vol. 2, 382–422. 'Romantics on the Fringe' is a better designation for the second group.

25 My interest in this literary phenomenon explains why I have not included

Victor Hugo in my list of writers. His prose gives sublimity to depths and achieves mythic proportion. In any case his work spans too many decades and would cause my chronological framework to explode.

George Sand could more meaningfully have been included in my inquiry into the distanciating sort of romantic prose. As an adolescent she invented a religion for herself, pretty much in the manner in which she wrote novels later (of which one at least, *Spiridion*, bears closely upon religious themes). On the autobiographical accounts and on *Spiridion*, see 'Un roman panthéiste,' in Pierre Macherey, *A quoi pense la littérature?* (Paris: PUF, 1991), 37–51.

26 From *La vie de Marianne* to *Adolphe* numerous eighteenth-century novels start with a preface narrating how the 'editor' discovered the manuscript he offers to the public, thus claiming to offer an account of real events. How many readers were duped by this practice? *La Nouvelle Héloïse* starts with two prefaces raising the issue explicitly: is the correspondence a fictitious or a 'true' one? Rousseau accepts full responsibility for the book he presents to the public but his tortuous prefaces elude the factual question.

27 Facts on what (following the German historian who first broached the subject) is called the 'Leserevolution' in France may be culled from Roger Chartier, *Les origines culturelles de la Révolution française* (Paris: Seuil, 1990), 99–115 and from Robert Darnton 'First Steps toward a History of Reading,' in *The Kiss of Lamourette: Reflections in Cultural History* (New York: Norton, 1990).

28 Chartier, *Les origines culturelles*, 113–15.

29 *Voyage autour de ma chambre* by Xavier de Maistre (1794) is a good example of the book written for this sort of reading. Composed during the forty-two days of the author's political detention, it narrates in a rather disconnected manner forty-two days of wandering around his cell. It invites as readers all those who are confined, 'the unhappy, the sick and the bored' (chap. 2); recollecting his own reading, the author remembers as many travels to 'another world' (chap. 36). See Daniel Sangsue, *Le récit excentrique: Gautier–de Maistre–Nerval–Nodier.* (Paris: Corti, 1987), 163–222. For more on eccentric stories, see chap. 3, pp. 72–3 below.

30 It is true that most university libraries today will have as much learned secondary material on *La princesse de Clèves* as on the Gospel of Mark or the *Nicomachean Ethics*. But Madame de la Fayette would be very surprised to see what her book has led to.

31 Hans Frei, *Eclipse of the Biblical Narrative*, 118

32 Hans Robert Jauss (with other German colleagues) has launched a school of 'reception criticism' that tries to focus on the peculiarities related to the

reception of books as works of art. It puts forward the idea that literature is socially influential because it puts forward 'communicational models.' It is thus situated between the formalists, who pay no attention to the social context of literature, and the marxists, who see literature as just another part of the ideological system. See H.R. Jauss, *Toward an Aesthetic of Reception* (Minneapolis: University of Minnesota Press, 1982) and 'A Sketch of a Theory and History of Aesthetic Experience,' in *Aesthetic Experience and Literary Hermeneutics* (Minneapolis: University of Minnesota Press, 1981).

33 Chartier documents that those who turned royalists and those who turned jacobins during the Revolution were reading the same books during the 1770s and 1780s. *Les origines culturelles*, 87, 107.

34 Michel de Certeau, 'Une pratique sociale de la différence: Croire,' in *Faire croire*, ed. André Vauchez (Rome: Ecole française de Rome, 1981), 363–83. See also Michel Certeau, 'Croire/faire croire,' in *L'invention du quotidien*, vol. 1, *Arts de faire* (Paris: Union générale d'éditions, 1980).

35 'Profession de foi du vicaire savoyard,' in *Emile, Oeuvres complètes*, vol. 4 (Paris: Gallimard, 1969) 568.

36 Thus rational critique will never catch up with all these fleeting beliefs. Moderns, in Cioran's view, define themselves by the beliefs they repudiate, rather than by those they subscribe to (*La tentation d'exister* [Paris: Gallimard, 1956], 121). But this does not contradict De Certeau's point: What we call beliefs is what we don't believe in any more. And we believe even when we believe we don't believe.

37 See Jean Pouillon, 'Remarques sur le verbe croire,' in *La fonction symbolique: Essais d'anthropologie*, ed. Michel Izard and Pierre Smith (Paris: Gallimard, 1979), 43.

38 See Béatrice Didier, *Stendhal autobiographe* (Paris: PUF 1983), 167, with references to Hegel (p. 202) and Chateaubriand (p. 245).

39 'De la gloire,' *Essais*, II, 16 in *Oeuvres complètes* (Paris: Gallimard, 1962), 603.

40 *Pensées*, no. 159 in *Oeuvres complètes* (Paris: Gallimard, 1954), 1130.

41 For an attempt to redress the balance, see the book by Bernard Plongeron on the leader among the jurors, *L'abbé Grégoire ou l'Arche de la Fraternité* (Paris: Letouzey & Ané, 1989).

42 See Claude Langlois, 'Permanence, renouveau et affrontements,' in *Histoire des catholiques en France*, ed. François Lebrun (Toulouse, Privat, 1980). 321–406.

43 On this whole topic, see *Civilisation chrétienne: Approche historique d'une idéologie XVIIIè–XXè siècle*, ed. J.-R. Derré et B. Plongeron (Paris, Beauchesne, 1975).

44 American readers will undoubtedly be familiar with De Tocqueville's handling of these issues.

45 See Frank Paul Bowman, 'Théologie et esthétique: le divin, le sublime et le laid,' *Le Christ romantique* (Geneva, Droz, 1973) 221–75. The discussion of the priests who found the romantic aesthetic Christian is on pp. 246–9.

46 That the Restoration lost its literary-political battle, and got no help from our four post-revolutionary writers, should not obscure the fact that Chateaubriand, Nodier, Vigny, and Nerval all kept some loyalty to classical taste and kept literary links (personal also in the case of Chateaubriand) with the eighteenth century. None of them effected quite as radical a break as Hugo.

47 The preoccupation from 1800 on with 'terminating' the revolution and putting an end to civil war in France took many different forms; but the persistence of such moderate anti-revolutionary concerns could not displace the ideology of the rights of man, as a canon, and a promise.

48 Paul Bénichou entitled his book on the new writer (which he finds in the period between 1750 and 1830) *Le sacre de l'écrivain* (Paris: José Corti, 1973). The metaphor harks back to the old royal sanctity; the subtitle makes clear the brand-new context: *Essai sur l'avènement d'un pouvoir spirituel laïque dans la France moderne.*

49 1831, cited in Balzac *L'illustre Gaudissart: La muse du département* (Paris: Garnier, 1970), 64.

50 *Emile*, bk 2 in *Oeuvres complètes*, vol. 4 (Paris: Gallimard, 1969), 384.

CHAPTER 1

1 See Ernst Cassirer, 'Kant and Rousseau,' in *Rousseau, Kant and Goethe* (New York: Harper and Row, 1963).

2 See 'Readers Respond to Rousseau: The Fabrication of Romantic Sensitivity,' in Robert Darnton, *The Great Cat Massacre and Other Episodes in French Cultural History* (New York: Vintage Books, 1985).

3 Jean-Jacques Rousseau, *Contrat Social*, in Oeuvres complètes III: 351. (Roman numerals in the following notes refer to the volumes published in the Pléiade edition, *Oeuvres complètes* 4 vols, (Paris: Gallimard, 1959–69.)

4 Jean-Jacques Rousseau, *Emile*, bk 4; IV: 586.

5 Jean-Jacques Rousseau, *Discours sur les sciences et les arts*, III: 6.

6 Jean Starobinski, *Jean-Jacques Rousseau: La transparence et l'obstacle* (Paris: Gallimard, 1971), 344.

7 There is here a clear break from the Enlightenment mainstream. Most enlightened minds tried to reintegrate evil within a rational cosmic process. Evil was only 'apparently' evil or, it was hoped, clearly on its way

out, since human beings were 'clearly' becoming more rational. But to Rousseau society has created an apparent order which masks a real disorder. Evil is a moral scandal to be overcome by conversion and by radical social reorganization. See B. Baczko, *Rousseau: Solitude et communauté* (Paris: Mouton 1974), 185–9, 299.

8 Jean-Jacques Rousseau, *Confessions*, bk 1; I: 18–20. See Starobinski, *La transparence et l'obstacle*, 18–21.

9 Jean-Jacques Rousseau, *Lettre à Christophe de Beaumont*, IV: 939. Starobinski, appropriately, emphasizes that the famous sentence on 'man who reflects' being 'a depraved animal' does not mean that the human being is thereby morally guilty; *La transparence et l'obstacle*, 245.

10 Jean-Jacques Rousseau, *Préface to Narcisse*, II: 969.

11 Pierre Burgelin, *La philosophie de l'existence de Jean-Jacques Rousseau* (Paris: PUF, 1952), 556.

12 Baczko, *Rousseau*, 385.

13 Henri Gouhier, *Les méditations métaphysiques de Jean-Jacques Rousseau* (Paris: Vrin, 1970), 20, 30.

14 Schiller, Letter 3 in *Aesthetic Education of Mankind*, cited in Baczko, *Rousseau*, 77.

15 Rousseau, *Confessions*, bk 8; I: 351.

16 Burgelin, *La philosophie*, 260, 311. Burgelin rightly adds (p. 318) that for Rousseau as for Kant divided man remains entirely responsible.

17 Rousseau, *Contrat Social*, III: 288.

18 See R. Polin, *La politique de la solitude* (Paris: Sirey 1971), 70, 282.

19 He never travelled to either Corsica or Poland, and when he sought refuge in a Jura valley in Switzerland, he had stones thrown at him.

20 Starobinski, *La transparence et l'obstacle*, 47.

21 *Gesammelte Schriften* 20: 58–9, cited in E. Cassirer, *The Question of J.-J. Rousseau* (Indianapolis: Indiana University Press, 1963), 72.

22 Rousseau, *Emile*, bk 4; IV: 587–8. See also 593–4.

23 This is Baczko's interpretation in *Rousseau*, 102, 130, 390. On this view, Kant misunderstood the matter when he claimed that Rousseau justified Providence, or certainly masked the difference between this new justification and the older ones.

24 See the opening discussion, 'A Discourse on Eden,' in Paul A. Cantor, *Creature and Creator: Myth-making and English Romanticism* (Cambridge University Press, 1984). In Genesis, Adam wakes up from the hands of God with speech and reason. Rousseau's original man lacks both endowments.

25 How fictitious it is becomes apparent if one asks why Rousseau chooses to

see in social rivalry the source of infinite desire; why not trace this back to embodiment? The theoretical power of new fictions may also be discerned in Freud's account of the origins in *Totem and Taboo*.

26 See 'Metaphor,' in Paul de Man, *Allegories of Reading* (New Haven: Yale University Press, 1979).

27 Jean Starobinski, 'La mise en accusation de la société,' in Université de Neuchâtel, *J.-J. Rousseau: Quatre études* (Neuchâtel: Baconnière, 1978).

28 Rousseau, *Rousseau juge de Jean-Jacques*, 2nd dialogue; I: 815–16.

29 Rousseau, *Emile*, bk 4; IV: 568.

30 'Experience' argues Paul de Man is always both a fictitious discourse and an empirical event. See 'Excuses,' in *Allegories of Reading*.

31 Rousseau, Second preface of *La Nouvelle Héloïse*, II: 15–16.

32 *Confessions*, bk 4; I: 175. See also Françoise Barguillet, *Rousseau ou l'illusion passionnée. Les rêveries du promeneur solitaire* (Paris: PUF, 1991), 148.

33 See Madeleine B. Ellis, *Rousseau's Venetian Story: An Essay upon Art and Truth in Les Confessions* (Baltimore: Johns Hopkins Press, 1966) for an analysis of Rousseau's autobiographical pages placed next to everything that can be known from other sources about his year in Venice. The author's conclusion is that it takes art to render psychological realities.

34 J. Starobinski, 'Jean-Jacques Rousseau et le péril de la réflexion,' *L'oeil vivant* (Paris: Gallimard, 1961).

35 See Marc Eigeldinger, *Jean-Jacques Rousseau et la réalité de l'imaginaire* (Neuchâtel: Baconnière, 1962).

36 H.R. Jauss 'Rousseau's *Nouvelle Héloïse* and Goethe's *Werther* within the Shift of Horizons from the French Enlightenment to German Idealism,' in *Question and Answer: Forms of Dialogic Understanding* (Minneapolis: University of Minnesota Press, 1986), 180.

37 Rousseau, *Confessions*, bk 4; I: 171–2; *Emile*, bk 5; IV: 821; *Nouvelle Héloïse*, pt 6, letter 8, II: 693.

38 *Confessions*, bk 1; I: 25–6.

39 Fourth promenade, I: 1035.

40 Rousseau, *Confessions*, bk 9; I: 402–3. See Marc Eigeldinger, 'L'ambiguïté de l'écriture,' in *Jean-Jacques Rousseau: Univers mythique et cohérence* (Neuchâtel: Baconnière, 1978), 29–47.

41 For suggestive work on the history of sincerity, see Lionel Trilling, *Sincerity and Authenticity* (Cambridge: Mass.: Harvard University Press, 1971) and the summer 1979 issue of *Daedalus* entitled 'Hypocrisy, Illusion and Evasion,' especially the opening article by Judith Shklar, 'Let Us Not Be Hypocritical? See also Michel Despland, 'Can Conscience Be Hypocriti-

cal? The Contrasting Analyses of Kant and Hegel,' in *Harvard Theological Review* 68/3–4 (1975).

42 Rousseau, *Rousseau juge de Jean-Jacques*, 2nd dialogue; I: 19. See also Robert Darnton, *The Great Cat Massacre*, 227.

43 *Du bonheur public*, III: 510.

44 Rousseau, *Correspondance complète*, R.A. Leigh, ed. (Oxford: The Voltaire Foundation at the Taylor Institution, 1964–) vol. 23, 42.

45 Rousseau, *Confessions*, bk 1; I: 5.

46 Baczko, *Rousseau*, 166.

47 Part of the power of *La Nouvelle Héloïse* comes from its hovering between the cultivation of social and of private virtues. We see at Clarens a happy little society – presumably complete; there are workers on the estate. Its leading figures are both men and citizens. Yet the idyll of innocence lost and innocence restored takes place far from European society at large; moreover, the ladies and gentlemen who head the Alpine haven enjoy a happiness in their leisure which is different from that of its humbler denizens. The happiness of these united beautiful people is quite free from the requirements of ordinary citizenship. The élite of Clarens enjoy spiritual authenticity because they are the élite: all they do is show themselves as they are; the servants do the work.

48 See H.R. Jauss, 'Rousseau's *Nouvelle Héloïse* and Goethe's *Werther*,' in *Question and Answer*, 161. Attentive readers of the novel learn in the end that not all was well in Julie's secret heart: her posthumous letter calls her own virtuousness an illusion.

49 Locating the priest in Savoy makes a subtle promise of authenticity: he is rural and French-speaking, but not under the authority of the king of France: he is thus not embroiled in the corrupting ecclesiastical politics of gallican France.

50 *Emile*, bk 4; IV: 558.

51 Ibid., bk 5; IV: 777.

52 The many letters Rousseau received in 1761 from readers of La *Nouvelle Héloïse* have been preserved and are frequently referred to. For a detailed account see Claude Labrosse, *Lire au XVIIIè siècle: La Nouvelle Héloïse et ses lecteurs* (Lyon: Presses Universitaires de Lyon, 1985).

53 Darnton, *The Great Cat Massacre*, 232, 243.

54 Ibid., 233.

55 Rousseau wrote his *Lettre à M. D'Alembert* to argue that Genevans who had no theatre were more moral than Parisians who had many. Literature is not the best way to teach virtue.

56 Malesherbes transmitted to Rousseau the list of wished-for modifications

and deletions. See Rousseau/Malesherbes *Correspondance*, with preface and notes by Barbara de Negroni (Paris: Flammarion, 1991), 97–121.

57 For a complete analysis of ecclesiastical response to style and content see Philippe Lefebvre, *Les pouvoirs de la parole: L'Eglise et Rousseau 1762–1848* (Paris: Cerf, 1992).

58 Rousseau, *Confessions*, bk 1; I: 5.

59 The same point may be made by looking at the contrast with his one great literary precedent. When he wrote his *Confessions*, Augustine presupposed God's great and prior book, and its record of the all-encompassing history of the world, from Creation to Last Judgment; God as Author was the ultimate reference for the saint's narration of his own, brief, local record of sinfulness and of salvation by grace. Rousseau divorces his own authorship from any transcendent authority.

60 Stendhal, *Mémoires d'un touriste* (Paris: Maspéro, 1981), vol. 2, 135.

61 Starobinski cites Jean Hyppolite's summary of Hegel's analysis in *La transparence et l'obstacle*, 234, 238.

62 For a careful analysis of the *askesis* involved in this sort of writing see Françoise Barguillet, *Rousseau ou l'illusion passionnée*.

63 See Roddier's introduction in *Les Rêveries*, ed. Henri Roddier (Paris: Garnier, 1960), lxii–lxxxii.

64 Cantor, *Creature and Creator*, 21.

65 Ibid., 239; also 246, 328. See also the comments of K. Barth, *Protestant Theology in the 19th Century* (London: SCM Press, 1972), 212 and 225–9 on the completely new discovery in the realm of anthropology: goodness is in the heart, the heart being simply the man himself, discounting everything he produces or which confronts him as alien existence or as the work of alien hands.

66 Starobinski, *La transparence et l'obstacle*, 225, 23. Reading and writing thus emerge as systematic compensation for difficulties repeatedly encountered in the work of social communication.

67 Paul de Man, 'Excuses,' in *Allegories of Reading* 278–301. The good priest from Savoy raises this to the level of explicit principle: 'My vices make me a slave; remorse makes me free.' *Emile*, bk 4; IV: 586.

68 Jean Guéhenno, cited in Eigeldinger, *Jean-Jacques Rousseau: Univers mythique et cohérence*, 231.

69 Gouhier, *Méditations*, 218.

70 Rousseau, *Nouvelle Héloïse*, pt 6, letter 11; II: 714.

71 Rousseau, Letter of 11 November 1764, *Correspondance complète*, vol. 22, 41.

72 Letter to Moultou, 7 June 1762, in *Correspondance complète*, vol. 11, 36.

73 Rousseau, *Lettre à d'Alembert* (Paris: Garnier-Flammarion, 1967), 57.

74 Rousseau, *Emile*, bk. 4; IV: 608, 610. Page 609 cites Charron on the fact that one receives one's religion from other men.

75 Baczko, *Rousseau*, 233, 249.

76 Starobinski, *L'oeil vivant*, 137.

77 Starobinski, 'La mise en accusation de la société,' 37.

78 See M. Eigeldinger, *Jean-Jacques Rousseau: Univers mythique et cohérence* (Neuchâtel: Baconnière, 1978), 163. The author also draws a contrast with Plato, who uses myth to supplement reason without contradicting it; with Rousseau myth soars freely (see p. 311).

79 In letter 5 of *Lettres écrites de la montagne* (*Oeuvres complètes*, III, 783) Rousseau states he never dreamt of giving 'a method for fathers and mothers,' only a system of education to be discussed by the wise.

80 Rousseau, *Emile*, bk 4; IV: 624–5.

81 Rousseau, *Lettre à Christophe de Beaumont*, IV: 960.

82 Rousseau, letter 3 *Lettres écrites de la montagne*: 753–4.

83 Rousseau, *Morceau allégorique*, IV: 1053–4.

84 The contrast between the two Christs is echoed in a contrast between two exegeses. An orthodox exegesis assimilates much erudition but still states what ought to be believed, what authority has to be acknowledged. Rousseau launches an exegesis that lets the texts speak to the heart. Jesus is divine, the gospels sacred, because what they say carries with itself the marks of its own truth. 'The content of the texts provides the criterion of their authenticity. Exegesis is a matter of reflection, not erudition.' (Starobinski, *Transparence*, 88. See also 100–1.) Rousseau thus is another one of the rationalist exegetes. He, however, does not measure up the content of the gospels to a rationalist dogma. His is a more literary sort of exegesis: the text is to stir the conscience of a good man.

85 This is what Pierre Maurice Masson argued in the three volumes of his *La religion de Jean-Jacques Rousseau* (Paris: Hachette, 1916; repr. Genève: Slatkine, 1970).

86 Gouhier, *Méditations métaphysiques*, 113.

87 Rousseau, *Emile*, bk 4; IV: 581.

88 Rousseau, *Lettre à Christopher de Beaumont*, IV: 996.

89 Rousseau, *Contrat Social*, III: 460–9.

90 Rousseau, *Contrat Social*, III: 381.

91 Rousseau, *Lettres philosophiques* (Paris: Vrin, 1974), 192.

92 *Confessions*, bk 4; I: 41.

93 R.I. Boss, 'Rousseau's Civil Religion and the Meaning of Belief: An Answer to Bayle's Paradox,' *Studies on Voltaire and the 18th Century* 84 (1971), 162.

94 Irony, the most precious device for writers who wish to be understood, is rather rare in his writings.

95 Rousseau, *Emile*, bk 5; IV: 849.

96 H.R. Jauss 'Rousseau's *Nouvelle Héloïse* and *Goethe's Werther*,' 192.

97 Paul Bénichou, 'Jean-Jacques Rousseau: De la personne à la doctrine,' in *L'écrivain et ses travaux* (Paris: J. Corti, 1967). Or, as George Bataille put it: each type of conquest is 'the deed of a man fleeing a threat,' *L'expérience intérieure* (Paris: Gallimard, 1954), 56.

98 Jean Starobinski, 'Lire Rouseau,' in *Les Confessions et autres écrits autobiographiques* (Lausanne: La Guilde du Livre, 1962), viii, ix.

99 Ibid., x, xii.

100 Maurice Blanchot, 'Jean-Jacques et la littérature,' *Nouvelle Revue française* (June 1958), 1057–66.

101 The change can be illustrated by the very shift in the meaning of the agricultural metaphor originally behind the word culture. The Renaissance uses the metaphor of cultivation or culture to speak of an activity aimed at those who are in need of a tutor's attention. Thomas Elyot, for instance, draws a lengthy comparison between good parents and able gardeners. (*The Governor*, bk 1, chap. 4). We are still in a world with droughts and garden pests. At the end of the eighteenth century, the affirmation of creative freedom in history seems to have made a clean sweep of such usage. Culture is something the self does for itself, as is illustrated by this passage from Goethe's autobiography: 'to labour for his own moral culture is the simplest and most practicable thing which man can propose to himself; the impulse is inborn in him while in social life both reason and love prompt or rather force him to do so.' (*Dichtung und Wahrheit*, bk 16, 321). The discovery of historical culture is thereby seen as the prelude to a rationally grounded human self-creating. Goethe speaks of *Bildung*: what he visualizes is not a garden but an artist with a lump of clay. See also my two articles, 'La notion moderne de culture,' in M. Despland, J-C. Petit, and J. Richard, *Religion et culture: Colloque du Centenaire Paul Tillich* (Québec: Presses de l'Université Laval, 1987), 225–38 and 'La civilisation moderne et la morale,' in Pierre Fortin, ed., Colloque de Rimouski, *L'Ethique à venir* (Rimouski: UQAR, 1987), 257–74.

102 Cantor, 'A Discourse on Eden,' in *Creature and Creator*, 13.

103 *Emile*, bk 2; IV: 304.

104 Darnton calls 'possibilism' the sense of boundless possibility which was 'the bright side of popular emotion' during the Revolution; Robert Darnton, *The Kiss of Lamourette: Reflections on Cultural History* (New York: Norton, 1990), 17.

105 Hoelderlin, 'Rousseau'; French translation in *Oeuvres* (Paris: Gallimard, 1967), 774; V. Hugo, *Océan-tas de pierres* (Paris: Albin Michel, 1942), 350.

106 Allan Bloom, 'The Education of Democratic Man: Emile,' *Daedalus* (1978),

135–53, reprinted in *Jean-Jacques Rousseau*, ed. and intro. Harold Bloom (New York: Chelsea House, 1988).

107 This sincerity of his belief is crucial. Ever since the early Renaissance there have been decodings of Christian truths that undertook to show the 'real' truth. But such decodings were done on the basis of philosophies rival to Christianity, mainly Epicureanism or Platonism. With Rousseau people who see themselves as disciples of Christ feel the need of decoding.

108 Rousseau, *Emile*, bk4; IV: 581.

109 Kant, *On History* (New York: Bobbs-Merrill, 1963), 60.

110 Quoted in Starobinski, *L'oeil vivant*, 185.

111 For a passionate attack on Hegel's procedures see Eric Voegelin, 'On Hegel – A Study in Sorcery,' in *The Study of Time*, ed. J.T. Fraser, F.C. Haber, and G.H. Mueller (Heidelberg, Berlin, New York: Springer Verlag, 1972), 418–51.

112 Theodore Ziolkowski, 'Religion and Literature in a Secular Age: The Critic's Dilemma,' *The Journal of Religion* 59, pt 1 (January 1979), esp. 25–8.

113 M.H. Abrams, *Natural Supernaturalism: Tradition and Revolution in Romantic Literature* (New York: W.W. Norton 1971), 68.

114 Soren Kierkegaard, *Training in Christianity* (Princeton University Press, 1967) 249.

115 The refutation is found in *Essai sur l'indifférence*, vol. 1 (Paris: Tournachon-Mdin, 1817) chap. 5.

116 Paul Hoffmann, 'Le problème de la bonne foi dans la Profession de foi du Vicaire savoyard,' *Revue d'histoire et de philosophie religieuses* 67, pt 1 (1987), 19–36.

CHAPTER 2

1 Chateaubriand is a political liberal, i.e., he is in sympathy with the affirmation of the rights of man and looks for a political régime that will allow the unhindered exercise of them. See Louis Girard, *Les libéraux français* (Paris: Aubier, 1983), 5. The case was made in the past that he was only a façade liberal until 1824 (ibid., 53–3). This view we hope to correct.

2 As early as 1804 *Le génie du christianisme* was published in an abbreviated edition for young readers.

3 He became ambassador of France (in London in 1822 and Rome in 1828–9), minister of foreign affairs (1822–3), and architect of a successful war to restore a Bourbon in Spain, and, perhaps more practically, persuade Napoleon's army that it could win battles again.

4 As a witness of the seriousness of his religious quest, we have the testi-

mony of Joubert, his close friend during the crucial years 1800–4. Joseph Joubert's *Carnets*, 2 vols (Paris: Gallimard, 1938) reflect the depth of the dialogue between the two.

5 Rousseau was an important (and early) influence on Chateaubriand. See Charles Dédéyan, *Chateaubriand et Rousseau* (Paris: Sedes, 1973). See also Jean Roussel, *Jean-Jacques Rousseau en France après la Révolution 1795–1830* (Paris: A. Colin, 1972), 139–80, 359–94.

6 *Essai sur les révolutions* (1797, 1802), ed. Maurice Regard (Paris: Gallimard, 1978), 382, 428.

7 Pierre Moreau, *Chateaubriand* (n.p. Desclée de Brouwer, 1965), 30.

8 *Essai sur les révolutions*, 116.

9 The accounts he gives of his political choices have been submitted to close scrutiny, and many sins have been found, of omission and commission. Henri Guillemin wrote a book to get all the skeletons out of the closet and found many cases where our author preferred a beautiful account of his life to a true one. In the end Guillemin admits that he still loves him any way. See *L'homme des Mémoires d'outre-tombe* (Paris: Gallimard, 1964).

In 1804 Chateaubriand committed himself to the political opposition by leaving the service of the First Consul after the summary military execution of the Duke of Enghien, thereby making plausible what he wrote in 1831, namely, that he had always been unimpressed by slaughterers of human flesh (*Etudes historiques*, [Paris: Garnier, n.d.], 59). The posthumous memoirs keep linking the name of Napoleon to the number of Frenchmen (three million) who died in Napoleon's imperial uniforms, not the republican or royalist ones (*Mémoires*, vol. 1, 871). For a biography in English see George D. Painter, *Chateaubriand: A Biography* (London: Chatto and Windus, 1977).

10 *Le génie du christianisme* (Paris: Gallimard, 1978), 681. He goes on: 'One cannot portray faithfully the interior of our homes and even less the bottom of our hearts.'

11 *Mémoires d'outre-tombe* (Paris: Gallimard, 1959), vol. 1, 171, 292.

12 The new poetic problem comes to a head in the epic genre. There death on a vast scale is subsumed in a greater, providential order. Chateaubriand's boundless admiration goes to four epic poets: Homer, Virgil, Tasso, and Milton. He is one of the moderns seeking to emulate them; his two major literary efforts are epic poems in prose, on Indians in the American forests and Christians in the Roman Empire: *Les Natchez* (written in the 1790s, published in 1826) and *Les martyrs* (1809).

13 Neither does he join the major architect of the subsequent Catholic

reaction, Joseph de Maistre, who reintroduces the horrors of history into a providential order by affirming that the bloodshed of the Revolution was regenerative chastisement.

In 1809 François Guizot blamed him for putting a notion of vicarious atonement at the centre of *Les martyrs*. He replied that his text is quite orthodox: his martyrs expiate but do not redeem. But in 1831, in the *Etudes historiques*, he came round to Guizot's view and deplored the continuation after Christ's sacrifice of 'confused views of expiation.' In the meantime, Joseph de Maistre had published *Les soirées de Saint-Petersbourg* and Chateaubriand clearly recoiled before such excesses of sacrificial mystique.

14 Manuel de Diéguez, *Chateaubriand ou le poète face à l'histoire* (Paris: Plon, 1963).

15 Note for instance his pages on the Jacobins and on the literary merit of the Marseillaise. *Essai sur les revolutions*, 79–81, 116–18.

16 *Essai sur les revolutions*, 318; *Itinéraire de Paris à Jerusalem* (Paris: Garnier-Flammarion, 1968), 169.

17 Maurice Regard, notes in *Essai*, 1400.

18 The most complex response will not be elaborated until *Les mémoires d'outre-tombe* (1848).

19 Pierre Moreau (*Chateaubriand*, chap. 1), 32–6, has the best answers to the problems raised by Chateaubriand's muddled location in time (1798 or 1799) of his conversion. It was not a conversion that changed the entire man; something slowly ripened between 1797 and 1799, but even then the conversion was not complete. 'The *Génie* is not the book of a convert; writing it converted the author'. For a fuller study, see his book *La conversion de Chateaubriand* (Paris: Alcan 1933). One might also say that as a prospective author of a second book, Chateaubriand decided to be on the Christian side but still had to figure out what it meant to be on this side.

20 An adapted Protestant edition was published in London in 1813 both in French and in translation, *The Beauties of Christianity*. All the translators had to do was omit the too specifically Catholic passages. A complete Catholic translation (by Charles I. White) was published in Baltimore (1856) under the title *Genius of Christianity*. Selections from it are available in *Romance and the Rock: Nineteenth-Century Catholics on Faith and Reason*, ed. and intro. Joseph Fitzer (Minneapolis: Fortress Press, 1989), 25–59.

21 *Génie*, 1096–1108.

22 A shy, less subjective precedent may be found in the 'tableaux' which the Protestant apologist Jacques Abbadie added to his more argumentative

passages in his *Traité de la vérité de la religion chrétienne*, 3 vols, 1684–9 (Despland, *La religion en Occident*, 410).

23 *Génie*, 694–5.

24 *Génie*, 1031, 1049, 1071, 1092. Such pages invite the reader to rally round a new flag. (There is even a new Constantine to hold it: the second 1803 edition is dedicated to Napoléon, then premier consul.) Chateaubriand seems to believe at this point that a new public, civilized Christian order is about to emerge for the welfare of all.

25 Camille Jullian, *Notes sur l'histoire de France au XIXème siècle* (1897) Genève, Paris: Slatkine, 1979), viii.

26 Barbéris is a leading marxist critic. It is ironic that it took this author to start rehabilitating Chateaubriand as a political liberal and as an emancipatory writer. We will refer frequently to him.

27 The best-known examples are those of Delisle de Sales and Rétif de la Bretonne. Michel Delon, in 'Savoir totalisant et forme éclatée,' *Dix-huitième siècle* 14 (Paris: Garnier, 1982), 13–26 showed how this innovation introduces a tension between 'truth' and 'my truth,' between omniscient discourse and fragmentary vision. The disruption of the accepted borders between genres indicates a crisis: the very status of writing is questioned.

28 Barbéris in *A la recherche d'une écriture* (Paris: Mame, 1974) adds that one can also discern in the treatise itself features that undermine its ostensible argument and thus prepare for the shift to an overt piece of fiction. Thus the *Génie* finds a literary procedure to express the ambivalence toward religion that remained uncontrolled in the *Essai*.

For an English translation of the two fiction pieces, see *Atala and René*, trans. Rayner Heppenstall, intro. Robert Baldick (London: Oxford University Press, 1963).

29 See Pierre Barbéris, *René de Chateaubriand: Un nouveau roman* (Paris: Larousse, 1973).

30 We find here confirmation of one of Roland Barthes's theses: he argued that modern works enshrine duplicity; they provide pleasure, i.e., culturally comforting reading, and a (personal) enjoyment that detaches the reader from his cultural moorings. See *Le Plaisir du texte* (Paris: Seuil, 1973), 15, 25.

31 *Génie*, 534, 716, 883.

32 P. Barbéris, *Chateaubriand: Une réaction au monde moderne* (Paris: Larousse, 1976), 140.

33 The aesthetics of the sublime prepared the ground for the romantic discovery of the generating power of the imagination (see Paul Crouzet, *La poétique de Stendhal* [Paris: Flammarion, 1983], 155). From the end of the

eighteenth century, a new meaning appears for the term 'world.' Besides the (real) world of common sense and astronomers and the (corrupt) world of the theologians, there appears the inner world which individuals create through their dreams and in which they live.

34 M. Milner and C. Pichois, *Littérature française*, vol. 7 (Paris: Arthaud, 1985), 91. On the contention between the two analogies see Richard Rorty, *Philosophy and the Mirror of Nature* (Princeton University Press, 1979). On the shift in the romantic theory of art see M.K. Abrams, *The Mirror and the Lamp* (New York: Norton, 1958).

35 The expressions 'arts' and 'the arts' acquire new meanings at the end of the eighteenth century. Literature, music, painting, sculpture, architecture, theatre, and dance become grouped together to constitute, collectively, *art* (see R. Williams, *Culture and Society* [Harmondsworth: Penguin, 1961], 15). Grouped together, these activities are distinguished from the 'mechanical arts'; they are conceived as creative and as achieving uniquely significant human products. They are beautiful and alone express the individual. The term 'aesthetic,' still used in *The Critique of Pure Reason* to refer to the mental organization of sense perception, shifts its meaning to refer to that new whole of artistic capabilities and activities.

36 *Mémoires d'outre-tombe*, vol. 1, 94–6.

37 Quoted in P. Moreau, *Chateaubriand*, 44–5.

38 The Romantics did not discover this space. We already find it quite graphically laid out in *Don Quixote*, in the famous scene of Master Pedro's puppet show. A realistic narrative places the Don (and the readers) in an inn, with ordinary people, about to watch a puppet show. The show starts: it is a story of a knight, a princess, and Moorish captors. The imagination of the Don heats up, he draws his sword, sets out in hot pursuit, and destroys the puppet theatre. The line between fiction and truth has been erased in this excessively imaginative and dynamic mind. But what happens in us, as we sit in our armchairs, laughing at the ridiculous behaviour of the Don? We too lend reality to a story which is only a fiction winning its way into our minds through the unusual medium of the printed page. As Ortegay Gasset puts it, both the Don and the reader move into 'the hollow interior of an aesthetic body' (Jose Ortega y Gasset, *Meditations on Don Quixote* [New York: Norton, 1963], 133–4). The difference is that most readers do not draw their swords; all they do is enjoy the text. With them the occurrence remains confined in their interior aesthetic space. What the Romantics did is explore systematically and exploit the potentialities of this inner space.

39 Georges Poulet, *Les métamorphoses du cercle* (Paris: Flammarion, 1979), 170, 212, 523, and *Trois essais de mythologie romantique* (Paris: Corti, 1966), 9. See

also his introduction in Joseph Joubert, *Pensées*, ed. and intro. G. Poulet (Paris: Union genérale d'éditions, 1966), x, xiv, where Poulet shows how Joubert consistently describes the activities of the mind by means of spatialization.

40 His authorship entirely verifies his friend Joubert's observation that an acquired style is good only when it is the result of many previous 'rêveries.' *Pensées*, 135.

41 Letter of 6 March 1801.

42 'Le siècle' is temporal-historical as well as worldly. Through their life course Christians have become children of a very specific age, children of *this* age. The connotations are purely chronological and factual, and not negative as in the New Testament.

43 *Essai sur les révolutions*, 257.

44 See the notes by Maurice Regard in *Essai sur les révolutions*, 1389–1397.

45 *Essai sur les révolutions*, 259.

46 *Itinéraire*, 107, 381.

47 *A la recherche d'une écriture*, 483.

48 It was the Contess de Boigne. See Jean-Paul Clément, *Chateaubriand politique* (Paris: Hachette, 1986), 13.

49 Abbé Boulogne. See notes in *Génie*, 1651.

50 Aug. F. Thomas Dufossé. See notes in Génie, 1648.

51 See Moreau, *Chateaubriand*, 66.

52 Sainte-Beuve, *Chateaubriand et son groupe littéraire* (1849; 2nd ed. Paris: Lévy 1872), vol. 1, 297, 304, 343.

53 Marcel Proust, *Contre Sainte-Beuve* (Paris: NRF, 1954), 127.

54 To this, he made an obvious retort: 'Is Christianity less true, when it appears more beautiful?' he asked in his defence of the *Génie*. *Génie*, 1104–8.

55 'It is certain,' wrote Joubert, 'that he likes the errors more than the truths of which his book is filled, because the errors are more his. He is more the author of them.' Joubert, *Carnets*, 26, cited in Jean Roussel, *Jean-Jacques Rousseau en France après la Révolution 1795–1830* (Paris: Colin, 1972), 368.

56 Joubert left a momentous one-liner on the subject of the Génie: 'There is some tit in this brain.' See *Pensées*, 131.

57 *Défense du Génie*, 1102. It is significant that what is 'proved' is the power not the truth of religion.

58 Reboul, intro. to *Le génie du christianisme* (Paris: Garnier-Flammarion, 1966), vol. 1, 32–4.

59 *Itinéraire de Paris à Jérusalem*, 39, 41, 43. Did the travel produce the images, or did the images lead to the travel?

60 *Génie*, 956.

61 *Génie*, 487. See Stéphane Michaud, *Muse et madone: Visages de la femme de la Révolution française aux apparitions de Lourdes* (Paris: Seuil, 1985), 29–32.

62 The feeling of the sublime, next to that of the beautiful, had served to map out the properly aesthetic domain of the soul, but Kant had carefully distinguished the sublime from the religious: the former senses the contrast between self and universe; the latter acknowledges and venerates a transcendent reality. See J. Vieillard-Baron, 'Phénoménologie de la conscience religieuse,' in *Dix-huitième siècle* 14 (1982), 177–84. Kant's discussion is in par. 28 of the *Critique of the Faculty of Judgement*.

63 *Le poète face à l'histoire*, 84, 94.

64 See P. Foucher, *La philosophie catholique en France au XIXè siècle* (Paris: Vrin, 1955), 14.

65 Moreau, *Chateaubriand*, 25.

66 Cited in Moreau, *Chateaubriand*, 47.

67 Reboul, Intro. to *Le génie*, 34; Moreau, *Chateaubriand*, 34.

68 Schleiermacher for instance, labels the inferior religions 'aesthetic' and the higher, moral ones 'teleological.' This does not prevent him from being blamed by Ritschl for his 'aestheticism.' Kierkegaard establishes a hierarchy between the aesthetic, the moral, and the religious but his authorship shows this Christian hard at work on an aesthetic undertaking.

69 *Génie*, 470 and 1097. One can argue that this defence is disingenuous; what options were open however to a Catholic layman in an age when the hierarchy was intellectually somnolent while surrendering nothing of its claim to exclusive authority?

70 An interesting rapprochement here could be made with Kierkegaard, who took great pains to reflect on his vocation as religious writer and stressed that he was 'without authority.' See the famous entry in the Journal (X2.a.475) where he links his renunciation of authority to the fact, among others, that there is too much of the poetical in him (W. Lowrie, *Kierkegaard* [New York: Harper and Row, 1962], 274ff and 386ff).

71 *Itinéraire*, 174.

72 *Essai sur les révolutions*, 1826 preface, p. 23. There is a clear contrast on this point between him and the early theoretician of liberalism. Benjamin Constant found that ancient liberty consisted in participation in collective power and that this was impossible in modern conditions where freedom consisted in 'peaceful enjoyment of private independence.' *De la liberté chez les modernes* (Paris: Livre de Poche, 1980), 501. For Chateaubriand modern freedom also has a political dimension.

73 *Itinéraire*, 174.

74 *Essai sur les révolutions*, 28.

75 He voiced his disagreement in an 1828 encyclopaedia article, cited in Charles Dédéyan, *Chateaubriand et Rousseau* (Paris Sedes, 1973), 47.

76 It is idle to ask whether this political gesture was sincere or calculated. When he resigned in 1804, Chateaubriand made a public gesture, knowing that in time he could be punished – or rewarded — for it.

77 The *Mémoires d'outre-tombe* frequently refer to the process of osmosis between dreams and realities. See the texts cited and analysed in *Littérature française*, eds. M. Milner and C. Pichois, vol. 7, (Paris: Arthaud, 1985), 277–280. For an English version, see *Memoirs of Chateaubriand*, selected, trans., and with an intro. by Robert Baldick (London: H. Hamilton, 1961).

78 A rapprochement on this point can be made with the Jansenist Royer-Collard, the Calvinist Guizot, and the aristocratic de Tocqueville. All these political liberals saw the necessity for a slow, social transformation. The habits of freedom had to transform democracy; revolutionary passions had to be replaced by democratic ones.

79 See the comment in *La vie de Rancé* (1845): 'Whoever is dedicated to the future has a novel in the depths of his life, to give birth to legend, the mirage of history.' (Paris: Garnier-Flammarion 1969), 68. Chateaubriand illustrates a necessity that Ernest Renan was to express perfectly: What one says of oneself is always poetry (Ernest Renan, *Souvenirs d'enfance et de jeunesse* [Paris: Livre de Poche, 1967] 7). The 'liberties' taken with brutal truth in this autobiography are thus not propaganda aimed at others, but stem from intimate necessity. There can be no self except the one one constructs for oneself, no plans for the future except those shaped by a desirous heart.

80 Here I follow the interpretation of the *Mémoires d'outre-tombe* put forward by André Vial in *Chateaubriand et le temps perdu* (Paris: Juillard, 1963).

81 From the 1820 on, he kept himself informed of the work of the new social statisticians. There is in this romantic hailer of the nineteenth century a clear continuity with the enlightened respect for facts. He quickly spotted the young de Tocqueville and introduced him to the salon of Madame Récamier, where the newcomer met all the best brains.

82 *Mémoires d'outre-tombe*, vol. 1, 1006–10.

83 See Pierre Barbéris, *A la recherche d'une ecriture*, 297. See also *Mémoires d'outre-tombe*, vol. 2, 357.

84 Ibid., 202, 205, 217, 302. The polemic against the liberals heightens after 1830. On Louis-Philippe, Chateaubriand is vitriolic. From 1834–6 references to the misled – and massacred – people appear under his pen. Ibid., 227.

85 Louis Girard labels 'libéralisme global' this new position, which promptly became a class ideology. See *Les libéraux français* (Paris: Aubier, 1983), 268.

86 *Génie*, 824, 1053.

87 *Mémoires d'outres-tombe*, vol. 2, 920.

88 All the relevant texts (of the politician and on politics) have been gathered by Jean-Paul Clément, with intro. and notes in *Chateaubriand politique* (Paris: Hachette, 1987).

89 Pascal wrote: 'Violence and truth have no power over each other.' *Lettres provinciales in Oeuvres* (Paris: Gallimard, 1954), 805.

90 *A la recherche d'une écriture*, 240–9.

91 *Mémoires d'outre-tombe*, vol. 2, 1087. The cardinals did not take his advice and elected a conservative pope, Pius VIII.

92 *Etudes historiques* (1831) (Paris: Garnier, n.d.), 87–102.

93 *Mémoires d'outre-tombe*, vol. 1, 468.

94 *Mémoires d'outre-tombe*, vol. 2, 930–3.

95 See Pierre Moreau, 'La religion de Chateaubriand,' *Table ronde* 241 (February 1968), 19.

96 *Etudes historiques*, 92–3. See the discussion in Pierre Moreau, *Chateaubriand*, 68–72.

97 *Mémoires d'outre-tombe*, vol. 2, 932.

98 On this oscillation between fight and flight see R. Binion, 'Notes on Romanticism,' in *Journal of Psychohistory* 11 no. 1 (summer 1983).

99 To write, the writer must *descend* from the sublime. This is the great discovery of Stendhal. See Paul Crouzet, *La poétique de Stendhal: Forme et société* (Paris: Flammarion, 1986), 11, 35. Literature thus follows an adventure parallel to that of the self. Freedom without policy is empty.

100 The Venus of Milo is beautiful because she is admired. Chateaubriand does not need social approbation to find Pauline de Beaumont beautiful. As the emotions of beauty become less socialized, aesthetics becomes closer to erotics. See Crouzet, *La poétique de Stendhal*, 185. I should add that Chateaubriand blamed Rousseau for letting his sincerity extend to intimate revelations about women he knew. See Dédéyan, *Chateaubriand et Rousseau*, 52–6. Chateaubriand fully adhered to classical norms of taste and discretion.

101 *Mémoires d'outre tombe*, vol. 2, 5.

102 These political views emerged progressively: on the prospects of democracy among the moderns, the 1827 edition of *Essai sur les révolutions* revises the pessimism of the 1798 text. See for instance 301.

103 We accept the judgment formulated in 1928 by Victor Giraud: Chateau-

briand's Christianity was rather aesthetic at first but became rather social. What we can see now is that it could not become social in the new democratic sense without being aesthetic at first. *Le christianisme de Chateaubriand*, 2 vols. (Paris: Hachette, 1925, 1928).

104 M. Crouzet, *La poétique de Stendhal*, 61, 281–2.

105 *Génie*, 461 (1827 preface).

106 Romantic literature thus picks up in a new era the old task of art: humanize emotional tumult, channel anti-social emotions, suggest a new hypothesis to the individual in need of organization, and struggle to unify disruptive desires. See Roger Bastide, *Art et société* (Paris: Payot, 1977), 27, 93–4, 185–7.

107 With romantic literature, as de Tocqueville well saw, the beautiful image offered to human contemplation is the magnificent image of human energy. Imagination focuses on the inner tumult, and strives to bring it under the sway of beauty. These sensibilities, adds de Tocqueville, are deeply linked to democratic institutions, and he lists *René* among his examples. *De la démocratie en Amérique*, vol. 2 (Paris: Garnier-Flammarion, 1981), 1, 17. Paul Crouzet adds that this democratic literature cultivates a narcissistic fascination with self (*Le poétique de Stendhal*, 221).

108 In the course of the nineteenth century, religion, instead of being public and integrative, became private and associational. It came to inhabit society rather than the state. See G.A. Kelly, *Hegel's Retreat from Eleusis* (Princeton University Press, 1978), 174. Religion, which declined on the state and political levels, revived as it assured social or factional unity. See Hugh McLeod, *Religion and the People of Western Europe* (Oxford University Press, 1981), v.

109 Note that they also open up (albeit unsatisfactorily) the modern agenda on gender and Incarnation. Sainte-Beuve, of course, and many others, were too prudish to explore this territory in public writing.

Joubert, a good Platonist, referred to the two Aphrodites of Plato's *Symposium* to explain the ambiguous charm of *Atala*. 'There is in this work a Venus that will be felt by all, heavenly for some, terrestrial for others.' Letter quoted in *Atala* (Paris: Garnier 1962), xxvii. The osmosis between the spheres of the two Aphrodites, or the link between aesthetics and erotics, is very apparent in the three versions of Chateaubriand's description of the Holy Week Tenebrae office in the Sistine Chapel. The first version is found in an intimate letter to Juliette Récamier. Written right after the ceremony, it is a tender effusion. Revised for the *Mémoires*, the text conveys mainly a feeling of history. A further revision published in an

1831 pamphlet is made to serve the ends of Christian proselytizing. See the texts and a discussion in Jean d'Ormesson, *Mon dernier rêve sera pour vous* (Paris: J.C. Lattès, 1982), 298–9.

110 See the discussion of Chateaubriand in Jean Roussel, *Jean-Jacques Rousseau en France*, 165–76, 359–94 esp. 383, 388. Chateaubriand contrasts the style of Buffon with that of Rousseau in *Génie*, 692–6. Christianity gives to the former a sense of decorum, and to the latter charm, abandon, and love.

See also G.A. Kelly's comments on *Emile* in *Idealism, Politics and History: Sources of Hegelian Thought* (Cambridge University Press, 1969). The chimaera made alive by Rousseau provides Kelly with a thread for his argument: the chimaera is rationalized by Kant, dogmatized by Fichte, and cancelled and preserved by Hegel.

111 Moreau, *Chateaubriand*, 35–6.

112 *Essai sur les révolutions*, 26.

113 *Mémoires d'outre-tombe*, vol. 2, 936.

114 Albert Thibaudet launched the reversal of Buffon's formula. See *Histoire de la littérature français* (Paris: Stock, 1936), 37.

115 Pierre Barbéris, *Chateaubriand*, 141. This is also illustrated by Kierkegaard's authorship. One might add that it also prevents the progressive coopting of religion. Chateaubriand is not the sort of messianic liberal France knew in the 1850s (Hugo, Quinet) who sang the advances of liberal democracy against all forces of darkness and saw the triumphant march of freedom as both inevitable and anti-fatalistic.

116 *Lycidas*, line 152.

117 *Mémoires d'outre-tombe*, vol. 2, 923.

CHAPTER 3

1 Claude Langlois stressed that the division on the Civil Constitution was the first breach in the happy revolutionary unity that had reigned since 1789: on this issue, the majority of the National Assembly imposed its will on the minority and accepted an uncompromising struggle. See Langlois's afterword, 'La déchirure,' 319–37, in the French translation (*La Révolution, l'Eglise, la France*, [Paris: Cerf, 1986]) of Timothy Tuckett, *Religion, Revolution and Regional Culture in Eighteenth-Century France: The Ecclesiastical Oath of 1791* (Princeton University Press, 1985).

On the durable impact of these oppositions, see Michel Despland, 'A Case of Christians Shifting Their Moral Allegiance: France 1790–1914,' in *Journal of the American Academy of Religion* 52, pt 4 (1984).

2 Charles Nodier, *Portraits de la Révolution et de l'Empire* ed. Jean-Luc

Steinmetz, 2 vols (Paris: Tallandier, 1988). The second volume gives a valuable bibliography of Nodier's works, with the modern editions (447–51).

3 Nodier's major essays on books are available in Charles Nodier, *L'amateur de livres*, intro. by Jean-Luc Steinmetz (Bordeaux: Le Castor Astral, 1993). See also Didier Barrière, *Nodier l'homme du livre. Le rôle de la bibliophilie dans la littérature* (Bassac: Plein Chant, 1989); pp. 300–8 has a bibliography on book sciences.

4 Nodier, *Portraits*, vol. 1, 244.

5 For a recent biography, see Georges Zaragoza, *Charles Nodier: Le dériseur sensé* (Paris: Klincksieck, 1992).

6 See 'Le premier Nodier et les méditateurs,' in Paul Bénichou, *Le sacre de l'écrivain 1750–1830* (Paris: Corti, 1973), 208–19.

7 The main source on this world is still Auguste Viatte, *Les sources occultes du romantisme: Illuminisme – théosophie: 1770–1820*, 2 vols (Paris: Champion, 1969). Robert Darnton showed the frequent connections between such illuminism and new pseudo-scientific theories on fluids and magnetism. See *Mesmerism and the End of Enlightenment in France* (Cambridge, Mass.: Harvard University Press, 1968), 68–71. The spread of such ideas leads him to speak of an epidemic. As the line between science and pseudo-science was not strictly drawn, 'science' could free itself from theology but not from fiction (p. 12).

8 On Saint-Martin, see Léon Cellier, 'Présence de Saint-Martin,' in *Parcours initiatiques* (Neuchâtel: Baconnière, 1977). *L'homme de désir* has been reprinted, with an introduction by Robert Amadou (Monaco: Editions du Rocher 1979). Chateaubriand met Saint-Martin; besides complaining about the supper he was offered, he declared that, while the teacher spoke French, he could not understand a word of what he said. See 'Chateaubriand et Saint-Martin,' in *Parcours initiatiques*, 45–57. See also *Mémoires d'outre-tombe*, vol. 1, 473–4; Chateaubriand adds there the story of the abbé who tried to show he could kill a canary by 'magnetic' mental concentration.

9 See the methodological observations in Frank Paul Bowman, 'Une lecture politique de la folie religieuse ou "théomanie",' in *Romantisme* 24 (1979), 75–87. Nodier collected all the books he could find by the few early modern mad writers; see 'Bibliographie des fous,' in *L'amateur de livres*, 63–89.

10 'De l'amour et de son influence,' in Charles Nodier, *Rêveries* (Paris: Plasma 1979), 109. See also the preface by Hubert Juin. This book gathers ten articles Nodier wrote between 1830 and 1833.

11 In *Portraits*, vol. 2, 257–422.

12 In *Portraits*, vol. 1, 167–228.

13 Ibid., 187.

14 Ibid., 289–378.

15 In *Portraits*, vol. 2, 231.

16 Ibid., 80–1.

17 Ibid., 298, 345.

18 Letter of 19 December 1829, in *Europe* 614 no 5 (June–July 1980), 65.

19 *Portraits*, vol. 2, 88. In his 1946 preface to the collected works of Saint-Just, Malraux (writing under a pseudonym) analyses the modernity of this revolutionary actor by showing how his action lay purely in his words. *Oeuvres choisies* (Paris: Gallimard, 1968), 9–53.

20 *Portraits*, vol. 1, 232–4, 237, 277, 373.

21 See the introduction by Jean-Luc Steinmetz to the 1988 edition of *Portraits de la Révolution et de l'Empire*, and the article by Michel Delon, 'Nodier et les mythes révolutionnaires,' in *Europe*, 614 no 5 (June–July 1980), 31–43.

22 In *Portraits*, vol. 1, 57–166.

23 Ibid., 166.

24 Ibid., 109, 132.

25 Eckart Schroeder-Buys, 'Charles Nodier und die Revolution,' in *Lendemains* 25/26 (1982), 52–70.

26 *Jean Sbogar* (Paris: Editions France-Empire, 1980), 150, 153–4, 155–6, 157, 158–9.

27 *L'amateur de livres*, 63. Quoted in Daniel Sangsue, *Le récit excentrique: Gautier–De Maistre–Nerval–Nodier* (Paris: Corti, 1987), 41.

28 See the introduction by Daniel Sangsue to Charles Nodier, *Moi-même* (Paris: Corti, 1985).

29 'Amélie,' in *Souvenirs de jeunesse*, with a preface by Hubert Juin (Paris: Aubier, 1992), 113.

30 Sangsue, *Le récit excentrique*, 252.

31 *Histoire du roi de Bohême* (Paris: Plasma, 1979), 75.

32 Hubert Juin, in his preface to the 1979 reprint of *Histoire du roi de Bohême*, vii–xx.

33 Pierre Barbéris, *Balzac et le mal du siècle*, vol. 2, *1830–3. Une expérience de l'absurde: de la prise de conscience à l'expression* (Paris: Gallimard, 1971), 930–4.

34 Didier Barrière, *Nodier l'homme du livre*, 185. Since pagination, illustrations, design, and layout are essential, quality reprints (details ibid., 287–9) are the only editions worth reading besides the 1830 original (see note 3).

35 All his tales are available in a standard edition, *Contes* (Paris: Garnier,

1961; revised 1987), with introduction and notes by Pierre-Georges Castex. References below are to the 1961 edition.

36 *La fée aux miettes*, in *Contes*, 168, 170.

37 See Jean-Luc Steinmetz, 'Aventures du regard,' in *Le champ d'écoute: Essais critiques* (Neuchâtel: Baconnière, 1985) 31–5.

38 What bibliophiles love, writes Nodier, is 'the silent conversation of great minds, which does not require the expense of reciprocity'; *L'amateur de livres*, 91.

39 *La fée aux miettes* in *Contes*, 290.

40 Such is the suggestion by Steinmetz in his notice on *La fée aux miettes* in Charles Nodier, *Smarra, Trilby et autres contes*, with preface, bibliography and notes by Jean-Luc Steinmetz (Paris: Garnier-Flammarion, 1980), 214.

41 J.-L. Steinmetz in his preface, 'Le veilleur de nuit,' to *Smarra, Trilby et autres contes*, 23.

42 The writing of the tale may have been occasioned by a 1829 exchange in a magazine on new methods of treatment of the insane. Nodier found the 'philanthropic' proposal unacceptably cruel. See the introduction by Castex to *La fée aux miettes* in *Contes*, 156–9.

43 Nodier, *Contes*, p. 36, 42.

44 See Michel Picard, *Nodier: La fée aux miettes; Loup y es-tu?* (Paris: PUF, 1992) for an analysis of the completely regressive nature of eroticism in the tale.

45 Printed in *Rêveries*, 59–84.

46 Ibid., 63, 65.

47 *Histoire d'Hélène Gillet*, in *Contes*, 330.

48 *Paul ou la ressemblance*, in *Contes*, 644.

49 Quoted by Hubert Juin in *Lectures du XIXème siècle*, vol. 1 (Paris: Union générale d'éditions 1976), 20.

50 See Auguste Viatte, *Les sources occultes du romantisme: Illuminisme – théosophie: 1770–1820*, 2 vols. (Paris: Champion, 1969), vol. 2, 145–67.

51 *L'amour et le grimoire*, in *Contes*, 516–46. Nodier salutes Champollion's achievement in deciphering hieroglyphs in 1822 (521). But it is possible to surmise that undeciphered hieroglyphs gave him a bigger frisson.

52 Nodier's last tale tells the story of the odd friar and his unusual book, *Franciscus Columna*, in *Contes*, 882–903; see also 'Bibliographie des fous,' in *L'amateur de livres*, 67–9.

53 *La fée aux miettes*, *Contes*, 334.

54 In *Rêveries*, 85–110.

55 *Correspondance croisée de Victor Hugo et Charles Nodier*, ed. Jacques Rémi-Dahan (Bassac: Plein Chant, 1987), 137.

56 Ibid., 102–3, 107–8.

57 'Préliminaires,' in *Jean Sbogar*, 17.

58 Castex, in Nodier's *Contes*, 839–47.

59 At that time Catholic apologists spread the idea of a primitive revelation, granted by God to Adam and to all peoples, and subsequently corrupted everywhere, save in the Catholic Church. But Nodier has in mind a more esoteric kind of knowledge. Also his sources are not high Scripture but low folklore.

60 'De la palingénésie humaine et de la résurrection' (1832), printed in *Rêveries*, 215.

61 Printed in *Portraits*, vol. 2, 114–164.

62 Ibid., 114.

63 Emile Lehouck, 'Discours autobiographique et tradition romanesque dans *Suites d'un mandat d'arrêt*,' in *Charles Nodier: Colloque du deuxième centenaire Besançon 1980* (Paris: Belles Lettres, 1982), 31–9.

64 'Lettre à Christophe de Beaumont,' in *Oeuvres complètes*, vol. 4, 548–9.

65 *La fée aux miettes*, in *Contes*, 283.

66 Quoted by Hubert Juin in his preface to *Souvenirs de jeunesse: Mademoiselle de Marsan* (Paris: Aubier, 1992), 15.

67 See Hermann Hofer, 'La pensée mystique et religieuse de Charles Nodier,' in *Romantisme et religion*, M. Baude and M. M. Münch, eds. (Paris: PUF, 1980), 185–94.

68 Quoted by Lehouck, 'Discours autobiographique,' in *Charles Nodier*, 31.

69 The deed was not as spectacular as one might think from the painting standing in the hall of the Académie de Médecine; careful experimentation went on during a long period of time and the insane were released little by little.

70 'Bibliographie des fous,' in *L'amateur de livres*, 87. The major modern folly Nodier decries is the belief in material progress; he thereby brings again water to the mill of all conservative social critics.

71 'Piranèse, contes psychologiques, à propos de la monomanie réflective,' in *Oeuvres complètes* (Paris: Renduel, 1832–7), vol. 11, 167–204. See the article by Bryan G. Rogers, 'Nodier et la monomanie réflective,' in *Romantisme 27* (1980), 15–29. To many Romantics, *I Carceri* evoked internal jails, and inner, engulfing abysses, namely, the ability selves have of making their own mazes and getting trapped in them. See Georges Poulet, 'Piranèse et les poètes romantiques français,' in *Trois essais de mythologie romantique* (Paris: Corti, 1985), 135–87.

72 Anne-Marie Roux, 'Nodier et "l'effet de folie",' in *Romantisme 27* (1980), 33, 40.

73 Jean Roudaut, 'Nodier: la poésie ou la mort,' in *Magazine littéraire* 258 (Octobre 1988), 41–3.

74 'De l'amour et de son influence comme sentiment sur la société actuelle,' in *Rêveries*, 97.

75 'Clémentine,' in *Souvenirs de jeunesse*, 80.

76 See Béatrice Didier, *Ecrire la Révolution: 1789–1799* (Paris: PUF, 1989), 195–206.

77 See Tzvetan Todorov, *The Fantastic: Structural Approach to a Literary Genre* (Cleveland: Press of Case Western Reserve University, 1973). Todorov points out that the beliefs toyed with are far from being only those traditionally labelled 'supernatural.' As the discussions of magnetism show, scientific minds then did not know the precise limits of the possible.

78 'Rien n'est vrai que le faux,' quoted in Juin, 'Charles Nodier,' *Lectures du XIXème siècle*, vol. 1, 23.

79 See Miriam S. Hamenachem, *Charles Nodier: Essai sur l'imagination mythique* (Paris: Nizet, 1972), 10.

80 The notion of the magic book, encyclopaedic or perfect, containing or offering the whole science of the world, was a subject of much reflection in German romaniticism, with Novalis especially; on him, see Walter Moser, *Romantisme et crises de la modernité: Poésie et encyclopédie dans le "Brouillon" de Novalis* (Longueil, Qué.: Le Préambule, 1989).

81 See Barrière, *Nodier l'homme du livre*, 50, 90.

82 Ibid., 68.

83 At the same time Joubert (1754–1824) embodied the opposite attitude: as he read a book, he tore off the pages that seemed of no interest to him; all the books that made it into his library were much thinner than when they left the bookstore.

84 'De l'alphabet typographique' (1836), reprinted (with other articles on the printer's art) in *Critiques de l'imprimerie*, texts selected and introduced by Didier Barrière (Paris: Editions des cendres, 1989), 69.

85 He reminded his readers that Erasmus (and all the great humanists) had a great obsession with the quality of the text and did not trust anybody else with it. See his article 'Les inconvénients d'une faute d'impression' (1837), in Barrière (ed.), *Critiques de l'imprimerie*, 85. Nodier deplores the fact that most writers among his contemporaries do not care about what printers do with their text.

86 'De quelques phénomènes du sommeil' (1831), in *Rêveries*, 114, 127.

87 See Barbéris, *Balzac et le mal du siècle*, vol. 2, 1417–21. Both books by Balzac in that list contain features characteristic of the 'eccentric' novel. See also

George Castex, 'Nodier et l'école du désenchantement,' in *Horizons romantiques* (Paris: Corti, 1983), 35–43.

88 *Revue des deux mondes* (1 September 1839), quoted in Pierre Macherey, *A quoi pense la littérature?* (Paris: PUF, 1981), 222–3.

89 'Thérèse,' in *Souvenirs de jeunesse*, 71.

90 In 1829 Hugo created a sensation by publishing *Le dernier jour d'un condamné*. The force of the text comes from its eccentric qualities: we do not hear a traditional narrative from the man about to be executed, or an account of his youth or his crime, or a story of his trial. The reader is locked up inside the consciousness of the prisoner on the morning of the execution. As Hugo documented in his 1832 preface, simply to evoke that internal monologue provoked the anger of those who believed in the justice (or necessity) of the death penalty. See Sangsue, *Le récit excentrique*, 164–7.

91 'Suites d'un mandat d'arrêt,' *Portraits*, vol. 2, 114.

92 H.R. Niebuhr, 'Faith in our History,' in *The Meaning of Revelation* (New York: Macmillan, 1960), 73–81.

93 Sangsue, *Le récit excentrique*, 274.

94 'De las cosas mas seguras, la mas segura es dudar,' in *Histoire du roi de Bohême*, 80.

95 Jean-Marie Le Sidaner, 'Le peuple de Nodier,' *Europe*, 43–5.

96 Steinmetz, preface in *Smarra, Trilby et autres contes*, 37.

97 Sainte-Beuve, 'Charles Nodier,' in *Revue des deux mondes* (1 May 1840); reprinted in *Oeuvres* (Paris: Gallimard, 1951), vol. 2, 297–333.

CHAPTER 4

1 *Correspondance croisée de Victor Hugo and Charles Nodier* (Bassac: Plein Chant, 1987), 167. Nodier also once wrote, equally sententiously, that societies will begin again, as they began before, thanks to charming stories (in the review of *Han d'Islande*, ibid., 131).

2 Review of Hugo, *Odes et ballades* (1827), in *Correspondance croisée*, 137.

3 See Pierre Rosanvallon, *Le moment Guizot* (Paris: Gallimard, 1985), 18.

4 For an overview of the intellectual achievements of Vigny's contemporaries, see Alan B. Spitzer, *The French Generation of 1820* (Princeton University Press, 1982).

5 See Bernard Plongeron, *L'abbé Grégoire ou l'arche de la fraternité* (Paris: Letouzey et Ané, 1989).

6 This failure was to receive its most brilliant analysis in Edgar Quinet, *La*

Révolution (1865, reprinted with an excellent preface by Claude Lefort [Paris: Belin, 1987]). See also François Furet, *La gauche et la révolution au milieu du XIXème siecle* (Paris: Hachette, 1986), 51–72.

7 Reprinted in 1985, with an introduction by Pierre Rosanvallon (Paris: Hachette).

8 On Saint-Simon, with Fourier and Comte as well, see Frank E. Manuel, *The Prophets of Paris* (1962; repr. New York: Harper and Row, 1965); see also D.G. Charlton, *Secular Religions in France 1815–1870* (London: Oxford University Press, 1963).

9 See Georges Matoré, *Le vocabulaire et la société sous Louis-Philippe* (1951; repr. Genève: Slatkine, 1967).

10 'Avertissement' in *Promenades dans Rome, voyages en Italie* (Paris: Pléïade, 1973), 597.

11 Paul Bénichou, *Les mages romantiques* (Paris: Gallimard, 1988), 113.

12 *Journal d'un poète*, 19 February 1840, in *Oeuvres complètes*, vol. 2 (Paris: Gallimard, 1948), 1128–9. All references to this work are to this volume of the Pléiade edition.

13 Vigny worked on the first two simultaneously and published fragments from both in the *Revue des deux mondes*. He worked on the third one from 1832 on. All three works respond in some manner to the bourgeois revolution of 1830. He wrote only one other major prose work, the historical novel *Cinq-Mars*, published in 1826, when the Restoration was still going strong.

14 Such insertion of an apparently alien document became a frequent romantic literary ploy. Kierkegaard used it to great effect, most notably in *Stages on Life's Way* trans. W. Lowrie, (1845; Princeton University Press, 1940).

15 Doctor Noir, in *Stello*. See *Stello; Daphné*, ed. François Germain (Paris: Garnier, 1970), 187. All references are to this edition.

16 For a general introduction to Vigny's life, the temper and tenor of his work, see Paul Viallaneix, *Vigny par lui-même* (Paris: Seuil, 1964).

17 *Servitude et grandeur militaires*, ed. François Germain (Paris: Garnier, 1965), 31–2. All references are to this edition. There is an English translation by Marguerite Barnett, *The Military Condition* (Oxford University Press, 1964).

18 *Journal d'un poète* 11 August, 1830; *Oeuvres complètes*, vol. 2, 916.

19 *Sevitude*, bk 1, chap. 1, 5–16.

20 Reason, writes Vigny, must attack all fanaticisms; such is the task of every writer.

21 Three times, Vigny speaks out against Joseph de Maistre: here, in *Servi-*

tude, p. 67, in the poem *La prison*, and in *Stello*, as we shall see below. The opposition went deep, and had something to do with his objections to the Christians' God, whom he sees as requiring blood.

22 *Servitude*, 65.

23 *Servitude*, 214–19.

24 See Bénichou, *Les mages romantiques*, 180–5.

25 *Servitude*, 193.

26 The unknown sacrifices of soldiers are also contrasted with the constant public posturing and persistent ambition of lawyers.

27 On the fear of speech and the praise of silence, see Paul Viallaneix, *Vigny par lui-même*, 94–109.

28 There is an English translation of this work, *Stello: A Session with Doctor Noir*, trans. Irving Massey, with introduction and notes (Montréal: McGill-Queen's University Press, 1963).

29 In giving him his name Vigny probably thought of his close friend Dr Esprit Blanche, a pupil of the great Pinel and one of the leaders in that first generation of compassionate French alienists who tried to bring some humanity to the care and 'treatment' of the mentally insane. Gérard de Nerval was hospitalized in his clinic.

30 *Stello*, 147.

31 See chap. 32, 147–52. Commentators agree that Vigny, who lets his doctor voice sentiments of horror before the bloodthirsty behaviour of revolutionary crowds, promptly adds a correction attacking a leading anti-revolutionary ideologue, since he does not want to bring grist to the mill of the reactionary anti-republicans.

32 *Stello*, 146.

33 See also the portrait of Napoléon, who is compared to a motor in a machine, in *Servitude*, bk 3, chap. 5, 153–67.

34 The recourse to three stories also formally checks the tendency toward duality and deadlock: the drama moves on and progress is conceivable.

35 Note that Vigny does not leave the poet as alone as he left the soldier with a conscience. Stello has the company of the doctor. The form of *Servitude*, however, also gave a friend to the model officer: the writer who labels his story a story of grandeur.

36 Viallaneix, *Vigny par lui-même*, 38.

37 F. Germain in his preface to *Servitude*, xxvi, lviii.

38 As Marc Eigeldinger puts it, *Stello* fully brings out the divorce patent after 1830 between poetry and bourgeois prosaicity. See his introduction to *Stello* (Paris: Garnier-Flammarion, 1985). Vigny thus announces the Baudelaire of post-1848.

39 *Journal d'un poète*, 912.

40 Vigny's clearest philanthropic involvement is on behalf of starving poets, a class of the needy that became identifiable in the 1830s; there was a wave of young intellectual suicides after 1832.

41 Commentators discern in *Stello*, as in *Servitude*, echoes of the sentiments so frequently expressed in the 1820s and 1830s (a generous, hopeful ideology which received theoretical expression in the works of Saint-Simon): imagination is useful to society; a new élite is emerging, made of poets, scholars, and intelligent rulers. The formal context of the doctor's presentation of a better alternative makes it clear, however, that we do not have here another utopian doctrinaire statement, but a tentative affirmation which requires a truly liberal view of social interaction.

42 *Stello*, 191.

43 There is much, he writes in *Journal d'un poète*, to be said against life, but the only criticism that really makes its point is silence, 11, 969.

44 The contribution of Vigny to French poetry is the philosophical poem, a sort of short epic where symbols convey rich thought content.

45 Fernande Bartfeld, 'Le lecteur de Stello comme malade ou bourreau,' *Romantisme* 23 (1979), 55–63.

46 On the notion of open work, see Umberto Eco, *The Open Work*, trans. Anna Cancogni (Cambridge, Mass.: Harvard University Press, 1989).

47 Marc Eigeldinger, intro. to the Garnier-Flammarion ed. 11–12 (see n 38). F. Bartfeld, 'Le lecteur de Stello,' 62, adds that *Stello* wants to be a satirical novel, and that these two objectives cannot be pursued at once.

48 While I argue that *Stello* represents a successful overcoming of authorial doubts about authorial vocation, it is, from another critical standpoint, a work much darker than *Servitude*. Frederick Jameson analyses all the men/women and adult/children relationships in the earlier work and notes that the human impossibilities imposed by modern society are prefigured in the notorious difficulties soldiers encounter in their love and family lives. But the crises in the lives of couples and families exposed throughout *Servitude* end on a positive note. See 'L'inconscient politique,' in G. Falconer and H. Mitterand, *La lecture socio-critique du texte romanesque* (Toronto: Hakkert, 1975), 39–48. *Stello* is in a more anarchist vein. Couples and families are impossible. In the first story, the poet is alone and the only sexuality is that of the king and his mistress, playful and sterile. In the second, the poet can only have a clandestine affair with the wife of another. In the third, he yearns in vain after a married woman devoted to her husband. Stello and the doctor of course can only be single and unattached.

49 On the project, see the introduction by François Germain in the Garnier edition of *Stello; Daphne*, 213–74. Vigny planned, as usual, three stories on three religious reformers, Julian, Melanchthon, and J.-J. Rousseau. Of the history of the project, the background reading, and the succession of plans, the fullest account is in G. Bonnefoy, *La pensée religieuse et morale d'Alfred de Vigny* (Paris: Belles-Lettres, 1927). Vigny also planned, briefly, a third consultation on women and on love.

50 Christians, Vigny adds, have a particularly terrifying and mutilating notion of God, 'mutilating' because of the requirement for chastity.

51 See F. Germain, 'Vigny et la religion,' in *Stello; Daphné*, 214–20.

52 *Journal d'un poète*, 1 October 1834, 1013–14. I presume that he planned to do that strictly for himself, since there are no signs whatever of any attempt at a literary construction.

53 Raymond Schwab, *La renaissance orientale* (Paris: Payot, 1950), 402.

54 In his journal in 1837, Vigny once used the word *théosophe* to describe this new sort of student focusing on religious matters. *Oeuvres complètes*, vol. 2, 1053, 1081. He wisely gave it up; the illuminist meaning was glued to the word.

55 *Stello; Daphné*, 298.

56 Vigny here seems to act on the pronouncement of Chateaubriand to the effect that the confrontation of cultures and the conflicts of religions offer to the Muse one of the richest, most fecund and dramatic topics (*Mémoires d'outre-tombe*, Pléiade edition, vol. 1, 465.) There is a big difference, however; in *Les martyrs*, Christianity is the true, the superior religion and it prevails over Hellenism for the right reasons.

57 On Vigny's orientalism, see Vera A Summers, *L'orientalisme d'Alfred de Vigny* (Paris: Champion, 1930; repr. Slatkine 1976). The author stresses Vigny's appreciation of the Hebrew Bible.

58 This is the only point where our reading must accept a hypothesis because of the unfinished nature of the text. Note then that here the 'narration' is the cause of the disease, rather than cure. Note also that our text is unsatisfactory in that we do not see the doctor 'cure' Trivulce, nor get any hint as to how he might go about it.

59 See Frank Paul Bowman, 'A Romantic View of the Hellenist Past: Vigny's *Daphné*,' in W.G. Langlois, *The Persistent Voice* (New York: New York University Press, 1971). The procedure is reminiscent of that found in the *Symposium*: Plato makes us believe that we get what Socrates said at third hand and Diotima at fourth. Here again, it is religious affirmations that are conveyed only through a weak(?), unreliable(?) chain of tradition.

60 Literature keeps pace with the learned specialists. A heated debate on

hellenistic syncretism and the relationships with early Christianity raged in France ever since the 1820s. See Frank Paul Bowman, *Le Christ des barricades 1789–1848* (Paris: Cerf, 1987), 146–54. The controversy was renewed with the publication of Etienne Vacherot, *Histoire critique de l'ecole d'Alexandrie* (3 volumes, 1846–1850). The leading Catholic attack came from Alphonse Gratry, *La sophistique contemporaine* (Paris: C. Douniol, 1851).

61 'They find generally more good faith among pagans than among heretics' (*Stello; Daphne*, 311). Christian Antioch is a city that consumes treasures (both literal and figurative) and produces none.

62 The construction of this 'treasure' explains why Vigny never bothered to complete his synopsis of the teachings of the world religions. Dead clothes are for mummies, not for live human beings.

63 Bowman, *Le Christ des barricades*, 52.

64 This was also the conclusion Constant arrived at in his (posthumously published) *Du polythéisme romain, considéré dans ses rapports avec la philosophie grecque et la religion chrétienne* (Paris: Béchet âiné, 1832).

65 See L. Retat, *Religion et imagination religieuse: leurs formes et leurs rapports dans l'oeuvre d'Ernest Renan* (Paris: Klincksieck, 1957), appendix 2, 'Daphné d'Alfred de Vigny: à propos d'un nouvel arianisme.'

66 From Madame de Stael on, it had become a commonplace to compare the revolutionary urban crowds to the Barbarians that stormed the Empire to create a new world. See details in *Stello; Daphné*, 432–3. In 1848, Fréderic Ozanam urged his fellow Catholics to move over to the Barbarians. Quite a few did, but mainly only for a while.

67 This figure is modelled on the socialist Lamennais. Sainte-Beuve had declared that *Paroles d'un croyant* (1834) was an apocalypse of hatred. Vigny's papers indicate that he wanted to develop this scene more. But, as Bénichou points out (*Les mages romantiques*, 207), Vigny was more at ease with the world of Julian than with the moderns. The conflict between Hellenism and Christianity can be the object of historical contemplation, of some nostalgic repose; contemporary conflicts afford no rest.

68 He thus breaks company decisively with Victor Hugo and his constant confidence that fatality can be swayed or overcome. See Viallaneix, *Vigny par lui-même*, 130, 143.

69 See Michel Despland, 'The French Response to D.F. Strauss *Das Leben Jesu*,' in American Academy of Religion, *Papers of the Nineteenth-Century Theology Working Group* (Berkeley: Graduate Theological Union, 1986), 85–98.

70 See the *Journal d'un poète*, 30 January 1837, 1056: 'Christianity gets weaker every day, showing under its worn gown the ever-living platonism.'

71 See F. Germain, *Stello; Daphné* 268–9.

72 Ronald Grimsley, 'Kierkegaard, Vigny and the poet,' *Revue de littérature comparée* (January–March 1960), reprinted in his *Soren Kierkegaard and French Literature: Eight Comparative Studies* (Cardiff: University of Wales Press, 1966), 58–60. There is no indication that Kierkegaard read Vigny, but we know that he read *the Revue des deux mondes* in the 1830s; see the 'Introduction' in *Kierkegaard and French Literature.*

73 Reviewing *Stello's* impact a few years later, Vigny notes that many liked the book as book, but, alas, few hearts were changed. Preface ('Dernière nuit de travail') to *Chatterton* (Paris: Garnier-Flammarion, 1968), 25.

74 Preface to *Chatterton*, 26–30.

75 Those familiar with Kierkegaard will recognize here his own stated intent as writer. More on him in Louis Mackey, *Kierkegaard: A Kind of Poet* (Philadelphia: University of Pennsylvania Press, 1971).

76 *Stello; Daphné*, 207. This metaphor is also used (1848–9) by Kierkegaard, *Armed Neutrality and An Open Letter*, ed. and transl. Howard V. and Edna H. Hong (New York: Simon and Shuster, 1968). The expression was common in the Scandinavian countries during the Napoleonic wars.

77 Marc Eigeldinger,*Vigny* (Paris: Seghers, 1965).

78 *Journal d'un poète*, 1130.

79 Ibid., 928.

80 Se François Germain, 'Vigny ou la croyance difficile,' in *Les amis d'Alfred de Vigny* 2, (March 1969), 4–15. See also Bénichou, *Les mages romantiques*, 149.

81 The best nineteenth-century writers did just that. Emile Durkheim and René Girard have since then, each in his own way, confirmed the strength of the links.

82 The difference between *Daphné* and *Les martyrs* on the Christians of the hellenistic era is thus not so much that Vigny painted a different picture but that he painted his picture differently. With Vigny, the two urban crises, in fourth-century Antioch and nineteenth-century Paris, are used to illumine and raise questions about each other. Vigny does not give us a Christian city one can feel nostalgic about. He keeps us in the present. Chateaubriand also did this in the *Mémoires d'outre-tombe.*

83 For the elaboration of this distinction, see Vincent Descombes, 'L'équivoque du symbolique,' in *Confrontations* (Paris: Aubien, 1980). English translation in *Theory Culture and Society* 3, pt 3 (1986), 69–83.

84 V. Descombes argues we should do likewise, or else our notion of the symbolic will remain hopelessly ambiguous.

CHAPTER 5

1 The three volumes of *Oeuvres complètes*, edited by Jean Guillaume and Claude Pichois, are available in the Pléiade collection (Paris: Gallimard). I have quoted from vol. 2 (1984). Vol. 1 became available in 1989, vol. 3 in 1993. For a brief, updated bibliography on secondary material see Michel Collot, *Gérard de Nerval ou la dévotion à l'imaginaire* (Paris: PUF, 1992), 26.

2 Quoted by Léon Cellier in *Gérard de Nerval*, 3rd ed. (Paris: Hatier, 1974), 77.

3 'We must fathom in a work,' says Jean Starobinski, 'the specific nature of a desire, of a power (a genius) who tried to attain and confirm his own self by giving birth to his work.' See 'Le sens de la critique,' in *La relation critique* (Paris: Gallimard, 1970). After citing this quotation, Raymond Jean adds, 'This initial *desire* is doubtless one of the most decisive elements in enabling us to understand the connection between living and writing established by a literary act.' *Lectures du désir* (Paris: Seuil, 1977), 9.

4 Aristide Marie, *Gérard de Nerval le poète et l'homme* (Paris: Hachette, 1914, repr. 1955) remains the basic text.

5 See Nerval's comments in 'La Bibliothèque de mon oncle,' *Les illuminés* (*Oeuvres complètes*, vol. 2, 885–6; see also the note on 1713–14). His uncle also seems to have collected libertine and subversive works.

6 See *Aurélia* (1855), in Nerval, *Aurélia et autres textes autobiographiques*, ed. Jacques Bony (Paris: Garnier-Flammarion, 1990), 292–3. Celtic antiquities were very popular for a time. The Académie celtique was founded in 1805. Many in France believed at that time that Celtic was the primitive language in which God delivered his original revelation to humankind. This theory was more flattering to national pride than contemporary linguistic theory, which was beginning to see in Sanskrit the common source of all Indo-European languages. See Jacques Solé, *Les mythes chrétiens* (Paris: Albin Michel, 1979), 257.

7 For further details of Nerval's esoteric readings and their influence see Jean Richer, *Nerval; expérience et création* (Paris: Hachette, 1963).

8 See Jean-Claude Fizaine, 'Les aspects mystiques du romantisme français,' *Romantisme* 11 (1976), 7.

9 For an explanation of his financial difficulties, the degradation involved in producing copy, and the difference between writing for money and writing for art, see the chapters 'Cadre économique' and 'Journaliste ou écrivain?' in Raymond Jean, *Lectures du désir*, 46–59.

10 See in particular 'Les nuits d'octobre' (1852) and 'Promenades et souvenirs' (1854–5).

11 See Georges Poulet, 'Piranèse et les poètes romantiques français,' in *Trois essais de mythologie romantique* (Paris: Corti, 1966; repr. 1985), 135–87.

12 Pierre Gascar, in *Gérard de Nerval et son temps* (Paris: Gallimard, 1981), 60–4 comments on the extraordinary number of duels and suicides in this society so often at the mercy of fickle success and misfortune.

13 Here Restif de la Bretonne was his model and predecessor. See 'Les confidences de Nicholas,' in *Les illuminés*, in *Oeuvres complètes*, vol. 2, 946–1074.

14 Nodier, in contrast, is an admirer of German letters and praises Germany as the 'refuge of soul.' ('De l'amour et de son influence comme sentiment sur la société actuelle,' in *Rêveries* [Paris: Plasma, 1979], 101.)

15 Michel Carle, *Du citoyen à l'artiste: Gérard de Nerval et ses premiers écrits* (Les Presses de l'Université d'Ottawa, 1992), 116–17. Carle demonstrates that in Nerval's case it is liberalism that led him to romantic inventiveness (105); he also provides a satisfactory solution to the issue raised by the constant presence of political allusions in Nerval's works.

16 See Pierre Gascar, *Gérard de Nerval et son temps*, 218. There are also indications that he was badly rattled in 1834 when he saw in Naples the painting of Judith with the severed head of Holophernes by Artemisia Gentileschi. See Jacques Bony, 'Nerval et la peinture italienne,' in *L'imaginaire nervalien: l'espace de l'Italie*, ed. Monique Streiff Moretti (Naples: ESI, 1988).

  On 31 March 1841, Nerval wrote a letter offering his services to the ministry in charge of national archaeology. He believed he could prove that the Merovingians had really been Hindus, Persians, and Trojans.

  Some members of the literary community saw his madness as a sign of a reprehensible disorder and predicted the demise of his career as a writer. Others idealized his condition, not realizing the suffering it caused. In this vein, Nerval continued to play with the idea that the madman is 'visited' or 'elected,' transported far from the artificial world.

17 For a discussion of the increase in cases of religious madness during the first half of the nineteenth century, see F.P. Bowman, 'Religion, Politics and Utopia in French Romanticism,' in the *Australian Journal of French Studies* 13, pt 3 (1974), 307–24, and 'Une lecture politique de la folie religieuse ou "théomanie",' in *Romantisme* 24 (1979), 75–87. Bowman concedes that it is impossible to draw a line between religious eccentricity and religious madness. The cases he examines share utopian and apocalyptic dreams of justice and unity; they also idealize women or the androgynous. He thus finds the connections between socialist content and

religious content, in particular the same re-eschatologization, that Henri Desroches found in early religious socialism.

In the final analysis, however, Nerval bears little resemblance to the other writers, none of whom could be classed as first-rate. If Nerval is to be placed within a group, it must be in the generation of young Romantics who were brutally excluded from power in 1830. See François Gaillard, 'Nerval, ou les contradictions du romantisme,' *Romantisme* 1&2 (1971), 128–38.

18 Gascar, *Gérard de Nerval et son temps*, 204, 295.
19 Michel Jeanneret, *La lettre perdue: Ecriture et folie dans l'oeuvre de Nerval* (Paris: Flammarion, 1978), 153.
20 Jeanneret, *La lettre perdue*, 5, 58.
21 Readers can gain a sense of the pathos in Nerval's life by reading some of his letters to his father; he never got any recognition from his parent, who never even came to visit him in the hospital. Nerval's correspondence is chronologically distributed through the three volumes of *Oeuvres complètes*.
22 Sarah Kofman, *Nerval, le charme de la répétition: Lecture de Sylvie* (Lausanne: L'Age d'homme, 1979), 27, 31.
23 Jeanneret, *La lettre perdue*, 110.
24 Four of Nerval's works were in some stage of the process of publication at the time of his death. Léon Cellier edited them in one volume: Nerval, *Promenades et souvenirs: Lettres à Jenny. Pandora. Aurélia* (Paris: Garnier-Flammarion, 1972). We will refer to Cellier's preface, 11–49; the title will be abbreviated *Promenades*.

   More recently, Jacques Bony edited three of these, along with three other pieces, to offer under one cover all the autobiographical works Nerval worked on since 1840. *See Aurélia. Un roman à faire. Les nuits d'octobre. Petits chateaux de Bohême. Pandora. Promenades et souvenirs* (Paris: Garnier-Flammarion, 1990); our references to *Aurélia* will be to this edition, abbreviated *Aurélia*. Bony's introduction (7–36) defends the view (8) that Nerval undertook to assemble an autobiographical account of himself, using as models Rousseau's *Confessions* at first, and, increasingly as time went on, his *Rêveries d'un promeneur solitaire*.
25 See Gabrielle Malandain, *Nerval ou l'incendie du théâtre: Identité et littérature dans l'oeuvre en prose de G. de Nerval* (Paris: Corti, 1986), 247–8.
26 See Françoise Gaillard, 'Nerval, ou les contradictions du romantisme,' *Romantisme* 1&2 (1971) 128–38.
27 In this respect Nerval can be compared to Vigny; his search for artistic regeneration is, however, more poignant because more radical. Nerval is

thus to be contrasted with Nodier, whose views on politics do not add up to a whole, or, if they do, they add up to an imbecilic one.

28 *Isis*, in Nerval, *Les filles du feu. Les chimères*, ed. Léon Cellier (Paris: Garnier-Flammarion, 1965), 194. In 'Quintus Aucler,' in *Les illuminés*, in *Oeuvres complètes*, vol. 2, 1135–6, he openly deplores the death of religions and prefers the blasphemies of Byron and the impiety of Shelley to the indifference of these 'children of the century,' because they were at least still religious feelings.

29 *Le voyage en Orient*, in *Oeuvres complètes*, vol. 2, 475, 517. In 'La Bibliothèque de mon oncle' he distanced himself from this 'indigestible and unhealthy food for the soul,' which he had, however, so eagerly devoured in the past.

30 The narrator of a book of travel can allow himself to take each instant as it comes. See Jean-Pierre Richard, 'Géographie magique de Nerval,' in *Poésie et profondeur* (Paris: Seuil, 1955), 15. Nodier also published his travels, in particular a *Promenade de Dieppe aux montagnes d'Ecosse* (1821). Jacques Bony notes that Nerval's ambulatory urges have something frenetic about them and that when narrating his travels he tries to get out of an internal labyrinth; see 'Introduction' to *Aurélia* (Paris: Garnier-Flammarion 1990), 16.

31 See Gérald Schaeffer, *Le voyage en Orient de Nerval: Etude des structures* (Neuchâtel: Baconnière, 1967), 32, 65. Parts of Nerval's book may be found in English in *Journey to the Orient*, selected and translated from the French and with an introduction by Norman Glass (New York: New York University Press, 1972).

32 This particular poet allowed himself every licence in writing his book. He changed his itinerary, and presented things he had only read about as things he had seen.

33 Gascar, *Nerval et son temps*, 187–90.

34 Readers of Kierkegaard will recall that *Fear and Trembling* (1843) was written to communicate with Régine Olsen, after the author had broken his engagement to her.

35 *Le voyage en Orient*, in *Oeuvres complètes*, vol. 2, 237–40.

36 Jeanneret in his preface to Nerval, *Le voyage en Orient* (Paris: Garnier-Flammarion, 1980), 16–17.

37 These promethean themes exist in several of Nerval's works; the subject establishes himself as the sole master. He succeeds in his desire to assume the role of creator; he recreates the world and makes it better than it was under Jehovah. Domination through transcendence is therefore eliminated. See Jeanneret, *La lettre perdue*, 117–19.

38 Jeanneret correctly points out that Nerval by articulating his alternative

'simply added to the list of possible religions. While they are all believable, none are absolute.' *Le voyage en Orient,* ed. M. Jeanneret, 17. On the different religions Nerval encountered in the Orient, and 'the degree and modalities of belief he granted the manifestations of transcendence that each religion explained in its own fashion,' see Max Milner, 'Religions et religion dans *Le voyage en Orient* de G. de Nerval,' *Romantisme* 50 (1985), 41–52. Milner considers him a sceptic who lets himself be swayed by emotion.

39 *Le voyage en Orient,* in *Oeuvres complètes,* vol. 2, 385–96.

40 Ibid., 364.

41 Ibid., 385–96, 525–62, 671–773. The first story is made up of different scholarly dissertations. The second comes from Silvestre de Sacy (in *La religion des Druzes*). The third was not adapted from anything he read, but contains a vast amount of masonic material; ultimately it is 'the elaboration of a personal dilemma, which is both conscious and unconscious' (Ibid., notes, 1588).

42 See Schaeffer, *Le voyage en Orient de Nerval,* 33, 59, 99, 184.

43 Schaeffer sees this as a result of the author's conquest of identity rather than of the formulation of his own beliefs. He claims that this was how Nerval reshaped the reality of 'the Oriental Renaissance' into a cosmic venture. See Schaeffer *Le voyage en Orient de Nerval,* 49, 279, 295, 383, 390, 396. Nerval's timing was perfect. In 1844 the quarrel between liberal scholars (Quinet, Michelet, etc.) and the Catholic party, which accused the universities of pantheism, raged in Paris. See Brian Juden, 'Nerval et la crise du panthéisme,' in *Cahiers de l'Herne* 37 (1979), *Gérard de Nerval,* 275–87.

44 See Jeanneret, *La lettre perdue,* 26–7. Said showed how frequently the accounts of the Orient given by nineteenth-century Europeans are only opportunities to express Western phantasms. See Edward Said, *Orientalism* (New York: Random House 1979). Said endorses (179–84) the frequently expressed opinion that Nerval, in spite of his personal agenda, confronted the real Orient more than most literary travellers; his book, he writes, breaks beyond the limits 'imposed by orthodox Orientalism.'

45 Milner, 'Religions et religion dans *Le voyage en Orient* de Gérard de Nerval,' 47.

46 See Schaeffer, *Le voyage en Orient de Nerval,* 64, 491. See also Malandain on the rise of a free voice in *Le voyage en Orient*: this voice 'represents,' 'enacts' the romantic (i.e., modern) subject, which assumes and mediates its subjectivity and its desire for reality through writing *Nerval ou l'incendie du théâtre,* 56.

47 'Quintus Aucler,' in *Les illuminés,* in *Oeuvres complètes,* vol. 2, 1157, 1159.

48 Ibid., 1119–26.
49 See Cellier, *Gérard de Nerval*, 108.
50 'Quintus Aucler,' in *Les illuminés*, in *Oeuvres complètes*, vol. 2, 1158, 1079, 1137.
51 Malandain, *Nerval ou l'incendie du théâtre*, 17–29.
52 'Jacques Cazotte,' in *Les illuminés*, in *Oeuvres complètes*, vol. 2, 1082.
53 'Les confidences de Nicolas,' in *Les illuminés*, in *Oeuvres complètes*, vol. 2, 1020–1. Restif was obliged to 'exhibit his soul' to earn his living.
54 Ibid., 1073–4.
55 'Jacques Cazotte,' in *Les illuminés*, in *Oeuvres complètes*, vol. 2, 1093–7. Nerval also quotes from a text, supposedly from 1763, that presents a vision of horror: a gruesome machine cuts bodies into pieces, while the victims remain alive and continue speaking (1097–9). The text may be a hoax by la Harpe; see the note on p. 297 in Nerval, *Oeuvres*, ed. Henri Lemaître (Paris: Garnier, 1986).
56 'Les confidences de Nicolas,' in *Les illuminés*, in *Oeuvres complètes*, vol. 2, 1074.
57 Ibid., 1074.
58 Raymond Jean, *Lectures du désir*, 39. See also his reading of the story in *La poétique du désir* (Paris: Seuil, 1975), 193–224.
   Octavie has been subjected to psychocritical readings that found the same network of obsessive images as in the sonnets in *Les chimères*. See Charles Maurron, *Des métaphores obsédantes au mythe personnel: Introduction à la psycho-critique* (Paris: Corti, 1980), 64–80. Maurron adds, 'the force of unconscious processes is so strong in Nerval, and their expression in dreams or delirium mirroring clear thought is so obvious, that we read this author as pyschocriticism would have us read all others' (p. 367).
59 See publication details in Nerval, *Oeuvres*, ed. Lemaître, 639, 641, and 827–31.
60 *Octavie*, in *Les filles du feu*, 183.
61 Marie-Jeanne Durry, *Gérard de Nerval et le mythe* (Paris: Flammarion, 1956), 67–70. Durry is, of course, referring to Nerval's literary work rather than to what he wrote to earn a living. His serious writing took up almost all of his time from 1850 on.
62 Nerval mentions this beginning in *Aurélia*, 256.
63 For an English version, see *Daughters of Fire: Sylvie, Emilie, Octavie*, trans. James Whitall (London: Heinemann, 1923).
64 *Octavie*, in *Les filles du feu*, 185.
65 Ibid., 185.
66 An echo of *Ruines* by Volney.

67 See Jeanneret, *La lettre perdue*, 68. The figure of Isis plays an important role in Nerval's work and should be placed in perspective. As Jurgis Baltrusaitis has shown, in *La quête d'Isis: Essai sur la légende d'un mythologie* (Paris: Flammarion, 1985), the 'Egyptian tale' blossomed and was spread under the aegis of scholarship. Its apologists found traces of the cult of Isis throughout Gaul and obstinately tried to prove that all cults stemmed from Egypt. Although Champollion's egyptology halted growth of the legend, the story did continue to circulate. Nerval distanced himself from this type of literature; here too, he refused to become a 'believer.'

68 *Sylvie*, in *Les filles de feu*, 111. Reality is threatening even when there is no question of a rival; the chapter on Restif in *Les illuminés* shows us young Nicolas's terror when the actress smiles at him off-stage; she lives and smiles 'an instant for him alone.' *Oeuvres complètes*, vol. 2, 949.

69 It is impossible in a summary to do justice to the complexity of the story's structure, the atmosphere created by the leaps in time, and the slowing down or acceleration of the passing of time. For a recent English version see *Selected Writings*, trans. Geoffrey Wagner (Ann Arbor, Mich.: Ann Arbor Paperbacks, 1970). The book contains *Sylvie*, *Aurélia*, and some poems.

70 *Sylvie* is the story of the stagnation of a subject enslaved by the self.

71 Malandain, *Nerval ou l'incendie du théâtre*, 65.

72 Kofman, *Nerval ou le charme de la répétition*, 81–90.

73 Malandain, *Nerval ou l'incendie du théâtre*, 147.

74 Jean, *Lectures du désir*, 20.

75 Léon Cellier, *De 'Sylvie' à 'Aurélia': Structure close et structure ouverte*, Archives des Lettres modernes, 131 (1978), 35–6.

76 Jean, *Lectures du désir*, 10–12.

77 For a history of the varying appreciation offered to Nerval's ocuvre, see Raymond Jean, *Nerval* (Paris: Seuil, 1964; repr. 1978), 5–13.

78 Cellier, ed., in *Promenades et souvenirs: Lettres à Jenny, Pandora, Aurélia* (Paris: Garnier-Flammarion, 1972), 26. See also Jean, *Nerval*, 109–21, and *La poétique du désir*, 253–303.

79 See Jacques Bony, introduction to *Aurélia*, 27.

80 In 1841 Nerval was treated by Dr Esprit Blanche. In 1853 he was under the care of Dr Emile Blanche, son of the former, who inherited his father's dossiers. The two doctors were in the line of the great French alienists who endeavoured to care humanely for the mentally ill. Esprit Blanche was a pupil of Philippe Pinel.

There are, of course, many steps between the notation of dreams and the construction of an autobiographical narrative. The form Nerval created hinges on subtle shifts between the I of the afflicted person and the I of the narrator.

81 *Aurélia*, 258.

82 'The fixing of fantasies in writing is a kind of magic execution of these monsters that seduce and destroy those who surrender to them. Writing is a sign of victory, the indication of a transfer of power, a passage from passivity to activity,' Kofman, *Nerval, le charme de la répétition*, 27.

83 *Aurélia*, 260.

84 Ibid., 270.

85 Ibid., 277.

86 Ibid., 281.

87 Ibid., 285.

88 Ibid., 287.

89 Malandain, *Nerval ou l'incendie du théâtre*, 166–7.

90 *Aurélia*, 295.

91 Ibid., 295–7.

92 Ibid., 302. Describing his discovery of the pleasures of imagination and of writing, Chateaubriand says that he stood at his window and pronounced an incantation meant to dominate the world (*Mémoires d'outre-tombe*, bk 3, chap. 13). His madness was purely literary and his observed behaviour never gave alarm to his friends. Nerval, however, was diagnosed as a 'theomaniac'; delusion about being a messiah coloured his sense of being a writer able to produce a 'great' book.

93 Ibid., 308.

94 Bowman clearly explains that the ending of *Aurélia* is political, as is, I would add, the ending of *Le voyage en Orient*. See Frank Paul Bowman, 'Mémorables d'*Aurélia*: signification et situation générique,' in *French Forum* 11–12, (May 1986), 169–181. Saturnin had been wounded in Algeria, in a war against Muslims. What was then called the Oriental question took the form of a confrontation between Russia (wishing to protect the Christians of the Orient) and Muslim Turkey (occupying the Holy Sites). The situation eventually led to the Crimean War. For Nerval, fraternity is the solution to 'both personal and political salvation' (p. 174).

 Along the same lines, Gaillard has shown that the dreams of *Aurélia* express the impossibility of living within a social structure, where space and culture are hermetic (Françoise Gaillard, 'Nerval ou les contradictions du romantisme').

95 *Aurélia*, 251.

96 'Géographie magique de Nerval,' in *Poésie et profondeur* (Paris: Seuil 1955), 85.

97 Callot, *Gerard de Nerval ou la dévotion à l'imaginaire*, 7, 80, 95–101.

98 Milner, 'Religions et religion dans *Le voyage en Orient* de G. de Nerval,' 50.

99 Malandain also notes that, in *Aurélia*, the relation of the narrator to the audience is maintained and reaffirmed right up to the end (*Nerval ou l'incendie du théâtre*, 178).

100 See Cellier, *De 'Sylvie' à 'Aurélia'*, 8.

101 Durry, *Gérard de Nerval et le mythe*, 61.

102 It was the 'esoteric' stories of *Le voyage en Orient* rather than the pleasant Parisian vignettes recounted in the first person that served as a model and enabled him to write himself. Ibid., 126.

103 See Gaillard, 'Nerval, ou les contradictions du romantisme,' 129. I would agree with Gaillard that in *Aurélia* Nerval clearly breaks with esoteric or romantic 'revelations' that offer irrationalism as the only answer that contrasts with the rationalism of the world.

104 *Le voyage en Orient* is 'the impossible book, the one that would reconcile all partners in the conflict,' writes Schaeffer in *Une double lecture de G. de Nerval: Les illuminés et Les filles du feu* (Neuchâtel: Baconnière, 1977), 15.

105 Jeanneret, *La lettre perdue*, 203. As I have consistently shown, affirmations of esoteric belief are always qualified in the text.

106 Malandain, *Nerval ou l'incendie du théâtre*, 154. See also 175–6 for comments on the doubles in *Aurélia*.

107 Chateaubriand and Vigny suffered the loss of a world, but were not deprived of the memory of their first years. Nerval tried in vain to spread over his life the enchantment of a lost childhood. See Yves Vadé, *L'enchantement littéraire: Ecriture et magie de Chateaubriand à Rimbaud* (Paris: Gallimard, 1990), 160, 174. Nostalgia presupposes that the lost object was once possessed. For Nerval's account of his childhood, see 'Juvenalia,' in *Promenades et souvenirs*, in *Aurélia*, 225–7.

108 See the dream of the trial ('Autre rêve' in *Les nuits d'octobre*) for his anxiety about his status as a writer; in this nightmare, impressive figures, none less than professors at the Sorbonne, accuse him of being '*fantaisiste*! realist!! essayist!!!', all capital crimes; *Aurélia*, 117.

109 'In country as in literature I belong to France and the French tradition,' manuscript note, quoted by Lemaître in his edition of *Oeuvres*, 761. See also the preface to *Choix de poésies allemandes* (1830): 'the French imagination is governed by individuals, while the German one governs individuals and their will,' quoted by Cellier in *Gérard de Nerval*, 25–6.

110 *Aurélia*, 257.

111 *Aurélia*, 160–2.

112 *Promenades et souvenirs*, in *Aurélia*, 224.

113 Yet Nerval wanted to be clear; he informs us that *Les chimères*, his most impenetrable text, is no more obscure than the metaphysics of Hegel or *Les mémorables* of Swedenborg ('Lettre à Alexandre Dumas,' preface to *Les filles du feu*, ed. Cellier, 30).

114 Schaeffer, *Le voyage en Orient de Nerval*, 504.

115 In fact, as Edward Said has shown in *Orientalism*, the 'objective' knowledge amassed by this kind of orientalist serves to legitimate colonizing invasion and exploitation by allegedly 'more developed' Europeans.

116 Milner points out the work's merits: 'In *Le voyage en Orient*, Nerval does not, like Benjamin Constant in *De la religion*, present his questions as philosophical and historical inquiries. Neither, like Ballanche, Quinet, or Lamartine, does he present them as mythic constructions able to sum up the history of humanity. Instead they are a series of existential experiences.' See 'Religions et religion dans *Le voyage en Orient* de Gérard de Nerval,' 41. Schaeffer observes that *Le voyage en Orient* ends with a 'creative synthesis, a source of great modern adventures, without renouncing the banalities of daily life, which are henceforth interwoven with the fantastic' (*Le voyage en Orient de Nerval*, 504).

117 Georges Poulet, 'Sylvie ou la pensée de Nerval,' in *Trois essais de mythologie romantique* (Paris: Corti, 1985), 78.

118 Jeanneret, *La lettre perdue*, 95.

119 According to Malandain, the power of Nerval's imaginary world has excluded 'more than in anyone else the experience of learning rules of social behaviour as a principle of reality.' At worst, this power leads the subject to deny all the merits of group codes and causes it to be swept into 'the narcissistic contemplation induced by the choice of object-image.' It should also be noted that this narcissistic contemplation in the individual theatre leaves the social theatre intact, thus playing into the hands of the controlling forces. Inside the intimate circle of narcissism, speech also remains within the exclusively self-perpetuating ideological universes (*Nerval ou l'incendie du théâtre*, 13, 92, 125, 150). The last – and most atrocious – of the nightmares in *Aurélia* (*Aurélia*, 307–8) is of the 'vast charnel house,' which depicts universal history in the bloody colours of the history of terror.

120 Malandain, *Nerval ou l'incendie du théâtre*, 102.

121 Jeanneret, *La lettre perdue*, 205, 212. In Nerval's work there is no exit from the text, no public engagement as in Kierkegaard, who published *Attack on Christendom* during the last months of his life. We must, however, recognize that there is a new text: the novel of initiation has become a religious confession. The idea of repetition also suggests a possible comparison between these two Romantics.

122 *Aurélia*, 262.

123 Ibid., 283.

124 See F.P. Bowman, 'Le statut littéraire de l'autobiographie spirituelle,' in *Le statut de la littérature: Mélanges offerts à Paul Bénichou*, ed. Marc Fumaroli (Genève: Droz, 1976), 317.

125 *Aurélia*, 293.

126 As Jeanneret says, 'It could prove that faith and language are only autonomous systems after all, and that signs operate like many of the other conventions of the mind' (*La lettre perdue*, 223). The subject writing *Aurélia* involves himself in a language and a faith; that is all. Success is not attained by choosing 'true' language, but by choosing a language that allows the subject to be involved.

127 Emile Blanche was convinced that shifting to the notion of a male God was a helpful step toward Nerval's cure.

128 Manuscript note, quoted by Lemaître in his edition of *Oeuvres*, 681. Since there are many women in *Le voyage en Orient*, the pictures of women (veiled and unveiled) on the covers of the two volumes of the Garnier-Flammarion edition are highly appropriate.

129 Stéphane Michaud, *Muse et madone: Visages de la femme de la Révolution française aux apparitions de Lourdes* (Paris: Seuil, 1985), 175.

130 Kofman, *Nerval, le charme de la répétition*, 52, 122, 113.

131 *Aurélia*, 299.

132 Ibid.

133 Ibid., 314.

134 Ibid., 284.

135 Malandain writes that in Nerval, the subject simultaneously has access to spiritual secrets and accepts the forms of these secrets as seductive and deceiving. 'What produces the division is the idea that a continuous movement of desire – deficiency, deception, achievement, desire – leads to the literary discovery of a living world. Today this idea still offers models to modernity for reflecting on, and even perhaps for remedying, its own inadequacies. The tension towards the *elsewhere* is substituted for the hope of a univocal, naïve definition of the powers of the subject and of his writing, a definition which is, in the end, reductionistic, because unrealistic' (*Nerval ou l'incendie du théâtre*, 56; translation by the author).

136 Durry, *Nerval et le mythe*, 50.

137 Letter to Alexandre Dumas, quoted in the preface to *Les filles du feu*, ed. Cellier, 24.

138 Julia Kristeva, *Soleil noir: Dépression et mélancolie* (Paris: Gallimard, 1987), 181.

139 See Jeanneret, *La lettre perdue*, 86.

CONCLUSION

1 *Confessions*, bk 8; I: 392.
2 *Confessions*, bk 17; I: 580.
3 See the list in Marie-Helène Cotoni, 'Voltaire, Rousseau, Diderot,' in Yvon Belaval and Dominique Sourel, eds., *Le siècle des lumières et la Bible* (Paris: Beauchesne 1986), 779–803.
4 *Emile*, in *Oeuvres complètes* IV: 625–6.
5 *Oeuvres complètes* III: 768.
6 On 'the religion of the Gospel' see Pierre Burgelin, *Jean-Jacques Rousseau et la religion de Genève* (Genève: Labor et Fides, 1962), 36–43. Cotoni cites a passage in which Rousseau refers to his own *Emile* as a book 'full of sweetness and peace' in terms which he usually employs to describe the Gospel. She also shows that he remembers biblical expressions on the sufferings of Christ when he wishes to describe his own. *Le siècle des lumières et la Bible*, 794.
7 *Emile*, in *Oeuvres complètes* IV: 415.
8 Is it significant that none of the books on Rousseau's religion includes a chapter on the Bible? See P. Burgelin cited in n6, Pierre Maurice Masson, *La religion de Jean-Jacques Rousseau* (Genève: Slatkine, 1970), and Christian Jaquet, *Le pensée religieuse de Jean-Jacques Rousseau* (Louvain: Bibliothèque de l'Université, 1975).
9 *Atala. René. Le dernier Abencérage* (Paris: Garnier, 1962), 6.
10 *Le génie du christianisme*, pt 2, 785–6.
11 Ibid., 761–86.
12 Ibid., 940–5.
13 A letter cited in Paul Bénichou, *Le sacre de l'écrivain* (Paris: Corti, 1973), 210.
14 Chateaubriand includes the Bible in such a list in *Génie* (761) but argues for its literary singularity. His pages on the Trinity (Ibid., 474–7) find evidence of the triune god in numerous ancient Scriptures. Later on however, he abstained from all such allusions; as knowledge of these Scriptures grew, he, unlike many others, stopped venturing on this ground and became a modest occidentalist.
15 'De quelques phénomènes du sommeil,' (1831) in *Rêveries*, (Paris: Plasma, 1979), 114.
16 Vera A. Summers, *L'orientalisme d'Alfred de Vigny* (Paris: Slatkine, 1976), chap. 1.
17 Such misogyny is not rare among Romantics, who oscillated between exaltation and denigration of the second sex. Bénichou has the right quip

on Vigny, he needed women too much not to hate them (see *Les mages romantiques*), 249.

18 Ibid., 192.

19 'The Old & New Testaments are the Great Code of Art' (Blake, in the margins of *The Laocoon*). This line provided Northrop Frye with one of his most famous titles, *The Great Code: The Bible and Literature* (New York and London: Harcourt Brace Jovanovich, 1982).

20 See, the conclusion, 'Anthologies of Desire,' in Thomas M. Kavanagh, *Writing the Truth: Authority and Desire* (Berkeley: University of California Press, 1987), 187–9.

21 Leo Strauss, *Persecution and the Art of Writing* (Westport Conn.: Greenwood Press 1959, repr. 1973), examining the works of medieval Jewish authors and of Spinoza remains an excellent introduction to the general issues.

22 See H.J. Hunt, *The Epic in Nineteenth-Century France* (Oxford: Blackwell, 1941).

23 Ernest Renan, *L'avenir de la science* (1848) (Paris: Calmann-Levy, 1890), chap. 2.

24 See the preface Roland Barthes wrote (1965) for the 10x18 edition, reprinted in *Le degré zéro de l'écriture* (Paris: Seuil, 1972).

25 'Du fantastique en littérature,' in *Rêveries*, 80.

26 *Les illuminés* in *Oeuvres complètes*, vol 2, 1074–5.

27 Gérald Schaffer, *Une double lecture de Gérard de Nerval: Les illuminés et Les filles du feu* (Neuchâtel: Baconnière, 1977), 24.

28 Michel Butor, 'Le voyage et l'écriture,' *Romantisme* 4 (1972), 17.

29 Chateaubriand was not just after sacred and historical sites: he cut short his stay in Jerusalem to make sure he arrived in time in Algesiras, Spain, where he had an appointment with Anne de Noailles. He did not plant any clues in the text to enable the reader to sense this secondary motif in the journey. He admitted it in a page of *Les Mémoires d'outre-tombe* (which disappeared from the final version) (see vol. 2, 1006–8). In contrast, Nerval opens his *Voyage en Orient* with chatter about love affairs. He too stays somewhat off the mark of perfect veracity: instead of erasing the record, he magnifies it.

30 See publication details in *Oeuvres*, ed. Lemaître, 504.

31 See the article by Raymond Mahieu, 'Ecrire en 1850: Angélique de Nerval,' in Graziella Pagliano and Antonio Gomez-Moriana, ed., *Ecrire en France au XIXe siècle* (Longueuil, Qué.: Editions du Préambule, 1989), 145–55.

32 Walter Moser, *Romantisme et crise de la modernité: Poésie et encyclopédie dans la 'Brouillon' de Novalis* (Longueuil, Qué.: Editions du Préambule, 1989) opens his study with a chapter on the rise of the fragment as literary form

in the romantic era: readers ordinarily forget the processes that produce texts except in the case of fragments (21).

33 Moser, *Romantisme et crise de la modernité*, 439.

34 Alexandre Vinet, *Philosophie morale et sociale*, vol. 2, (Lausanne: Bridel, 1916), 114–200. See also Bernard Reymond, *A la redécouverte d'Alexandre Vinet* (Lausanne: l'Age d'homme, 1990), 122–130.

35 Journal X4 A 185, 9 March 1851, in S. Kierkegaard, *Armed Neutrality* (New York: Simon and Shuster, 1969), 117.

36 Here are some of Nodier's titles: *Dictionnaire des onomatopées* (1808), *Essai sur la philosophie des langues, ou Théorie de l'alphabet naturel* (1822), *Notions élémentaires de linguistique ou Histoire abrégée de la parole et de l'écriture* (1834). This last was reviewed by Eckstein in *Journal de l'Institut historique* 1 (1834–5).

37 See the 'Présentation' by Max Milner, introducing the collection of articles on insanity and romantic writers in *Romantisme* 24 (1979), 3–5. Many Romantics are preoccupied with the problem of insanity because they see links between these phenomena and their own enigmatic relationship to language.

38 Paul Valéry, *Cahiers* (Paris: Editions CNRS, 1958), vol. 6, 108.

39 Rousseau makes very significant departures: he does not attempt to instruct his reader in any doctrine or wisdom, but he still tries to persuade – with his sincerity, rather than with the merits of any of his views. He is not Mentor showing anyone how to live, but Orpheus appealing to others with his unique sound. See Jean Terrasse, *De Mentor à Orphée: Essais sur les écrits pédagogiques de Rousseau* (Montréal: Hurtubise/HMH, 1992).

40 Already in the eighteenth century, Lessing's famous formula about the possession of truth being reserved to God while the endless pursuit of truth is the lot of man began shifting attention from the content of belief to the form of it. See *Lessing's Theological Writings*, ed. Owen Chadwick (Stanford University Press, 1957), 43.

41 Yves Vadé, *L'enchantement littéraire* (Paris: Gallimard, 1990), 96.

42 Ibid., 87, 463. Chateaubriand is clearly in the camp of those who do not believe at all. Likewise Vigny; but in his days the scientific method was walking a more definite and assured path.

43 Ibid., 194, 266, 472.

44 The illusion was first spread by the great sophists. But, as Jacques Derrida has pointed out, ('Mythologie blanche,' in *Marges* [Paris: Editions de Minuit, 1972], 227–324) even the most 'abstract' philosophers remain in the grip of metaphors.

45 Roland Barthes, 'Ecrivains et écrivants,' in *Essais critiques* (Paris: Seuil, 1964), 147–154.

46 Vadé, *L'enchantement littéraire*, 346–68.

47 F.P. Bowman, 'Illuminism, Utopia and Mythology,' in *The French Romantics*, vol. 1, 79.

48 W. Moser, *Romantisme et crise de la modernité*, 271.

49 Moser shows how Novalis undertakes a romantic chemistry; he demonstrates that when Novalis defines, he posits another state of affairs; he reinvents the world, by virtue of his discourse; see *Romantisme et crise de la modernité*, 327–34.

50 See Donald R. Kelley, *Foundations of Modern Historical Scholarship: Language, Law and History in the French Renaissance* (New York: Columbia University Press, 1970).

51 Moser, *Romantisme et crise de la modernité*, 83.

52 See P. Lacoue-Labarthe and J.L. Nancy, *L'absolu littéraire: Théorie de la littérature du romantisme allemand* (Paris: Seuil, 1978).

53 *Logic*, no. 212.

54 'Le livre, instrument spirituel,' in Mallarmé, *Oeuvres complètes* (Paris: Gallimard, 1945), 378. See also Maurice Blanchot, *Le livre à venir* (1959; Paris: Gallimard, 1971), 326–58.

55 'Jamais un coup de dé n'abolira le hasard,' in 'Un coup de dé,' in *Oeuvres complètes*, 457–77. See also Blanchot, *Le livre à venir*, 358.

56 'L'Or,' in Mallarmé, *Oeuvres complètes*, 398–9. See Vadé, *L'enchantement littéraire*, 87.

57 'De quelques phénomènes du sommeil,' in *Rêveries*, 127.

58 See Mark Taylor, *Erring: A Postmodern A/theology* (University of Chicago Press, 1984), 7, 15, 87, 76. Narrativity establishes identity for God-self-history-books.

59 'Igitur,' in *Oeuvres complètes*, 433

60 'On est détrompé sans avoir joui, il reste encore des désirs et l'on n'a plus d'illusions,' in *Le génie du christianisme*, pt 2, bk 3, chap. 9, 714.

61 Letter to Moultou, June 7 1762; *Correspondance complète*, vol. 11, 36.

62 *Les martyrs*, in *Oeuvres romanesques et voyages* (Paris: Gallimard, 1969), vol. 2, 115–16.

63 John Coulson, *Religion and Imagination: In Aid of a Grammar of Assent* (Oxford: Clarendon Press, 1981), 32.

64 Ibid., 61.

65 Ibid., 80.

66 'In France,' declared Stendhal, 'everything is uncertain.' Pierre Barbéris

correctly interprets: nothing is really defined in the new France; the USA is a democracy; the UK has a solid constitutional tradition, and the powers of the Holy Alliance (Russia, Austria, Prussia) are confident despotisms. See Pierre Barbéris, *Sur Stendhal* (Paris: Messidor/Editions Sociales, 1982), 19.

67 Montesquieu is the great theoretician of the need for art in daily life. See Starobinski, *Le remède est dans le mal* (Paris: Gallimard, 1989).

68 See Jean-Yves Guiomar, *La nation entre l'histoire et la raison* (Paris: La Découverte, 1990), 175–90.

69 Heinrich Heine, *De la France* (Paris/Genève: Slatkine, 1980), 340.

70 Ibid., 180.

71 See also the observations of Louis Dumont on France being the nation of consensus in 'Religion, Politics and Society in the Individualistic Universe,' in *Proceedings of the Royal Anthropological Institute for 1970* (London: 1971).

72 *Stello; Daphné*, 358.

73 Frank Paul Bowman, *Le discours sur l'éloquence sacrée à l'époque romantique* (Genève: Droz, 1980).

74 See Stephen Prickett, *Romanticism and Religion: The Tradition of Coleridge and Wordsworth in the Victorian Church* (Cambridge University Press, 1976).

75 See Michel Baude and Marc-Matthieu Münch, eds., *Romantisme et religion: Théologie des théologiens et théologie des écrivains* (Paris: PUF, 1980). The distinction made in the subtitle is highly appropriate but the articles unfortunately do not include an examination of literary forms.

76 See Michel de Certeau, *La faiblesse de croire* (Paris: Seuil, 1987), chap. 10 and 11.

77 F.P. Bowman, *Le Christ des barricades: 1789–1848* (Paris: Cerf, 1987), 112.

78 F.P. Bowman, *Le Christ romantique* (Genèva: Droz, 1973), 273.

79 Flaubert held an enormous grudge against the socialists on the grounds that they believed in magic: they tried to change the world by uttering the right formulas.

80 Pierre-Simon Ballanche, *Le vieillard et le jeune homme* (Paris: Alcan, 1929), 139.

81 Victor Hugo, 'Séance des cinq associations d'art et d'industrie,' in *Actes et paroles I; Oeuvres complètes*, vol. 10, *Politique* (Paris: Laffont, 1985), 158.

82 Quoted in D.G. Charlton, *The French Romantics*, vol. 1, 62.

83 *Mémoires d'outre-tombe*, vol. 1, 929.

84 *Brouillon*, no. 433; quoted in W. Moser, *Romantisme et crise de la modernité*, 368.

85 These are the titles of chapters 5 and 6 (Stanford, Calif.: Stanford University Press 1965).

86 'Fragments politiques,' in *Oeuvres complètes* (Paris: Gallimard, 1964), III: 511.

87 See Serge Moscovici, *La machine à faire des dieux* (Paris: Fayard, 1988), 431.

88 *Stello; Daphné*, 191.

89 'la vie affective ... et la sensibilité intellectuelle,' in *Oeuvres* (Paris: Gallimard, 1957), vol. 1, 611.

90 Madame de Stael, *Essai sur les fictions* (1795) (Paris: Ramsay, 1979), 43, 51.

91 See Michel Crouzet, *Le naturel, la grâce et le réel dans la poétique de Stendhal: Essai sur la genèse du romantisme* (Paris: Flammarion, 1986), 9–10.

92 Jay Caplan showed in detail how Diderot wrote novels designed to maintain in readers both detachment from the lives of fellow human beings and identification with them; see his *Framed Narratives: Diderot's Genealogy of the Beholder* (Minneapolis: University of Minnesota Press, 1985). In his afterword (97–115) Jochen Schulte-Sasse argues that the modern sort of literature (as aesthetic subsystem) has value because it offers a medium for reconciliation and nurtures the tension between the desire for unity and the impossibility of realizing it.

For the linkages between aesthetic and practical interests, see 'Reading for Life' in Martha Nussbaum, *Love's Knowledge: Essays on Philosophy and Literature* (New York and Oxford: Oxford University Press, 1990) 230–44.

93 Clifford Geertz, *The Interpretation of Cultures* (New York: Basic Books, 1973), 10.

94 See Peter Sloterdijk, *Thinker on Stage: Nietzsche's Materialism* (University of Minnesota Press, 1989).

95 Vadé, *L'enchantement littéraire*, 30.

96 F.P. Bowman's list of five great 'apologetic' novels of the 1830s adds Sainte-Beuve's *Volupté* and Guttinguer's *Arthur* to Balzac's three.

97 *Aurélia*, 291.

98 The nineteenth-century rise of both doctrines is examined simultaneously in Jaroslav Pelikan, *Christian Doctrine and Modern Culture*, vol. 5 of *The Christian Tradition* (University of Chicago Press, 1989), 241–52.

Works Cited

PRIMARY SOURCES

Chateaubriand, François René. *Atala and René*. Trans. Rayner Heppenstall with Intro. Robert Baldick. London: Oxford University Press, 1963.
- *Atala. René. Le dernier Atencérage*. Paris: Garnier, 1962.
- *Chateaubriand politique*. Ed. Jean-Paul Clément. Paris: Hachette, 1987.
- *Essai sur les révolutions: Le génie du christianisme* (1797, 1802). Ed. Maurice Regard. Paris: Gallimard, 1978.
- *Etudes historiques* (1830). Paris: Garnier, n.d.
- *Genius of Christianity*. Trans. Charles I. White. Baltimore: John Murphy, 1856.
- *Itinéraire de Paris à Jerusalem*. Paris: Garnier-Flammarion, 1968.
- *Les martyrs*. In *Oeuvres romanesques et voyages*. Paris: Gallimard, 1969.
- *Mémoires d'outre-tombe* (1848). Ed. Maurice Levaillant and Georges Moulinier. 2 vols. Paris: Gallimard, 1951.
- *Memoirs of Chateaubriand*. Selected, trans. and intro. Robert Baldick. London: H. Hamilton, 1961.
- *Les natchez* (1826). In *Oeuvres romanesques et voyages*. Paris: Gallimard, 1969.
- *La vie de Rancé* (1845). Paris: Garnier-Flammarion, 1969.

Nerval, Gérard de. *Aurélia et autres textes autobiographiques*. Ed. Jacques Bony. Paris: Garnier-Flammarion, 1990.
- *Daughters of Fire: Sylvie, Emilie, Octavie*. Trans. James Whitall London: Heinemann, 1923.
- *Les filles du feu: Les chimères*. Ed. Léon Cellier. Paris: Garnier-Flammarion, 1965.
- *Journey to the Orient*. Selections ed. and trans. Norman Glass. New York: New York University Press, 1972.

– *Oeuvres*. Ed. Henri Lemaître. Paris: Garnier, 1986.
– *Oeuvres complètes*. Ed. Jean Guillaume and Claude Pichois. Vol. 2. Paris: Gallimard, 1984.
– *Promenades et souvenirs: Lettres à Jenny. Pandora. Aurélia*. Ed. Léon Cellier. Paris: Garnier-Flammarion, 1972.
– *Selected Writings*. Trans. Geoffrey Wagner. Ann Arbor, Mich.: Ann Arbor Paperbacks, 1970.
– *Le Voyage en Orient*. Ed. Michele Jeanneret. Paris: Garnier-Flammarion, 1980.

Nodier, Charles. *L'amateur de livres*. Intro. Jean-Luc Steinmetz. Bordeaux: Le Castor Astral, 1993.
– *Contes*. Ed. Pierre-Georges Castex. Paris:Garnier, 1987; rev. 1987.
– *Correspondance inédite*. Ed. A. Estignard. Genève: Slatkine, 1973.
– *Critiques de l'imprimerie*. Texts selected and intro. Didier Barrière. Paris: Editions des cendres, 1989.
– *Histoire du roi de Bohême*. Paris: Plasma, 1979.
– *Jean Sbogar*. Paris: Editions France-Empire, 1980.
– *Moi-même*. Intro. Daniel Sangsue. Paris: Corti, 1985.
– *Portraits de la Révolution et de l'Empire*. Ed. Jean-Luc Steinmetz. 2 vols. Paris: Tallandier, 1988.
– *Smarra, Trilby et autres contes*. Preface, bibliography, and notes Jean-Luc Steinmetz. Paris: Garnier-Flammarion, 1980.
– *Souvenirs de jeunesse: Mademoiselle de Marsan*. Intro. Hubert Juin. Paris: Aubier, 1992.

Rousseau, Jean-Jacques. *Correspondance complète*. Ed. R.A. Leigh. Oxford: The Voltaire Foundation at the Taylor Institution, 1964 – .
– *Lettre à d'Alembert*. Paris: Garnier-Flammarion, 1967.
– *Oeuvres complètes*. Vol. I. Paris: Gallimard, 1959.
– *Oeuvres complètes*. Vol. II. Paris: Gallimard, 1964.
– *Oeuvres complètes*. Vol. III. Paris: Gallimard, 1964.
– *Oeuvres complètes*. Vol. IV. Paris: Gallimard, 1969.
Rousseau/Malesherbes. *Correspondance*. Preface and notes Barbara de Negroni. Paris: Flammarion, 1991.

Vigny, Alfred de. *Chatterton*. (1835). Paris: Garnier-Flammarion, 1968.
– *The Military Condition*. Trans. Marguerite Barnett. Oxford University Press, 1964.
– *Oeuvres complètes*. Ed. F. Baldensberger. 2 vols. Paris: Gallimard, 1948.
– *Servitude et grandeur militaires*. Ed. François Germain. Paris: Garnier, 1965.

- *Stello*. Ed. Marc Eigeldinger. Paris: Garnier-Flammarion, 1985.
- *Stello; Daphné*. Ed François Germain. Paris: Garnier, 1970.
- *Stello: A Session with Doctor Noir*. Trans. Irving Massey, with intro. and notes. Montréal: McGill-Queen's University Press, 1963.

Abbadie, Jacques. *Traité de la vérité de la religion chrétienne*. 3 vols. Amsterdam: 1684.
Arnold, Matthew. 'Equality.' in *Mixed Essays* (1879). Reprinted in vol. 8 of *Complete Prose Works*. Ann Arbor: University of Michigan Press, 1972.
Ballanche, Pierre-Simon. *Le vieillard et le jeune homme*. Paris: Alcan 1929.
Balzac. *L'illustre Gaudissart: La muse du Département*. Paris: Garnier, 1970.
Bayle. *Pensées diverses* (1683). Rotterdam: Reinier Leers, 1704.
Constant, Benjamin. *De la liberté chez les modernes*. Paris: Livre de Poche, 1980.
- *Du polythéisme romain, considéré dans ses rapports avec la philosophie grecque et la religion chrétienne*. Paris: Béchet âiné, 1832.
de Stael, Germaine. *Essai sur les fictions* (1795). Paris: Ramsay, 1979.
de Tocqueville, Alexis. *De la démocratie en Amérique*. 2 vols. Paris: Garnier-Flammarion, 1981.
Dinouart, abbé. *L'art de se taire* (1771). Preface Jean-Jacques Courtine and Claudine Haroche. Paris: Jérôme Millon, 1987.
Guizot, François. *Histoire de la civilisation en Europe*. Paris: Hachette, 1985.
Heine, Heinrich. *De la France*. Paris/Genève: Slatkine, 1980.
Hoelderlin. 'Rousseau.' In *Oeuvres*. Paris: Gallimard, 1967.
Hugo, Victor. *Océan-tas de pierres*. Paris: Albin Michel, 1942.
- 'Séance des cinq associations d'art et d'industrie.' In *Actes et paroles* 1. *Oeuvres complètes*. Vol. 10, *Politique*. Paris: Laffont, 1985.
Hugo, Victor, and Charles Nodier. *Correspondance croisée de Victor Hugo et Charles Nodier*. Ed. Jacques Rémi-Dahan. Bassac: Plein Chant, 1987.
Joubert, Joseph. *Carnets*. 2 vols. Paris: Gallimard, 1938.
- *Pensées*. Ed. Georges Poulet. Paris: Union générale d'éditions, 1966.
Kant, Immanuel. *On History*. Ed. L.W. Beck. New York: Bobbs-Merrill, 1963.
Kierkegaard, Soren. *Armed Neutrality and An Open Letter*. Eds. and transls. Howard V. Hong and Edna H. Hong. New York: Simon and Shuster, 1968.
- *Stages on Life's Way*. Trans. W. Lowrie. Princeton University Press, 1940.
- *Training in Christianity*. Trans. W. Lowrie. Princeton University Press, 1967.
Lessing, G. E. *Lessing's Theological Writings*. Ed. Owen Chadwick. Stanford University Press, 1957.
Mallarmé. *Oeuvres complètes*. Eds. H. Mondor and G. Jean Aubry. Paris: Gallimard, 1945.
Montaigne. *Essais*. In *Oeuvres complètes*. Ed. M. Rat. Paris: Gallimard, 1962.

Pascal. *Lettres provinciales*. In *Oeuvres complètes*. Ed. J. Chevalier. Paris: Gallimard, 1954.

– *Pensées*. In *Oeuvres complètes*. Ed. J. Chevalier. Paris: Gallimard, 1954.

Quinet, Edgar. *La Révolution* (1865). Preface by Claude Lefort. Repr. Paris: Belin, 1987.

Renan, Ernest. *L'Avenir de la science* (1848). Paris: Calmann-Levy, 1890.

– *Souvenirs d'enfance et de jeunesse*. Paris: Livre de Poche, 1967.

Saint-Just. *Oeuvres choisies*. Paris: Gallimard, 1968.

Saint-Martin. *L'homme de désir*. Intro. Robert Amadou. Monaco: Editions du Rocher, 1979.

Sainte-Beuve. *Chateaubriand et son groupe littéraire* (1849). 2nd ed. Paris: Lévy, 1872)

– *Oeuvres*. 2 vols. Paris: Gallimard, 1951.

Stendhal. *Mémoires d'un touriste*. 3 vols. Paris: Maspéro 1981.

– *Voyages en Italie*. Paris: Gallimard, 1973. ed. Paris: Lévy 1872), vol.1.

Vinet, Alexandre. *Philosophie morale et sociale*. 2 vols. Lausanne: Bridel, 1916.

SECONDARY SOURCES

Abrams, M.K. *The Mirror and the Lamp*. New York: Norton, 1958.

– *Natural Supernaturalism: Tradition and Revolution in Romantic Literature*. New York: Norton, 1971.

Baczko, Bronislav. *Rousseau: Solitude et communauté*. Paris: Mouton, 1974.

Baltrusaitis, Jurgis. *La quête d'Isis: Essai sur la légende d'un mythologię*. Paris: Flammarion, 1985.

Bann, Stephen. 'Romanticism in France.' In *Romanticism in National Context*. Eds. Roy Porter and Mikulas Teich, 240–59. Cambridge University Press, 1988.

Barbéris, Pierre. *Balzac et le mal du siècle*. Vol. 2, 1830–3. *Une expérience de l'absurde: de la prise de conscience à l'expression*. Paris: Gallimard, 1971.

– *Chateaubriand: Une réaction au monde moderne*. Paris: Larousse, 1976.

– *A la recherche d'une écriture*. Paris: Mame, 1974.

– *René de Chateaubriand: Un nouveau roman*. Paris: Larousse, 1973.

– *Sur Stendhal*. Paris: Messidor/Editions Sociales, 1982.

Barguillet, Françoise. *Rousseau ou l'illusion passionnée: Les rêveries du promeneur solitaire*. Paris: PUF, 1991.

Bartfeld, Fernande. 'Le lecteur de Stello comme malade ou bourreau.' *Romantisme* 23 (1979): 55–63.

Barrière, Didier. *Nodier l'homme du livre: Le rôle de la bibliophilie dans la littérature*. Bassac: Plein Chant, 1989.

Barth, K. *Protestant Theology in the 19th Century*. London: SCM Press, 1972.

Barthes, Roland. 'Ecrivains et écrivants.' In *Essais critiques*. Paris: Seuil, 1964.
− *Le degré zéro de l'écriture*. Paris: Seuil, 1972.
− *Le plaisir du texte*. Paris: Seuil 1973.
Bastide, Roger. *Art et société*. Paris: Payot, 1977.
Bataille, George. *L'expérience intérieure*. Paris: Gallimard, 1954.
Baude, Michel and Marc-Matthieu Münch, eds. *Romantisme et religion: Théologie des théologiens et théologie des écrivains*. Paris: PUF, 1980.
Bédouelle, Guy and Roussel Bernard, eds. *Les temps des réformes et la Bible*. Paris: Beauchesne, 1989.
Bénichou, Paul. 'Jean-Jacques Rousseau: De la personne à la doctrine.' In *L'écrivain et ses travaux*. Paris: Corti, 1967.
− *Les mages romantiques*. Paris: Gallimard, 1988.
− *Le sacre de l'écrivain: Essai sur l'avènement d'un pouvoir spirituel laïque dans la France moderne*. Paris: Corti, 1973.
− *Les temps des prophètes*. Paris: Gallimard, 1977.
Binion, R. 'Notes on Romanticism.' *Journal of Psychohistory* 11, no. 1 (Summer 1983): 43–64.
Blanchot, Maurice. 'Jean-Jacques et la littérature.' *Nouvelle Revue française* (June 1958): 1057–66.
Bloom, Allan. 'The Education of Democratic Man: Emile.' In *Daedalus* (1978): 135–43. Reprinted in *Jean-Jacques Rousseau*. Ed. and intro. Harold Bloom. New York: Chelsea House, 1988.
Bonnefoy, G. *La pensée religieuse et morale d'Alfred de Vigny*. Paris: Belles-Lettres, 1927.
Bony, Jacques. 'Nerval et la peinture italienne.' In *L'imaginaire nervalien: l'espace de l'Italie*. Ed. Monique Streiff Moretti. Naples: ESI, 1988.
Boss, R.I. 'Rousseau's Civil Religion and the Meaning of Belief: An Answer to Bayle's Paradox.' *Studies on Voltaire and the 18th Century* 84 (1971).
Bowman, Frank Paul. *Le Christ des barricades 1789–1848*. Paris: Cerf, 1987.
− *Le Christ romantique*. Genève: Droz, 1973.
− *Le discours sur l'éloquence sacrée à l'epoque romantique*. Genève: Droz, 1980.
− *French Romanticism: Intertextual and Interdisciplinary Readings*. Baltimore: The Johns Hopkins University Press, 1990.
− 'Illuminism, Utopia and Mythology.' in *The French Romantics*. Ed. D.G. Charlton. Vol. 1. Cambridge University Press, 1984.
− 'Une lecture politique de la folie religieuse ou "théomanie."' *Romantisme* 24 (1979): 75–87.
− 'Mémorables d'*Aurélia*: signification et situation générique.' *French Forum* 11–12 (May 1986): 169–181.
− 'Religion, Politics and Utopia in French Romanticism.' *Australian Journal of French Studies* 13:3 (1974): 307–24.

- 'A Romantic View of the Hellenist Past: Vigny's *Daphné*.' In W.G. Langlois. *The Persistent Voice*. New York University Press, 1971.

Burgelin, Pierre. *La philosophie de l'existence de Jean-Jacques Rousseau*. Paris: PUF, 1952.

Butor, Michel. 'Le voyage et l'écriture.' *Romantisme* 4 (1972): 4–19.

Cantor, Paul A. *Creature and Creator: Myth-making and English Romanticism*. Cambridge University Press, 1984.

Caplan, Jay. *Framed Narratives: Diderot's Genealogy of the Beholder*. Afterward by Jochen Schulte-Sasse. Minneapolis: University of Minnesota Press, 1985.

Carle, Michel. *Du citoyen à l'artiste: Gérard de Nerval et ses premiers écrits*. Les Presses de l'Université d'Ottawa, 1992.

Cassirer, Ernst. 'Kant and Rousseau.' In *Rousseau, Kant and Goethe*. New York: Harper and Row, 1963.

Castex, George. 'Nodier et l'école du désenchantement.' In *Horizons romantiques*. Paris: Corti, 1983.

Cellier, Léon. *Gérard de Nerval*. 3rd ed. Paris: Hatier, 1974.

- 'Présence de Saint-Martin,' and 'Chateaubriand et Saint-Martin.' In *Parcours initiatiques*. Neuchâtel: Baconnière, 1977.

- De 'Sylvie' à 'Aurélia': Structure close et structure ouverte. Archives des Lettres modernes, 131 (Paris, 1978).

Charlton, D.G., ed. *The French Romantics*. 2 vols. Cambridge University Press, 1984.

- *Secular Religions in France 1815–1870*. London: Oxford University Press, 1963; repr. 1970.

Chédozeau, Bernard. 'Les grandes étapes de la publication de la Bible catholique en français.' In *Le grand siècle et la Bible*. Ed. Jean Robert Armogathe. Paris: Beauchesne, 1985.

Cioran. *La tentation d'exister*. Paris: Gallimard, 1956.

Clément, Jean-Paul. *Chateaubriand politique*. Paris: Hachette, 1986.

Collot, Michel. *Gérard de Nerval ou la dévotion à l'imaginaire*. Paris: PUF, 1992.

Cotoni, Marie-Helène. 'Voltaire, Rousseau, Diderot.' In *Le siècle des lumières et la Bible*. Eds. Yvon Belaval and Dominique Sourel. Paris: Beauchesne, 1986.

Coulson, John. *Religion and Imagination 'In Aid of a Grammar of Assent.'* Oxford: Clarendon Press, 1981.

Crouzet, Michel. *Le naturel, la grâce et le réel dans la poétique de Stendhal: Essai sur la genèse du romantisme*. Paris: Flammarion, 1986.

Crouzet, Michel. *La poétique de Stendhal: Forme et société*. Paris: Flammarion, 1983.

d'Ormesson, Jean. *Mon dernier rêve sera pour vous*. Paris: J.C. Lattès 1982.

Darnton, Robert. *The Kiss of Lamourette: Reflections on Cultural History*. New York: Norton, 1990.

– *Mesmerism and the End of Enlightenment in France*. Cambridge, Mass.: Harvard University Press, 1968.

– 'Readers Respond to Rousseau: The Fabrication of Romantic Sensitivity.' In *The Great Cat Massacre and Other Episodes in French Cultural History*. New York: Vintage Books, 1985.

de Certeau, Michel. 'Croire/faire croire.' In *L'invention du quotidien*: Vol. 2 of *Arts de faire*. Paris: Union générale d'éditions, 1980.

– *La faiblesse de croire*. Paris: Seuil, 1987.

– 'Une pratique sociale de la différence: croire.' In *Faire croire*. Rome: Ecole française de Rome, 1981.

de Diéguez, Manuel. *Chateaubriand ou le poète face à l'histoire*. Paris: Plon, 1963.

de Man, Paul. 'Metaphor.' In *Allegories of Reading*. New Haven: Yale University Press, 1979.

Dédéyan, Charles. *Chateaubriand et Rousseau*. Paris: Sedes, 1973.

Delaura, David J. 'Religion, Poetry, and the Rise of Literary Humanism: The 19th Century Matrix.' *Journal of the American Academy of Religion* 47, pt 2, Supplement [June 1979]: 251–72.

Delon, Michel. 'Nodier et les mythes révolutionnaires.' *Europe* 614, no 5, (June–July 1980): 31–42.

– 'Savoir totalisant et forme éclatée.' *Dix-huitième siècle* 14 (Paris: Garnier, 1982): 13–26.

Derré, J.-R. and B. Plongeron, eds. *Civilisation chrétienne: Approache historique d'une idéologie XVIIIè-XXè siècle*. Paris: Beauchesne, 1975.

Derrida, Jacques. 'La mythologie blanche: La métaphore dans le texte philosophique.' In *Marges de la philosophie*. Paris: Editions de Minuit, 1972.

Descombes, Vincent. 'L'équivoque du symbolique.' In *Confrontations*. Paris: Aubier, 1980. English translation in *Theory Culture and Society* 3, pt 3 (1986): 69–83.

Despland, Michel, 'Can Conscience Be Hypocritical? The Contrasting Analyses of Kant and Hegel.' *Harvard Theological Review* 68, pt 3–4 (1975): 357–70.

– 'A Case of Christians Shifting Their Moral Allegiance: France 1790–1914.' *Journal of the American Academy of Religion* 52, pt 4 (1984).

– 'La civilisation moderne et la morale.' In Pierre Fortin, ed. Colloque de Rimouski. *L'Ethique à venir*. Rimouski: UQAR, 1987.

– 'The French Response to D.F. Strauss *Das Leben Jesu*.' In American Academy of Religion. *Papers of the Nineteenth-Century Theology Working Group*. Berkeley: Graduate Theological Union, 1986: 85–98.

– 'La notion moderne de culture.' In *Religion et culture: Colloque du Centenaire Paul Tillich*. Eds. M. Despland, J-C. Petit, and J. Richard. Québec: Presses de l'Université Laval, 1987.

– *La religion en Occident*. Montréal/Paris: Fides/Cerf, 1977.

Didier, Beatrice. *Ecrire la Révolution: 1789–1799.* Paris: PUF, 1989.

– *Stendhal autobiographe.* (Paris: PUF, 1983).

Dumont, Louis. 'Religion, Politics and Society in the Individualistic Universe.' *Proceedings of the Royal Anthropological Institute for 1970* (London: 1971): 31–41.

Durry, Marie-Jeanne. *Gérard de Nerval et le mythe.* Paris: Flammarion, 1956.

Eco, Umberto. *The Open Work.* Trans. Anna Cancogni and intro. David Robey. Cambridge, Mass.: Harvard University Press, 1989.

Eigeldinger, Marc. 'L'ambiguïté de l'écriture.' In *Jean-Jacques Rousseau: Univers mythique et cohérence.* Neuchâtel: Baconnière, 1978.

– *Jean-Jacques Rousseau et la réalité de l'imaginaire.* Neuchâtel: Baconnière, 1962.

– *Jean-Jacques Rousseau: Univers mythique et cohérence.* (Neuchâtel: a Baconnière, 1978.

– *Vigny.* Paris: Seghers, 1965.

Ellis, Madeleine B. *Rousseau's Venetian Story: An Essay upon Art and Truth in Les Confessions.* Baltimore: Johns Hopkins Press, 1966.

Fitzer, Joseph, ed. *Romance and the Rock: Nineteenth-Century Catholics on Faith and Reason.* Minneapolis: Fortress Press, 1989.

Fizaine, Jean-Claude. 'Les aspects mystiques du romantisme français.' *Romantisme* 11 (1976): 4–41.

Foucher, P. *La philosophie catholique en France au XIXè siecle.* Paris: Vrin, 1955.

Frei, Hans. *The Eclipse of the Biblical Narrative: A Study in Eighteenth- and Nineteenth-Century Hermeneutics.* New Haven and London: Yale University Press, 1974.

– 'The "Literal Reading" of Biblical Narrative in the Christian Tradition: Does It Stretch or Will It Break?' In *The Bible and the Narrative Tradition.* Ed. Frank McConnel. New York: Oxford University Press, 1986.

Furet, François. *La gauche et la révolution au milieu du XIXème siècle.* Paris: Hachette, 1986.

Gaillard, Françoise. 'Nerval, ou les contradictions du romantisme.' *Romantisme* 1&2 (1971): 128–38.

Gascar, Pierre. *Gérard de Nerval et son temps.* (Paris: Gallimard, 1981).

Gauchet, Marcel. *La révolution des droits de l'homme.* Paris: Gallimard, 1989.

Geertz, Clifford. *The Interpretation of Cultures.* New York: Basic Books, 1973.

Gengembre, Gérard. *A vos plumes citoyens! Ecrivains, journalistes, orateurs et poètes de la Bastille à Waterloo.* Paris: Gallimard, 1988.

Germain, François, 'Vigny ou la croyance difficile.' *Les amis d'Alfred de Vigny,* bulletin 2 (March 1969): 4–15.

Girard, Louis. *Les libéraux français.* Paris: Aubier, 1983.

Giraud, Victor. *Le christianisme de Chateaubriand.* 2 vols. Paris: Hachette, 1925, 1928.

Goethe. *Dichtung und Wahrheit*. Trans. J. Oxenford. New York: Horizon Press, 1969.

Gouhier, Henri. *Les méditations métaphysiques de Jean-Jacques Rousseau*. Paris: Vrin, 1970.

Grimsley, Ronald. 'Kierkegaard, Vigny and the poet.' *Revue de littérature comparée* (January–March 1960). Reprinted in *Soren Kierkegaard and French Literature: Eight Comparative Studies*. (Cardiff: University of Wales Press, 1966.

Guillemin, Henri. *L'homme des Mémoires d'outre-tombe*. Paris: Gallimard, 1964.

Guiomar, Jean-Yves. *La nation entre l'histoire et la raison*. Paris: La Découverte, 1990.

Hamenachem, Miriam. *Charles Nodier: Essai sur l'imagination mythique*. Paris: Nizet, 1972.

Hofer, Hermann. 'La pensée mystique et religieuse de Charles Nodier.' In *Romantisme et religion*. Ed. M. Baude and M. M. Münch. Paris: PUF, 1980.

Hoffmann, Paul. 'Le problème de la bonne foi dans la profession de foi du vicaire savoyard.' *Revue d'histoire et de philosophie religieuses* 67 pt 1 (1987): 19–36.

Hunt, H.J. *The Epic in Nineteenth-Century France*. Oxford: Blackwell, 1941.

Jameson, Frederic. 'L'inconscient politique.' In G. Falconer and H. Mitterand. *La lecture socio-critique du texte romanesque*. Toronto: Hakkert, 1975.

Jaquet, Christian. *Le pensée religieuse de Jean-Jacques Rousseau*. Louvain: Bibliothèque de l'Université, 1975.

Jauss, H.R. 'Rousseau's *Nouvelle Héloïse* and Goethe's *Werther* within the Shift of Horizons from the French Enlightenment to German Idealism.' In *Question and Answer: Forms of Dialogic Understanding*. Minneapolis: University of Minnesota Press, 1986.

– 'A Sketch of a Theory and History of Aesthetic Experience.' In *Aesthetic Experience and Literary Hermeneutics*. Minneapolis: University of Minnesota Press, 1981.

– *Toward an Aesthetic of Reception*. Minneapolis: University of Minnesota Press, 1982.

Jean Raymond. *Lectures du désir*. Paris: Seuil, 1977.

– *Nerval*. Paris: Seuil, 1964; repr. 1978.

– *Nerval par lui-même*. Paris: Seuil, 1988.

– *La poétique du désir*. Paris: Seuil, 1975.

Jeanneret, Michel. *La Lettre perdue: Ecriture et folie dans l'oeuvre de Nerval*. Paris: Flammarion, 1978.

Juden, Brian. 'Nerval et la crise du panthéisme.' *Cahiers de l'Herne* 37 (1979): 275–87.

Juin, Hubert. 'Charles Nodier.' In *Lectures du XIXème siècle*. Vol. 1. Paris: Union générale d'éditions, 1976.

Jullian, Camille. *Notes sur l'histoire de France au XIXème siècle* (1897). Genève, Paris: Slatkine, 1979.

Kavanagh, Thomas M. *Writing the Truth: Authority and Desire in Rousseau.* Berkeley: University of California Press, 1987.

Kelley, Donald R. *Foundations of Modern Historical Scholarship: Language, Law and History in the French Renaissance.* New York: Columbia University Press, 1970.

Kelly, G.A. *Hegel's Retreat from Eleusis.* Princeton University Press, 1978.

– *Idealism, Politics and History: Sources of Hegelian Thought.* Cambridge University Press, 1969.

Kofman, Sarah. *Nerval, le charme de la répétition: Lecture de Sylvie.* Lausanne: L'Age d'homme, 1979.

Kristeva, Julia. *Soleil noir: Dépression et mélancolie.* Paris: Gallimard, 1987.

Labrosse, Claude. *Lire au XVIIIè siècle: La Nouvelle Héloïse et ses lecteurs.* Lyon: Presses Universitaires de Lyon, 1985.

Lacoue-Labarthe, P. and J.L. Nancy. *L'absolu littéraire: Théorie de la littérature du romantisme allemand.* Paris: Seuil, 1978.

Langlois, Claude. 'Permanence, renouveau et affrontements.' In *Histoire des catholiques en France.* Ed. Francois Lebrun. Toulouse: Privat, 1980.

Laplanche, François. *L'Ecriture, le sacré et l'histoire: Erudits et politiques protestants devant la Bible en France au XVIIème siècle.* Amsterdam: APA-Holland University Press, 1986.

Le Sidaner, Jean-Marie. 'Le peuple de Nodier.' *Europe* 43, pt 5 (1980): 43–5.

Lefebvre, Philippe. *Les pouvoirs de la parole: L'eglise et Rousseau 1762–1848.* Paris: Cerf, 1992.

Lehouck, Emile. 'Discours autobiographique et tradition romanesque dans Suites d'un mandat d'arrêt.' In *Charles Nodier: Colloque du deuxième centenaire Besançon 1980.* Paris: Belles Lettres, 1982.

Lejeune, Philippe. *Le pacte autobiographique.* Paris: Seuil, 1975.

Lowrie, Walter. *Kierkegaard.* New York: Harper and Row, 1962.

Macherey, Pierre. *A quoi pense la littérature?* Paris: PUF, 1991.

Mackey, Louis. *Kierkegaard: A Kind of Poet.* Philadelphia: University of Pennsylvania Press, 1971.

Mahieu, Raymond. 'Ecrire en 1850: Angélique de Nerval.' In *Ecrire en France au XIXe siècle.* Eds. Graziella Pagliano and Antonio Gomez-Moriana. Longueuil, Qué.: Editions du Préambule, 1989.

Malandain, Gabrielle. *Nerval ou l'incendie du théâtre: Identité et littérature dans l'oeuvre en prose de G. de Nerval.* Paris: Corti, 1986.

Manuel, Frank E. *The Prophets of Paris.* New York: Harper and Row, 1962; repr. 1965.

– *Shapes of Philosophical History*. Stanford, Calif.: Stanford University Press, 1965.

Marie, Aristide. *Gérard de Nerval le poète et l'homme*. Paris: Hachette, 1914; repr. 1955.

Masson, Pierre Maurice. *La religion de Jean-Jacques Rousseau*. Genève: Slatkine, 1970.

Matoré, Georges. *Le vocabulaire et la société sous Louis-Philippe* (1951). Repr. Genève: Slatkine, 1967.

Maurron, Charles. *Des métaphores obsédantes au mythe personnel: Introduction à la psycho-critique*. Paris: Corti, 1980.

McLeod, Hugh. *Religion and the People of Western Europe*. Oxford University Press, 1981.

Michaud, Stéphane, *Muse et madone: Visages de la femme de la Révolution française aux apparitions de Lourdes*. Paris: Seuil, 1985.

Michel, Alain. 'La grandeur et l'humilité. La Bible dans l'esthétique littéraire en France.' In *Le grand siècle et la Bible*. Ed. Jean-Robert Armogathe. Paris: Beauchesne, 1989.

Milner, Max. 'Présentation.' *Romantisme* 24 (1979): 3–5.

– 'Religions et religion dans *Le voyage en Orient* de Gérard de Nerval.' *Romantisme* 50 (1985): 41–52.

– 'Romantics on the Fringe.' In *The French Romantics*. Ed. D.G. Charlton. Vol. 2. Cambridge University Press, 1984.

Milner, M. and C. Pichois, eds. *Littérature française*. Vol. 7. Paris: Arthaud, 1985.

Moreau, Pierre. *Chateaubriand*. N.p.: Desclée de Brouwer, 1965.

– *La conversion de Chateaubriand*. Paris: Alcan, 1933.

– 'La religion de Chateaubriand.' *Table ronde* 241 (February 1968): 19–31.

Moscovici, Serge. *La machine à faire des dieux*. Paris: Fayard, 1988.

Moser, Walter. *Romantisme et crise de la modernité: Poésie et encyclopédie dans le 'Brouillon' de Novalis*. Longueil, Qué.: Le Préambule, 1989.

Niebuhr, Richard R. *The Meaning of Revelation*. New York: Macmillan, 1960.

Nussbaum, Martha C. *Love's Knowledge: Essays on Philosophy and Literature*. New York: Oxford University Press, 1990.

Olender, Maurice. *Les langues du paradis: Aryens et Sémites, un couple providentiel*. Paris: Gallimard/Seuil, 1989.

Ortega y Gasset, Jose. *Meditations on Don Quixote*. New York: Norton, 1963.

Painter, George, D. *Chateaubriand: A Biography*. London: Chatto and Windus, 1977.

Pelikan, Jaroslav. *Christian Doctrine and Modern Culture*. Vol. 5 of *The Christian Tradition*. University of Chicago Press, 1989.

Picard, Michel. *Nodier: La fée aux miettes; Loup y es-tu?* Paris: PUF, 1992.

Plongeron, Bernard. *L'abbé Grégoire ou l'arche de la fraternité.* Paris: Letouzey & Ané, 1989.

Polin, Raymond. *La politique de la solitude.* Paris: Sirey, 1971.

Pouillon, Jean. 'Remarques sur le verbe croire.' In *La fonction symbolique: Essais d'anthropologie.* Ed. Michel Izard and Pierre Smith. Paris: Gallimard, 1979.

Poulet, Georges. 'Introduction,' to Joseph Joubert, *Pensées.* Paris: Union générale d'éditions, l966.

– *Les métamorphoses du cercle.* Paris: Flammarion, 1979.

– 'Piranèse et les poètes romantiques français.' In *Trois essais de mythologie romantique.* Paris: Corti, 1966; repr. 1985.

– 'Sylvie ou la pensée de Nerval.' In *Trois essais de mythologie romantique.* Paris: Corti, 1966; repr. 1985.

Prickett, Stephen. *Romanticism and Religion: The Tradition of Coleridge and Wordsworth in the Victorian Church.* Cambridge University Press, 1976.

Reardon, Bernard. *Liberalism and Tradition: Aspects of Catholic Thought in Nineteenth-Century France.* Cambridge University Press, 1975.

– *Religion in the Age of Romanticism.* Cambridge University Press, 1985.

Reboul, Pierre. 'Introduction' to *Le génie du christianisme.* Paris: Garnier-Flammarion, 1966.

Retat, L. *Religion et imagination religieuse: Leurs formes et leurs rapports dans l'oeuvre d'Ernest Renan.* Paris: Klincksieck, 1957.

Reymond, Bernard. *A la redécouverte d'Alexandre Vinet.* Lausanne: l'Age d'homme, 1990.

Richard, Jean-Pierre. 'Géographie magique de Nerval.' In *Poésie et profondeur.* Paris: Seuil, 1955.

Richer, Jean. *Nerval: expérience et création.* Paris: Hachette, 1963.

Riley, Patrick. *The General Will before Rousseau: The Transformation of the Divine into the Civic.* Princeton University Press, 1986.

Roddier, Henri. 'Introduction' to *Les Rêveries du promeneur solitaire.* Paris: Garnier, 1960.

Rogers, Bryan G. 'Nodier et la monomanie réflective.' *Romantisme* 27 (1980): 15–29.

Rorty, Richard. *Philosophy and the Mirror of Nature.* Princeton University Press, 1979.

Rosanvallon, Pierre. *Le moment Guizot.* Paris: Gallimard, 1985.

Roston, Murray. *Prophet and Poet: The Bible and the Growth of Romanticism.* London: Faber and Faber, 1965.

Roudaut, Jean. 'Nodier: la poésie ou la mort.' *Magazine littéraire* 258 (October 1988): 41–3.

Roussel, Jean. *Jean-Jacques Rousseau en France après la Révolution 1795–1830*. Paris: Colin, 1972.

Roux, Anne-Marie. 'Nodier et "l'effet de folie".' *Romantisme* 27 (1980): 31–45.

Said, Edward. *Orientalism*. New York: Random House, 1979.

Sangsue, Daniel. *Le récit excentrique: Gautier–De Maistre–Nerval–Nodier*. Paris: Corti, 1987.

Savart, Claude. 'Quelle Bible les Catholiques français lisaient-ils?' In *Le monde contemporain et la Bible*. Ed. Claude Savart and Jean-Noël Aletti. Paris: Beauchesne, 1985.

Schaeffer, Gérald. *Une double lecture de Gérard de Nerval: Les illuminés et Les filles du feu*. Neuchâtel: Baconnière, 1977.

– *Le voyage en Orient de Nerval: Etude des structures*. (Neuchâtel: Baconnière, 1967.

Schroeder-Buys, Eckart. 'Charles Nodier und die Revolution.' *Lendemains* 25/26 (1982): 52–62.

Schwab, Raymond. *La renaissance orientale*. Paris: Payot, 1950.

Scott, Nathan A., Jr. 'Arnold's Version of Transcendence: The Via Poetica.' *The Journal of Religion* 59, pt 3 [July 1979]: 261–84.

Shklar, Judith. 'Let Us Not Be Hypocritical.' In 'Hypocrisy, Illusion and Evasion,' *Daedalus* 108 (Summer 1979): 1–25.

Sloterdijk, Peter. *Thinker on Stage: Nietzsche's Materialism*. Minneapolis: University of Minnesota Press, 1989.

Smart, N, J. Clayton, P. Sherry, and S. Katz, eds. *Nineteenth-Century Religious Thought in the West*. 3 vols. Cambridge University Press, 1985.

Solé, Jacques. *Les mythes chrétiens*. Paris: Albin Michel, 1979.

Spitzer, Alan B. *The French Generation of 1820*. Princeton University Press, 1982.

Starobinski, Jean. 'Jean-Jacques Rousseau et le péril de la réflexion.' In *L'oeil vivant*. Paris: Gallimard, 1961.

– *Jean-Jacques Rousseau: La transparence et l'obstacle*. Paris: Gallimard, 1971.

– 'Lire Rousseau.' In Rousseau, *Les Confessions et autres écrits autobiographiques*. Lausanne: La Guilde du Livre, 1962.

– 'La mise en accusation de la société.' In Marc Eigeldinger, ed., *J.-J. Rousseau: Quatre Etudes*. Neuchâtel: Baconnière, 1978.

– *Le remède est dans le mal*. Paris: Gallimard, 1989.

– 'Le sens de la critique.' In *La relation critique*. Paris: Gallimard, 1970.

Steinmetz, Jean-Luc. 'Aventures du regard.' In *Le champ d'écoute: Essais critiques*. Neuchâtel: Baconnière, 1985.

Strauss, Leo. *Persecution and the Art of Writing*. Westport Conn.: Greenwood Press, 1959; repr. 1973.

Summers, Vera A. *L'orientalisme d'Alfred de Vigny*. Paris: Champion, 1930; repr. Slatkine, 1976.

Tackett, Timothy. *Religion, Revolution and Regional Culture in Eighteenth-Century France: The Ecclesiastical Oath of 1791.* Princeton University Press, 1985.
– *La Révolution, l'Eglise, la France: le serment de 1791.* Transl. Alain Spiess. Paris: Cerf, 1986.
Taylor, Mark. *Erring: A Postmodern A/theology.* University of Chicago Press, 1984.
Terrace, Jean. *De Mentor à Orphée: Essais sur les écrits pédagogiques de Rousseau.* Montréal: HMH, 1992.
Thibaudet, Albert. *Histoire de la littérature française.* Paris: Stock 1936.
Todorov, Tzvetan. *The Fantastic: Structural Approach to a Literary Genre.* Cleveland: Press of Case Western Reserve University, 1973.
Trilling, Lionel. *Sincerity and Authenticity.* Cambridge, Mass.: Harvard University Press, 1971.
Vadé, Yves. *L'enchantement littéraire: Ecriture et magie de Chateaubriand à Rimbaud.* Paris: Gallimard, 1990.
Valéry, Paul. *Cahiers.* Paris: Editions CNRS, 1958.
– *Oeuvres.* 2 vols. Paris: Gallimard, 1957.
Vial, André. *Chateaubriand et le temps perdu.* Paris: Juillard, l963.
Viallaneix, Paul. *Vigny par lui-même.* Paris: Seuil, 1964.
Viatte, Auguste. *Les sources occultes du romantisme: Illuminisme – théosophie: 1770–1820.* 2 vols. Paris: Champion, 1969.
Vieillard-Baron, J. 'Phénoménologie de la conscience religieuse.' *Dix-huitième siècle* 14 (1982): 167–90.
Voegelin, Eric. 'On Hegel – A Study in Sorcery.' In *The Study of Time.* Eds. J.T. Fraser, F.C. Haber, and G.H. Mueller. Heidelberg, Berlin, New York: Springer Verlag, 1972.
Williams, Raymond. *Culture and Society.* Harmondsworth: Penguin, 1961.
Zaragoza, Georges. *Charles Nodier: Le dériseur sensé.* Paris: Klincksieck, 1992.
Ziolkowski, Theodore. 'Religion and Literature in a Secular Age: The Critic's Dilemma.' *The Journal of Religion* 59, pt 1 (January 1979): 18–34.

Index of Subjects

Index of Authors